本研究得到教育部人文社会科学青年基金项目（项目名称：汉语对话中韵律趋同的实验研究 项目批准号：15YJC740105）和江苏师范大学博士学位教师科研支持项目（项目名称：英汉语篇韵律对比研究 项目批准号：15XWR008）的资助，特此感谢。

同济博士论丛
TONGJI Dissertation Series
总主编 伍 江 副总主编 雷星晖

夏志华 马秋武 著

汉语对话中韵律趋同的实验研究

Prosodic Entrainment in Mandarin Chinese Conversations: an Experimental Study

同济大学出版社
TONGJI UNIVERSITY PRESS

内 容 提 要

本书研究汉语对话中的韵律趋同现象，是会话交流中韵律语用功能实现的研究之一。本书通过实验手段，对自然会话进行分析，研究的主要目的是探索汉语韵律趋同的规律，同时在可行范围内，对英汉韵律趋同规律进行比较，从韵律的语用功能实现上找出两种语言的异同。

图书在版编目(CIP)数据

汉语对话中韵律趋同的实验研究 / 夏志华，马秋武著. —上海：同济大学出版社，2019.10
(同济博士论丛 / 伍江总主编)
ISBN 978-7-5608-8785-2

Ⅰ. ①汉… Ⅱ. ①夏… ②马… Ⅲ. ①汉语—韵律(语言)—研究 Ⅳ. ①H11

中国版本图书馆 CIP 数据核字(2019)第 225442 号

汉语对话中韵律趋同的实验研究

夏志华　马秋武　著

出 品 人　华春荣　　责任编辑　熊磊丽
责任校对　徐春莲　　封面设计　陈益平

出版发行　同济大学出版社　　www.tongjipress.com.cn
(地址：上海市四平路 1239 号　邮编：200092　电话：021-65985622)
经　　销　全国各地新华书店
排版制作　南京展望文化发展有限公司
印　　刷　浙江广育爱多印务有限公司
开　　本　787 mm×1092 mm　1/16
印　　张　16
字　　数　320 000
版　　次　2019 年 10 月第 1 版　　2019 年 10 月第 1 次印刷
书　　号　ISBN 978-7-5608-8785-2

定　　价　74.00 元

“同济博士论丛”编写领导小组

组　　　长: 杨贤金　钟志华

副　组　长: 伍　江　江　波

成　　　员: 方守恩　蔡达峰　马锦明　姜富明　吴志强
徐建平　吕培明　顾祥林　雷星晖

办公室成员: 李　兰　华春荣　段存广　姚建中

“同济博士论丛”编辑委员会

总序

在同济大学110周年华诞之际，喜闻“同济博士论丛”将正式出版发行，倍感欣慰。记得在100周年校庆时，我曾以《百年同济，大学对社会的承诺》为题作了演讲，如今看到付梓的“同济博士论丛”，我想这就是大学对社会承诺的一种体现。这110部学术著作不仅包含了同济大学近10年100多位优秀博士研究生的学术科研成果，也展现了同济大学围绕国家战略开展学科建设、发展自我特色，向建设世界一流大学的目标迈出的坚实步伐。

坐落于东海之滨的同济大学，历经110年历史风云，承古续今、汇聚东西，秉持“与祖国同行、以科教济世”的理念，发扬自强不息、追求卓越的精神，在复兴中华的征程中同舟共济、砥砺前行，谱写了一幅幅辉煌壮美的篇章。创校至今，同济大学培养了数十万工作在祖国各条战线上的人才，包括人们常提到的贝时璋、李国豪、裘法祖、吴孟超等一批著名教授。正是这些专家学者培养了一代又一代的博士研究生，薪火相传，将同济大学的科学研究和学科建设一步步推向高峰。

大学有其社会责任，她的社会责任就是融入国家的创新体系之中，成为国家创新战略的实践者。党的十八大以来，以习近平同志为核心的党中央高度重视科技创新，对实施创新驱动发展战略作出一系列重大决策部署。党的十八届五中全会把创新发展作为五大发展理念之首，强调创新是引领发展的第一动力，要求充分发挥科技创新在全面创新中的引领作用。要把创新驱动发展作为国家的优先战略，以科技创新为核心带动全面创新，以体制机制改革激发创新活力，以高效率的创新体系支撑高水平的创新型国家建设。作为人才培养和科技创新的重要平台，大学是国家创新体系的重要组成部分。同济大学理当围绕国家战略目标的实现，作出更大的贡献。

大学的根本任务是培养人才，同济大学走出了一条特色鲜明的道路。无论是本科教育、研究生教育，还是这些年摸索总结出的导师制、人才培养特区，“卓越人才培养”的做法取得了很好的成绩。聚焦创新驱动转型发展战略，同济大学推进科研管理体系改革和重大科研基地平台建设。以贯穿人才培养全过程的一流创新创业教育助力创新驱动发展战略，实现创新创业教育的全覆盖，培养具有一流创新力、组织力和行动力的卓越人才。“同济博士论丛”的出版不仅是对同济大学人才培养成果的集中展示，更将进一步推动同济大学围绕国家战略开展学科建设、发展自我特色、明确大学定位、培养创新人才。

面对新形势、新任务、新挑战，我们必须增强忧患意识，扎根中国大地，朝着建设世界一流大学的目标，深化改革，勠力前行！

万　钢

2017 年 5 月

论丛前言

承古续今，汇聚东西，百年同济秉持“与祖国同行、以科教济世”的理念，注重人才培养、科学研究、社会服务、文化传承创新和国际合作交流，自强不息，追求卓越。特别是近20年来，同济大学坚持把论文写在祖国的大地上，各学科都培养了一大批博士优秀人才，发表了数以千计的学术研究论文。这些论文不但反映了同济大学培养人才能力和学术研究的水平，而且也促进了学科的发展和国家的建设。多年来，我一直希望能有机会将我们同济大学的优秀博士论文集中整理，分类出版，让更多的读者获得分享。值此同济大学110周年校庆之际，在学校的支持下，“同济博士论丛”得以顺利出版。

“同济博士论丛”的出版组织工作启动于2016年9月，计划在同济大学110周年校庆之际出版110部同济大学的优秀博士论文。我们在数千篇博士论文中，聚焦于2005—2016年十多年间的优秀博士学位论文430余篇，经各院系征询，导师和博士积极响应并同意，遴选出近170篇，涵盖了同济的大部分学科：土木工程、城乡规划学(含建筑、风景园林)、海洋科学、交通运输工程、车辆工程、环境科学与工程、数学、材料工程、测绘科学与工程、机械工程、计算机科学与技术、医学、工程管理、哲学等。作为“同济博士论丛”出版工程的开端，在校庆之际首批集中出版110余部，其余也将陆续出版。

博士学位论文是反映博士研究生培养质量的重要方面。同济大学一直将立德树人作为根本任务，把培养高素质人才摆在首位，认真探索全面提高博士研究生质量的有效途径和机制。因此，“同济博士论丛”的出版集中展示同济大学博士研究生培养与科研成果，体现对同济大学学术文化的传承。

“同济博士论丛”作为重要的科研文献资源，系统、全面、具体地反映了同济大学各学科专业前沿领域的科研成果和发展状况。它的出版是扩大传播同济科研成果和学术影响力的重要途径。博士论文的研究对象中不少是“国家自然科学基金”等科研基金资助的项目，具有明确的创新性和学术性，具有极高的学术价值，对我国的经济、文化、社会发展具有一定的理论和实践指导意义。

“同济博士论丛”的出版，将会调动同济广大科研人员的积极性，促进多学科学术交流、加速人才的发掘和人才的成长，有助于提高同济在国内外的竞争力，为实现同济大学扎根中国大地，建设世界一流大学的目标愿景做好基础性工作。

虽然同济已经发展成为一所特色鲜明、具有国际影响力的综合性、研究型大学，但与世界一流大学之间仍然存在着一定差距。“同济博士论丛”所反映的学术水平需要不断提高，同时在很短的时间内编辑出版 110 余部著作，必然存在一些不足之处，恳请广大学者，特别是有关专家提出批评，为提高同济人才培养质量和同济的学科建设提供宝贵意见。

最后感谢研究生院、出版社以及各院系的协作与支持。希望“同济博士论丛”能持续出版，并借助新媒体以电子书、知识库等多种方式呈现，以期成为展现同济学术成果、服务社会的一个可持续的出版品牌。为继续扎根中国大地，培育卓越英才，建设世界一流大学服务。

伍　江

2017 年 5 月

前言

会话趋同是指参与者在对话中进行合作调整，以完成顺畅的交流。它普遍存在于会话交流中，主要表现为句法形式、词汇选择上的相似，发音、语速等韵律上的相仿，肢体表情的接近，等等。本书以其中的韵律趋同为研究重点。

具体而言，韵律趋同指双方在对话中调整其韵律表现，变得相似，以完成顺畅的交流。对话交流中，个体调整韵律表现以适应对方，这种调整过程复杂，涉及认知、心理、语言、社会等因素的综合作用，其中的规律值得探究。

本书研究汉语对话中的韵律趋同现象，是会话交流中韵律语用功能实现的研究之一。本书通过实验手段，对自然会话进行分析，研究的主要目的是探索汉语韵律趋同的规律，同时在可行范围内，对英汉韵律趋同规律进行比较，从韵律的语用功能实现上找出两种语言的异同。据此，本书提出了三个研究问题：韵律在普通话对话中是如何表现趋同的？社会因素如何影响韵律趋同？在跨语言比较中，英汉两种语言的韵律趋同规律有何异同？针对这些问题的分析构成了本书研究的主体：韵律趋同多层次分析、韵律趋同与社会因素关系的分析和韵律趋同跨语言比较分析（详见第4、5、6章）。

本书研究有如下两方面意义。

一、本书研究具有一定的理论意义

首先，汉语对话中韵律趋同研究印证和丰富了会话趋同研究的理论框架。现有的韵律趋同研究中已经涉及的语言主要有英语、荷兰语、瑞典语、日语等，极少涉及汉语。本书对于汉语会话中韵律趋同进行了较全面的研究，在印证已有的会话趋同理论的同时，首次提出会话中存在两类趋同，一类是绝对趋同，另一类是相对趋同。会话中两类趋同的提出丰富了已有的会话趋同理论，有助于会话趋同过程的描述，同时增进人们对该过程的理解。

其次，韵律趋同规律的跨语言比较具有语言类型学意义。本书比较了汉英两种语言中韵律趋同规律，帮助人们更深入理解不同类型语言中对话双方如何借助韵律手段实现会话趋同。从语言类型上来讲，英语和汉语属于两种不同类型的语言。在不同类型语言中进行韵律语用功能实现方式的比较具有语言类型学上的意义。

二、本研究具有一定的实践意义

首先，以本书结论为基础，可总结出有效的交流策略和方法，其具有实践指导意义。韵律趋同是对话双方在对话中韵律上的相互合作调整。本书关于时长、音高、音强韵律特征在不同层面上表现突出趋同的结论可以用来指导有效交流。

其次，本书的结论期待为语言合成带来些启发。让合成的语言和人类语言一样自然是言语工程研究的一大挑战。本书研究中所发现的对话趋同中韵律的调整是改进语言自然度的一个方面，所得出的研究结论也希望能为自然语言韵律合成研究带来些启发。

本书语料库和主要分析如下：

本书研究基于同济大学游戏语料库。该语料库包含115个即兴对话，每个对话平均时长为6分钟。这些即兴合作对话由本书研究设计的实验所引发。受试根据要求完成两类实验——图片排序和图片分类。70组受试者参加实验，每组两人，其中有14组根据要求参加了两次实验。

本书选取韵律的3个主要方面（时长、音高、音强），共计7个声学参数为变量，它们分别是：时长特征（语速），基频特征（基频最低值、基频平均值、基频最高值），音强特征（音强最低值、音强平均值以及音强最高值）。

IPU（停顿间隔单元，本书研究中停顿间隔设定为80毫秒）被认定为最小的数据提取和分析单元。通过软件SPPAS对语料进行IPU的自动识别和标注，然后对被识别的IPU边界进行人工核查。在标注好的语料上运行Praat脚本，并提取每个IPU单元上的7个声学参数为本书的分析数据。当韵律趋同分析涉及了更大单元时（即该单元包含多个IPU），本书计算IPU

的加权均值(以每个 IPU 的时长为权重),然后针对加权均值进行分析。

第 4 章的主要内容是多层次上韵律趋同的分析。从宏观到微观,本章在会话、话轮和声调单元三个不同层次上进行韵律趋同分析,其中每个层次上的分析主要从接近性、融合性和同步性三个角度展开。基于这些分析结果,本章针对相同角度不同层次上韵律趋同规律进行了从宏观到微观的跨层次比较分析。

通过接近性的比较分析发现,时长和音强特征在会话、话轮和声调单元三个不同层次上都表现出整体的相似性。通过融合性的比较分析发现,在话轮层次上,对话双方表现出显著的融合性,即随着对话的推进,两者的韵律表现越来越接近,但是在会话和声调单元层次上,均未发现类似的规律。通过同步性的比较分析发现,对于音高特征而言,即使整体的接近性和融合性不存在,对话双方在微观层次上也表现出了显著的同步性。

通过声调趋同分析发现,汉语对话中,混合性别对话者在声调产出上存在相对趋同,即混合性别对话者在声调的相对调域上存在趋同。

第 5 章的主要内容是韵律趋同与社会因素的分析,包含两方面:韵律趋同与性别关系的分析以及韵律趋同与角色关系的分析。

韵律趋同与性别关系的分析包括不同性别组合上的接近性分析和趋同程度分析。分析发现,在男女组合的对话中参与趋同的韵律参数最多,而在男男组合的对话中韵律参数最少;相同性别组合(女女组合和男男组合)中时长特征和音强特征上都有趋同表现,在混合性别组合(男女组合)中,包含以上两方面的韵律特征外(时长、音强),音频特征上也有趋同表现;男男组合的趋同度表现出最小的趋势。

韵律趋同与角色关系的分析包括角色影响检测和角色方向检测。在实验设计中,图片排序游戏中对话双方角色有区分(信息给予者和信息接收者),而图片分类游戏中对话双方角色无区分。角色影响检测结果表明角色对于韵律趋同程度有显著影响,即图片排序游戏中的韵律趋同程度显著大于图片分类游戏中的趋同程度。角色方向检测结果表明,对话双方在趋同的方向上的表现是:信息给予者更多地趋同于信息接收者。

第 6 章的主要内容是汉英韵律趋同跨语言比较分析。基于两种语言中相对应的研究部分，本章中的跨语言比较主要从宏观(会话层次)、微观(话轮层次)和不同性别组合上展开。

跨语言比较发现，两种语言在韵律趋同方式上表现出显著的相似性。比如，在会话层次，两种语言中韵律参数表现出相似的整体接近性；两种语言中体现话轮层次上接近性的韵律参数相同(它们是语速、音强均值、音强最高值)；在话轮层次上，两种语言表现出相似的融合性和同步性；混合性别组合的对话中，参与趋同的韵律参数最多，男男组合最少。

跨语言比较还发现，两种语言在韵律趋同程度上表现出不同。比如，话轮层次上，两种语言的融合程度不同；话轮和声调单元层次上，两种语言的同步程度不同；对于不同性别搭配而言，两种语言中，三种性别组合的韵律趋同程度不同。

对比还发现，现有的研究中，英语表现绝对趋同，而在本书研究中，汉语表现绝对趋同与相对趋同共存。

两种语言趋同方式的相似证明了，尽管隶属于不同类型的语言，汉语和英语利用相似的方式来实现音长、音高和音强上的趋同。而两种语言韵律趋同程度的差异，应该与两种语言类型上的差异有关。

综上所述，本书研究的主要发现有：

(1) 研究结果证实，汉语普通话的对话中，韵律的3个主要方面(时长特征、音高特征、音强特征)都有显著的趋同表现。

本书研究选取韵律的3个主要方面，共计7个声学参数为变量，它们分别是：时长特征(语速)，基频特征(基频最低值、基频平均值、基频最高值)，音强特征(音强最低值、音强平均值以及音强最高值)。第4、5、6章中三项主要分析(韵律趋同多层次分析、韵律趋同与社会因素关系的分析和韵律趋同跨语言比较分析)，证实了韵律的3个主要方面都有显著的趋同表现。

(2) 本书研究表明，汉语韵律在微观层次上的趋同表现比宏观层次上更明显。

首先，本书发现在宏观层次上表现趋同的韵律参数数量多于微观层次上的数量(详见第4章)。4项韵律参数在会话层次上表现趋同，而5项在声调单元上体现趋同。6项韵律参数在话轮层次上表现同步性，而7项在声调单元上表现出同步性。其次，本书研究还发现，对于音高特征而言，尽管在相对宏观层次上，其趋同表现不明显，而在相对微观层次上，它们表现出显著的趋同性。

(3) 韵律参数在不同层次上展现不同的趋同规律。

不论是在相对宏观还是微观层面上，音强特征表现出明显的趋同性；时长特征在相对宏观层次上表现更明显的趋同；音高特征在相对微观层次上表现更明显的趋同。通过第 4 章中的跨层次比较发现，音强特征几乎在分析的所有层次上都表现出显著的趋同性。时长特征在会话层面表现出的趋同性比话轮层面要更明显。音高特征在话轮和声调单元上表现出明显的同步性，而在会话层面上的同步性却不显著。

(4) 本书研究发现，随着对话的推进，话轮层面表现出融合性，即对话双方在韵律参数上的差距随着时间的推移而缩小，但是会话层面和声调单元层面并未发现这样的规律。

(5) 本书研究证明韵律趋同与社会因素具有紧密的联系。

对于性别特征而言，三种性别组合上体现出不同的韵律趋同规律。混合性别组合对话中参与趋同的韵律参数数量最多。从表现出趋同的韵律参数数量和趋同的程度上来讲，都是男性组合趋同最少。对于角色而言，本书研究证实角色影响会话中韵律趋同的程度，而且对话中信息提供者更多地趋向于信息接收者。

(6) 通过跨语言比较发现(详见第 6 章)，英汉两种语言在韵律趋同方式上存在显著共性，在韵律趋同程度上存在显著差别。

两种语言在韵律趋同方式上表现出显著的相似性。比如，在会话层次，两种语言中韵律参数表现出相似的整体接近性；两种语言中体现话轮层次上接近性的韵律参数相同；在话轮层次上，两种语言表现出相似的融合性和同步性；男女组合对话中参与趋同的韵律参数最多，而男男组合最少。

两种语言在韵律趋同程度上表现出不同。比如，话轮层次上，两种语言的融合程度不同；话轮和声调单元层次上，两种语言的同步程度不同；对于不同性别搭配而言，两种语言中，三种性别组合的韵律趋同程度不同。

(7) 本书首次提出会话中存在两类趋同，一类是绝对趋同，另一类是相对趋同。现有的研究中，英语表现绝对趋同，而在本书研究中，汉语表现绝对趋同与相对趋同共存。如汉语中，相对宏观单元上的韵律特征体现绝对趋同，混合性别对话者声调相对调域内体现相对趋同。

(8) 本书在汉语会话韵律趋同研究中使用的方法上具有参考价值。

本书中有参考价值的研究方法主要有两类：声调单元上相对趋同的分析方法和会话与话轮层次上绝对趋同的研究方法。

韵律趋同现象复杂，一项研究并不能涵盖其所有内容，本书研究在如下几方面存在，它们可成为后续的研究点。

第一，对于韵律趋同过程的研究需要进一步展开。由于韵律趋同性质难以捉摸，随着对话的进行，韵律趋同的过程在不断变化，是这研究的难点。在本书研究中，除了在话轮层次上，随着对话的推进对话双方在一些韵律参数表现上越来越接近以外，在会话层次和声调单元层次上均未发现类似规律。因此，后续需要进一步展开对于韵律趋同过程的研究。

第二，韵律趋同研究需囊括更多的社会因素。对于韵律趋同与社会因素的关系，本书研究着重于性别和角色这两个因素。事实上，与韵律趋同有关的社会因素众多，包括身份、年龄、性别、角色、区域、种族、环境，等等，这些都值得研究。研究难点在于如何在实验中凸显目标因素，同时控制其他因素。

第三，音高与韵律趋同的关系值得进一步研究。本书研究以二字组一声组合的声调单元为研究对象，从接近性、融合性和同步性三方面考察了音高和韵律趋同之间的关系，其他类型声调组合的韵律趋同研究需进一步展开。同时，对于汉语声调与语调的关系问题，现有研究多数是概念性描述，汉语本体研究还未给出明确清晰的答案，因此需要进一步展开相关研究，探索音高与韵律趋同之间的关系。

目 录

Chapter 1

Introduction

In conversation, the major goal of both interlocutors is to achieve mutual intelligibility. To reach this goal, both parties coordinate their communication ways. Therefore, conversations are considered as joint activities in which two interlocutors share or synchronize their mental states and performances. The joint nature of language processing in communication requires the interpersonal coordination in minds and actions (Brennan *et al*. 2010). This coordination is called entrainment.

Speech communication involves not only an exchange of propositional contents but also an interchange of emotions, attitudes, intentions, etc. of the speakers. Prosody is an effective tool to realize such pragmatic functions in interaction.

This book focuses on the prosodic entrainment and aims to explore how the prosody works in entrainment in Mandarin Chinese conversations, and to find out how prosodic entrainment in Chinese are different or similar to that in English.

1.1 Key Terms

1.1.1 Entrainment

Entrainment in speech means that speakers adapt their communicative behavior to their conversational partners. Social interaction involves participants' mutual coordination or adaptation. Many studies has focused on or touched this, and different terms are used for this phenomenon, such as entrainment (Brennan 1996; Cummins 2009; Van Der Wege 2009; Lee *et al.* 2010; Levitan & Hirschberg 2011; Levitan *et al.* 2012), alignment (Pickering & Garrod 2006), accommodation (Beňuš *et al.* 2011), convergence (Giles *et al.* 1991; Pardo 2006), synchrony (Edlund *et al.* 2009), mimicry (Couper-Kuhlen 1996; Pentland 2008) and chameleon effect (Chartrand & Bargh 1999). Other terms are also made but in less frequent use (De Looze *et al.* 2014). Child-directed speech or motherese (Fernald *et al.* 1989) is used to describe speakers' accommodation when having conversations with children; foreign talk or foreigness (Ferguson 1975; Zuengler 1991; Smith 2007) is used when talking with non-native speakers; Lombard effect (Summers *et al.* 1988; Zeine & Brandt 1988) is used on the occasion of accommodating to a noisy environment.

There is much evidence that entrainment is critical to humans' assessment of dialogue success, overall quality, and their evaluation of conversational partners. Goleman (2006) points out that humans' ability to synchronize their communicative behavior with that of their conversational partners is critical to successful communication.

Entrainment in speech happens at non-linguistic levels including gestures, facial expressions, body movements, etc. Chartrand & Bargh (1999) find in their studies of mannerism and facial expression entrainment that subjects display strong unintentional entrainment, and that greater entrainment leads subjects to report they liked the confederate more and that the overall interaction was progressing more smoothly. Some other studies also find out that the similar facial expressions and semblable body movements are used in conversations (Condon & Sander 1974; Meltzoff & Moor 1977; Maurer & Tindall 1983; Bavelas *et al.* 1986; Bernieri & Rosenthal 1991; Bernieri *et al.* 1994; Richardson *et al.* 2007; Shockley *et al.* 2007; Shockley *et al.* 2009; Hess & Blairy 2011).

Entrainment in speech happens at linguistic levels including phonetic elements, prosody, lexicon, syntax, etc. Pickering & Garrod (2004) claims that the automatic alignment at levels of linguistic representations is important both for production and perception in dialogues, and facilitated interaction. The adaptation of the interlocutors is found in lexicon (Brennan 1996; Pickering & Gorrod 2004; Nenkova *et al.* 2008; Branigan *et al.* 2011; Iwata & Watanabe 2013) and at the grammatical and syntactic structure of the speaking (Cleland & Pickering 2003; Haywood *et al.* 2005; Pickering & Ferreira 2008; Branigan *et al.* 2010). Reitter & Moor (2007) also find that degree of entrainment in lexical and syntactic repetitions occurring in the first five minutes of a dialogue significantly predicts task success in studies of the HCRC Map Task Corpus. The accommodation of the interlocutors is also found in pronunciation (Giles *et al.* 1991; Pardo 2006; Delvaux & Soquet 2007; Aubanel & Nguyen 2010; Bailly & Lelong 2010; Babel & Bulatov 2011).

Interlocutors in conversation also make prosodic adaptation (Natale 1975; Gregory & Hoyt 1982; Gregory *et al.* 1993; Stanford & Webster 1996; Gregory & Dagan 1997; Edlund *et al.* 2009; Levitan & Hirschberg 2011; De Looze & Rauzy 2011; De Looze *et al.* 2011; Levitan *et al.* 2012; Levitan 2013; De Looze *et al.* 2014). The present work focuses on prosodic entrainment in Mandarin conversations. The main reason for doing research on prosodic entrainment is the crucial roles prosody plays in speech communication.

1.1.2 Speech Prosody

Prosody plays crucial roles in interaction. Two definitions of speech prosody are relevant to its functions in interaction. One comes from Crystal (1969), and the other Firth (1957).

According to Crystal (1969), prosody is defined as "sets of mutually defining phonological features which have an essentially variable relationship to the words selected, as opposed to those features which have a direct and identifying relationship to such words". The prosodic phenomena are classified in two layers (Crystal 1969): primary (linguistic), and secondary (paralinguistic). The former includes pitch direction, pitch range, pause, loudness, tempo, rhythm. The latter includes voice qualifiers (for instance whisper, breathiness, creaky, etc.) and voice qualifications (Such as laughter, giggle, sobbing, or crying).

Most of the West European research tradition follows Crystal's definition. However, because this two-layer division in the classifications of prosodic phenomena is considered to be ambitious, some researchers have doubts on the validity of this definition. For example, one of the doubts comes from the problem of classifying pause between linguistic and paralinguistic phenomena.

Different from Crystal's linguistic and paralinguistic definition, some researchers (Kelly & Local 1989; Couper-Kuhlen 2000) accept a more extensive definition of prosody from Firth. Firth (1957) assumes that prosody is as all types of syntagmatic relationships between syllables, which is not determined by the structure of words and utterances, and that prosody includes syllable structures, stress or accentuation, tone, quality and quantity, and also phenomena like glottalization, aspiration, nasalization, whisper, etc. About Firth's definition, Selting (2010) supplies deeper illustration that all supra-segmental phenomena, which are produced by the interplay of pitch, loudness, duration, and voice quality can be understood as prosodic, and once they are used, they are independent of the language's segmental structure. By Firth's definition, prosody functions as signals for communication. This broader definition is useful for the research on prosody in interaction, in which increased interest has been put.

Why are the functions of prosody in interaction emphasized?

The main reason is that at the importance of prosody in interaction has been recognized and emphasized. A brief review of the research on prosody helps to illustrate how the emphasis is put on prosody in interaction.

In the early research, the perspective on prosody is structural not interactional. In the early part of last century, in the structural tradition, the research on prosody primarily was in structural terms. An analogy was made between prosodic phenomena and meaning-distinctive units (Such as phonemes) and meaning-bearing units (Such as morphemes) (Couper-Kuhlen 2009). Speech prosody have been considered as a part of language competence, analyzed in minimal pairs, and treated by phoneme-or morpheme-like elements with distinctive functions. Pike (1945) assumes that pitch levels in American

English distinguish meaning in much the same way as phonemes do in minimal words. Other researchers state that prosodic patterns are more similar to morphemes (Liberman & Sag 1974; Sag & Liberman 1975). Following this line, the term "intonational lexicon" appeared, which meant the semantics of particular tones or tone sequences could be represented in the similar way to that for morphemes and words.

With the development of linguistics, it is gradually known that the research on prosody from the perspective of structuralism has a number of limitations. The studies of prosody in structural tradition are valid only over sets of tonal configurations for single utterances. The prosody over global units and the non-compositional prosodic patterns, for example, paratone (Yue 1980), cannot be explained by the structural terms, and it is not feasible to put lexical analogy over the dynamic and temporal variations in prosody such as rhythm, tempo, and pause (Auer, Couper-Kuhlen & Muller 1999).

At that time, the pragmatic use of prosody in conversation has been recognized. Halliday (1967, 1970) is one of the first to do so. He assumes intonational distinctions such as tonality (division into tone groups), tonicity (placement of the tonic accent), and tone (a means for speakers to cut information into units), to mark information foci and to distinguish new from given information respectively. Almost at the same time, Bolinger (1965, 1972) argues against the view of intonation entailing discrete phoneme like pitch levels and predictable (Semantically determined) accent placement. In contrast, he proposes that intonation is the gesture of one's larynx (Bolinger 1986), and that the use of prosody is similar to mimetics, gestures and kinesics - all dimensions which reflect the embodiment of language when used in actual (face to face) communication. For example, although an organic source may be lacking in pause, a gestural function is identifiable for it in conversation. Bolinger also point out that intonation is a gradient phenomenon, and the pragmatic use of prosody in conversation should be emphasized, for example, "whatever it is that we find with the raised peak, there is more of it as that peak goes higher"(Bolinger 1961).

The study of conversation has made considerable influence on the study of prosody in interaction. Sacks and his colleagues (Sacks *et al.* 1974) advocate an "analytic mentality" for the discovery of social order in conversation. They assume (i) the importance of investigating natural data, (ii) a view of social interaction as an ongoing, sequentially organized and collaboratively achieved process, and (iii) the necessity for justifying one's analyses by showing the relevance of the categories to the participants themselves. Conversation analysts have "called attention to a whole host of phenomena which are often ignored in the study of discourse: hesitation particles, sound stretching, cut-offs, in-breaths, laughter, (micro-) pausing, stressing, and intonation" (Couper-Kuhlen & Selting 1996: 13). Till then, prosody has been emphasized in the study of language as a social phenomenon, and prosodic phenomena have been recorded in the transcripts of interaction. "Phonology for Conversation" is studied (Local, Kelly & Wells 1986; Kelly & Local 1989; Selting, 1992; Local & Walker 2004; Xia & Mu 2008; Selting, 2010; Xia 2012, 2013), in which phonetic features of spoken language are described in terms of their relevance to the organization of conversation.

Different from the conversation-analysis-based approach, one notable notion on prosody in interaction come from the work of Gumperz, who claims that participants in verbal interaction employ "empirically detectable signs" which *cue* conversational interpretation by evoking interpretative schemata or frames (Gumperz 1982). The process during which participants construct context through such cues in order to make utterances interpretable has been known as *contextualization* (Auer & Di Luzio 1992; Selting, M. 1996). According to Gumperz (1992), the contextualization cues affect participants' inference at three levels of generalization: (i) conversational management, e.g. in turn-taking and signaling degrees of informational relevance; (ii) sequencing, e.g. in cueing implication and disambiguating speaker intent in utterances; (iii) framing, i.e. in generating expectations about the nature of the interaction and in keying its mood or atmosphere. Some of the means which speakers use to contextualize language are prosodic features; others include code-switching and non-verbal elements such as body position, gesture and gaze (Auer 1992).

More recently, the Interactional Linguistics proposes the interactional approach to the research on prosody. This approach, advocated by Couper-Kuhlen & Selting (1996), is in fact inspired by contextualization theory coupled with the methodological procedures of conversation analysis. According to this approach, if the purpose is to investigate the prosodic phenomena as they function in genuine language communication, the structuralistic framework is thus of limited value. The reason is that prosodic effects are not symbolic signs but indexical. As index, prosodic signals function pragmatically, cueing inferences rather than symbolically representing aspects of linguistic reality. Different from the symbolic signs of language (words or morphemes), the meanings prosodic signals cue can't be specified out of context. Couper-Kuhlen (2009) states that prosodic effects never appear without words or word-like entities to carry them; these words and the discourse situation in which they are used provide a context for interpreting the prosody which accompanies them - vice versa; the prosody itself provides a context for interpreting its carrier, the words.

In summary, the research on prosody in interaction has filled a research gap since the mid-1980s, because data from natural social interaction had rarely been the basis for systematic studies of prosody before that time (Selting 2010). At present, prosody has been proved to be relevant and indispensable for the construction of social interaction. Researchers consider every-day talking as the primary source for the studies of linguistic and social processes in communication. The tasks for exploring basic principles of human being's communication will not be accomplished without the studies of prosody in interaction.

The present research, which focuses on prosodic entrainment in Mandarin Chinese conversation, is set in the framework of the researches on prosody in interaction.

Chinese is a tone language. It has different tone and prosodic systems from other types of languages. Several theories have set foundations for the research of prosody in Chinese.

Among these theories, super-positional view of prosody in Chinese should be mentioned at first. The super-positional view of Chinese prosody makes the earliest yet far-reaching influence. This outstanding contribution owes to Yuen Ren Chao, who proposed the "algebraic sum of big wave plus small wave" as the form of Chinese prosody (Zhao 1933). The main idea of this model is that (i) Chinese is a typical tone language; (ii) the contour of rising, falling or its combinations in pitch movement has been locally used as tones shapes, and these tones are lexically fixed for the identification of meaning; (iii) therefore, the prosody in Chinese is different from English which directly take the intonation contour, but appear as a complex combination of local tones and underlying intonation. This classical super-positional view of Chinese prosody has been improved by Gårding (1979), Fujisaki (1983, 2003), Zongji Wu (1998, 2003, 2004), Jiong Shen (1992, 1994, 1996), Jianfen Cao (2002), and Maocan Lin (2002, 2004, 2005).

Another is linear view. This view is originally based on the Auto-segmental Metric Phonology (AM Phonology) proposed firstly by Pierrehumbert (1980) and developed by Ladd (1996). The basic idea of this theory is that (i) different intonation are described as linear structured strings of L and H tones; (ii) the strings consist of one or more pitch accents, which are aligned with stressed syllables on the basis of the metrical pattern of the text, and two boundary tones at the end of the phrases regardless of the metrical structure of the text, which characterize the intonation of the end of the phrase; (iii) the phrase accent, which follows immediately after the pitch accent on the main phrase stress and controls the intonation from there to the boundary; (iv) local context-sensitive rules map the string of tones into the quantitative values which determine the fundamental frequency contour. The linear view is adopted in the modeling of Chinese prosody mainly in Lin's (2006) studies.

The third is parallel view. Proposed by Xu (2005), the framework of Parallel Encoding and Target Approximation (PENTA) is based on the recognition of two basic facts. One is that speech conveys communicative meanings, and the other is that it is produced by an articulatory system. In the model of PENTA, a communicative function stands for a relation between the intended communicative meaning and the physical implementation of the speech prosody. Different communicative functions may extend across different temporal intervals and they produce different encoding schemes. With the different encoding schemes, communicative functions are transmitted in parallel to the specifications of the target and/or the target approximation process. Therefore, the combined effects are implemented through the target approximation process, and consequently in surface F0 values and their timings, the dynamic changes are produced.

The present research follows the super-positional view, and treats the prosody of Chinese as the combination of local tones and underlying intonation. Through the acoustic parameters, the combined prosody is analyzed according to the design for entrainment.

1.1.3 Prosodic Entrainment

The importance of prosody in interaction and the ubiquity of entrainment in conversation call for intensive and extensive research on prosodic entrainment.

Specifically, prosodic entrainment means speakers adapt prosody to that of their interlocutors and become similar in conversation for better, smooth and successful communication (Levitan & Hirschberg 2011; Levitan *et al.* 2012).

This section focuses on functions of prosody involved in entrainment and realization of prosody in entrainment.

Main functions of prosody in communication are involved in entrainment. Prosody expresses text/discourse meaning, organizing meaning, and interpersonal meaning in entrainment.

Entrainment involves the discourse/textual meaning of prosody. The prosody in entrainment is realized at discourse level which is larger than a single sentence. Levitan & Hirschberg (2011) test conversation-level proximity and find that speakers are significantly more similar to their partners than to speakers with whom they are not paired in any conversation, and assume that the coordination in the conversation improves over the course of the conversation. De Looze *et al.* (2014) find that the prosodic accommodation changes dynamically over the course of a conversation and across conversations, and that the dynamics inform the naturalness of the conversation flow, the speakers' degree of involvement, and their affinity in the conversation.

Entrainment involves the organizing function in interaction. Prosodic entrainment is found to be realized at turn level, and it supplies cues for turn holding or yielding in the collaborative speaking context. Levitan & Hirschberg (2011) find that at the turn level, all the prosodic parameters examined in their research exhibit proximity and convergence, which indicates that entrainment is a dynamic process of continuous matching at turn exchanges, even in the prosodic feature that does not display conversation-level proximity. Beňuš, Gravano & Hirschberg (2011) have done research on the temporal alignment of turn-initial single words including mm, hm, um, okay, uh, or yeah, in English task-oriented dialogues, and find that the alignment in the prosodic forms is linked to the achievement of pragmatic goals by interlocutors, and that the degree to which temporal and metrical characteristics of interlocutors' speech become similar, and the directionality of this phenomenon is one aspect of turn-taking behavior that signals asymmetrical dominance relationships between the interlocutors.

The prosody in backchannels supplies good evidence for cooperation in interaction. Levitan, Granvano & Hirschberg (2011) have done research on the entrainment in speech preceding backchannels. They examined the pitch, intensity, duration, and voice quality and find that the similar prosodic patterns are used in the partners' backchannels, and that this similarity increases over the course of a dialogue, and that this similarity is associated with measures of dialogue coordination and task success. Backchannels or overlappings demonstrate coordination and adaptation of interlocutors in conversation and show that "conversation is not simply a start-stop interaction, and social interaction is a dynamic and joint activity" (De Looze *et al*. 2014). Prosody in backchannels supplies the evidence of continuous engagement by the interlocutors.

Prosody in entrainment is by nature related to the stance and interpersonal meaning of interaction. According to the definition of prosodic entrainment, prosodic entrainment means speakers adapt prosody to that of their interlocutors in conversation, and become similar in speaking for better smooth and successful communication (Levitan & Hirschberg 2011; Levitan *et al.* 2012). Therefore, the prosody in entrainment show cooperation in conversation, and it illustrates a collaborative stance and attitude.

Prosodic entrainment is important in social interaction. It assists the smooth expression and comprehension, and it reveals the alignment of cognitive, expressive, and comprehensive layers in interaction, by which communication is fulfilled accurately and effectively (Boylan 2004; Parrill & Kimbara 2006; Pickering & Garrod 2004, 2006). In addition, the accommodation in prosody improves interaction by establishing rapport (harmonious relation and mutual attention) and affiliation (Sheperd *et al.* 2001; Lakin & Chartrand 2003; Pickering & Garrod 2006; Tickle-Degnen & Rosenthal 2007; Miles *et al.* 2009; Kopp 2010; Chi-Chun, *et al.* 2010).

Prosodic accommodation varies according to the speakers' social status. For example, the participants having lower social status adapt more to the interlocutors having higher status (Giles *et al.* 1991). According to Speech Accommodation Theory (CAT; Giles *et al.* 1991), the benefits of adapting communication to accommodate others are to increase communication efficiency and gain social approval or shorten desired level of social distance. The interlocutors adapting to their partners have been evaluated more positively than those who do not, in terms of power, attractiveness and intelligence (Gallois & Callan 1988; Giles *et al.* 1991). Pardo (2006) has examined the degree to which interlocutors increased similarity in phonetic performances during conversational interaction, and find that both the role of a participant in the task and the sex of the pair of the talkers affected the degree of convergence. Levitan *et al.* (2012) have accomplished research on the relationship between prosodic entrainment and social behavior, and find that mixed gender pairs entrain more than same gender pairs, and entrainment is more important to the perception of mixed gender pairs than it is for the same gender pairs.

Prosody in entrainment plays crucial roles not only in expressing text/discourse meaning, organizing meaning, and interpersonal meaning but also in psychological and cognitive coordination of conversation. The prosodic entrainment is explained in a psychological model - Interactive Alignment Model. Studies show that prosodic adaptation is a subconscious method of obtaining social approval and acceptance (Matarazzo & Wiens 1967; Giles *et al*. 1991; Chartrand & Bargh 1999). Chartrand & Bargh (1999) point out that "the chameleon effect operates in a passive, non-goal dependent manner to create greater liking and ease of interaction". The social desirability test is adopted by Natale (1975) to study the speakers' prosodic accommodation, and it is found that those who have higher scores in the social desirability are more likely to accommodate their intensity level and timing patterns to those of their partners comparing with those with a low social desirability score.

In the research on human - computer interaction, prosodic entrainment has been proved to be an important aspect of interaction. The users' consistency to a machine increases when it adapts to their prosody (Suzuki & Katagiri 2007). The telephone system adapting its speaking-rate with the users' is evaluated more favorably (Ward & Nakagawa 2002). The prosodic adaptation is found to be such a crucial constituent of social interaction, usually considered as unconscious process, and accomplished automatically in the research of human computer interaction (Oviatt 1996; Coulston *et al*. 2002; Breazeal 2002; Bell *et al*. 2003). In spoken dialogue systems, various language technologies are used to facilitate and enhance human communication, but automatic systems which are able to identify and recreate social cues and behaviors is still a challenge and ongoing process. Therefore, the need of improving the naturalness in human-machine interaction motivates more work in this area. Before machines produce human-like communication, it is necessary to know comprehensively how human beings interact in real life. The present research is a study of this kind.

Since prosody plays such crucial roles in entrainment, how is it realized?

Prosody mainly covers 4 aspects: fundamental frequency, duration, intensity, and voice quality (Crystal 1969; Bolinger 1989; Ladd 1996; Cruttenden 1997). The studies of prosody in entrainment have been accomplished mainly from these 4 aspects.

Adaptation in pitch and intonation contours is found in interlocutors' speaking (Putman & Street 1984; Giles *et al.* 1991; Zebrowitz *et al.* 1992; Gregory *et al.* 1993; Stanford & Webster 1996; Gregory & Dangan 1997; Shepard *et al.* 2001; De Looze *et al.* 2011). The global pitch level (mean F0) adaptation is found in interviews of English in the research of Collins (1998). Pitch level and pitch range (median F0, and sd F0) accommodation is found in task-based conversations (Vaughan 2011; De Looze *et al.* 2011; De Looze & Rauzy 2011). Levitan & Hirschberg (2011) find the global level (conversation level) proximity by the measurement of pitch mean and pitch max, which means speakers are significantly more similar to their partners than to speakers with whom they are not paired in any conversation, and they also find local level (turn level) proximity, which means interlocutors exhibit similar pitch features at turn exchanges.

Adaptation in durational feature is found in interlocutors' speaking (Matarazzo & Wiens 1967; Webb 1972; Welkowitz & Kuc 1973; Street *et al.* 1983; Woodall & Burgoon 1983; Giles *et al.* 1991; Jaffe 2001; McGarva & Warner 2003; Kousidis *et al.* 2009; Edlund *et al.* 2009; De Looze *et al.* 2011). Pause duration of interviewee is found to be directly influenced by those of the interviewer in Matarazzo & Wiens's research (1967). The similar results are found in natural conversations of English and Swedish (Edlund *et al.* 2009; De Looze *et al.* 2011; De Looze & Rauzy 2011). Rhythm accommodation in conversational dyads is found by McGarva & Warner (2003). Levitan & Hirschberg (2011) find the accommodation in Speaking-rate at conversation level and turn level.

Adaptation in features of intensity is found in interlocutors' speaking (Black 1949; Natale 1975; Gregory & Hoyt 1982; Coulston *et al.* 2002; De Looze *et al.* 2011). Mean intensity adaptation is found in English interviews in Natale's research (1975). According to Levitan & Hirschberge (2011), the features of intensity are the most prominent in entrainment at both conversation and turn levels. Other studies also confirm the adaptation in intensity during interaction (Kousidis *et al.* 2009; Heldner *et al.* 2010; Vaughan 2011; De Looze *et al.* 2011; De Looze & Rauzy 2011).

Adaptation in voice quality is also found in interlocutors' speaking.

Levitan and her group (Levitan & Hirschberg 2011; Levitan *et al*. 2012) examined entrainment on voice quality: Jitter, Shimmer, Noise-to-harmonics ratio (NHR). In these researches, jitter describes varying pitch in the voice, and is perceived as a rough sound; shimmer describes fluctuation of loudness in the voice; noise-to-harmonics ratio is associated with perceived hoarseness. The results of the research show that shimmer and NHR exhibit significantly coordination over the course of the conversation.

From what are stated above, we can find that the studies of prosody in entrainment have been accomplished mainly from the 4 aspects of prosody. However, the research on adaptation in the features of fundamental frequency, duration, and intensity is much more than that in the features of voice quality. The present research examines the prosodic features from the former 3 aspects for the sake of relatively sufficient references from the previous studies. More detailed introduction of variables of the present research is supplied in Chapter 3.

1.2 Motivations

The present research aims to explore prosodic entrainment in Chinese conversations, and to make a cross-linguistic comparison of prosodic entrainment between English and Chinese. The motivation of this research comes mainly from 3 aspects.

Firstly, it is worth exploring intensively and extensively how prosody works in Chinese interaction.

Researches on functions of prosody in Chinese has already involved referential meaning of focuses, stresses, intonation of sentences, etc. (Wu 1981; Shen 1989; Shen 1994, 1996; Cao 2006; Jia 2009; Chen & Shi 2011), and organizing meaning of discourse prosody, which is realized over the speaking units larger than sentences in Chinese (Tseng *et al*. 2005; Li *et al*. 2007; Zheng 2010; Yang *et al*. 2011; Zhao *et al*. 2011).

Besides, more and more attention is paid to functions of Chinese prosody in spontaneous speaking. Some studies of prosody in Chinese conversations have been accomplished. Li (2002a) emphasizes the difference of prosodic research between read and spontaneous speech, and proposes C-ToBI as a prosodic labeling system for Chinese prosody; Hu, Xu & Huang (2002) find that a trained statistical model (CART) can identify the prosodic boundary location in Mandarin in their research on the prosodic boundaries in Chinese spontaneous speech corpus (ASCCD); Li (2002b) analyzes the correlation of prosodic parameters in Mandarin conversations under stressed and unstressed conditions respectively for synthesizing Mandarin and automatic prosodic labeling; Xiong (2003) finds that prosodic features of sentence boundaries and their communicative functions correlate with each other closely and prosodic features play important roles in determining the position and the type of sentence boundary by investigating prosodic features of sentence boundaries in a corpus of 973 Chinese telephone conversations; Wang (2005) points out that prosodic prediction, which is a process of prosodic chunking, is one of the major factors for the naturalness of speech synthesis in the analysis of the prosodic chunking of Chinese spontaneous speech; Yu, Huang & Tao (2008) set a Mandarin dialogue prosody model, and develop a prosody generation method for Mandarin dialogue speech synthesis in order to promote applications of text to speech systems.

In addition, interpersonal meaning of prosody in interaction is also studied in Chinese conversations. Various aspects of emotional intonation have been studied (Xu & Cai 2009; Zhong *et al.* 2011); Li (2005) has done an acoustic analysis on friendly speech over a Chinese dialogue corpus and finds that the acoustic patterns of pitch and duration of friendly declarative and interrogative utterances are different from those of the neutral utterances, and that tonal pitch is the most important means for a better expression of friendliness; Li *et al.* (2008) have done research on relationship between gestures and speech in spontaneous Chinese speech, and find that stress expression usually accompanies stronger hand gestures with compensatory hand and head gestures.

All these research on Chinese prosody in interaction are valuable. However, these studies involve only one-side or separated performances of speakers in prosody. The interaction between two sides is worth exploring in conversation. So the functions of prosody in Chinese conversations should be studied further (Liu 2001; Wang 2008; Li & Li 2010). Interlocutors' entrainment in prosody is a research point of this kind. The research on prosodic entrainment involves the two-side adaptation of interlocutors, which is different from the research on one side performances of the speakers in emotional intonation, discourse intonation, parotones, etc. in the previous studies.

Secondly, in the research on prosodic entrainment, more studies in Chinese are needed.

The languages in the previous studies of prosodic entrainment mainly are English (Natale 1975; Gregory & Hoyt 1982; Gregory & Dagan 1997; Levitan & Hirschberg 2011; De Looze *et al.* 2011; Levitan *et al.* 2012; Levitan 2013), and other languages involved are Dutch (Levelt & Kelter 1982), Swedish (Edlund *et al.* 2009), Japanese (De Looze *et al.* 2014), Arabic (Gregory *et al.* 1993), etc.

Different from the languages mentioned above, Chinese is a tone language. Tones are the use of pitch in language to distinguish lexical or grammatical meaning. In Mandarin Chinese, tones are distinguished by their distinctive shape, known as contour, with each tone having a different internal pattern of rising and falling pitch. Besides the function in tones, the features of F0 in Chinese also play their roles in forming intonation and expressing pragmatic meaning in communication. It is quite interesting to ask: How is pitch used to identify lexical meaning and at same time to show pragmatic meanings in interaction? How does Chinese prosody work in entrainment? What are the similarities or differences between Chinese and other types of languages in the use of prosody in entrainment?

Therefore, it is necessary to explore prosodic entrainment in Chinese conversations, and to make a cross-linguistic comparison between Chinese and other languages in order to find the similarities and differences in prosodic entrainment. In the present research, the comparison is accomplished with English.

Thirdly, the improvement in human-computer communication needs the research on prosody in interaction.

Developing automatic systems that can identify and understand social cues is a difficult and ongoing process, because a complete understanding of social, psychological, or linguistic interaction in communication has not been reached. The fine-grained adaptation is needed to improve the naturalness in human-machine interaction. According to Vinciarelli (2009), it is difficult and ongoing process to make automatic dialogue systems capable of recognizing and understanding social cues and behaviors; it is required to do work on the unsolved issues related to social cue extraction, temporal and spatial alignment of extracted data as well as measurement and output representation and interpretation. Before machine produces human-like communication, it is necessary to know comprehensively how human beings interact in life. The present research is one of the studies that explore how prosody works in interlocutors' alignment in Chinese conversation.

1.3 Research Questions

This research focuses on prosodic entrainment in Mandarin Chinese conversations. Three research questions are put forward.

1. How is prosody used to entrain in Mandarin conversation?

The analyses in Chapter 4 are made to answer this question. In this chapter, this question is decomposed into two questions:

Is prosodic entrainment in Mandarin conversation global or local? In Chapter 4, prosodic entrainment is analyzed from the global to the local at three levels, the levels of conversation, turn and tone units. Additionally, at the end of this chapter, cross-level comparisons of the results at these three levels are made in order to find out whether prosodic entrainment in Mandarin conversation is global, local or both, and how prosodic entrainment is made at these levels.

Is prosodic entrainment in Mandarin conversation convergent or constant as time goes on? Different from the static perspective in the the question above, this question focuses on the dynamic entrainment process in conversation. The analyses of entrainment process in Chapter 4 aim to find out whether two interlocutors are more similar when conversation goes on.

2. How do social factors affect prosodic entrainment in Mandarin conversation?

The analyses in Chapter 5 are made to answer this question. Social factors cover various aspects. It is difficult to control simultaneously several social factors in one experiment. This research focuses on two of them: gender and role. Therefore, two kinds of analyses are made in Chapter 5: the analyses of entrainment and gender, and the analyses of entrainment and role.

3. How is prosodic entrainment in Mandarin conversation differ or similar to that in English conversation?

The analyses in Chapter 6 aim to answer this question. The results of analyzing prosodic entrainment in Mandarin conversation in the present research are compared with those in English in previous research. The comparisons of prosodic entrainment between Chinese and English are accomplished mainly over conversational level, turn level, and gender aspects, on which the parallel work is available in these two languages.

1.4 Significance

This is a study of prosodic entrainment in Mandarin conversations. Significance of this research exists mainly in theoretical and practical sides.

Theoretical significance of the present research comes from two aspects.

Firstly, the study of prosodic entrainment in Mandarin conversation verifies and enriches the theoretical construction of entrainment. Chinese has different tone and prosodic systems from other types of languages. How prosody works in Mandarin Chinese verifies theories of entrainment based on the previous researches. In addition, classification of absolute and relative entrainment firstly proposed in the present research enriches the theoretical construction of entrainment. Both absolute and relative entrainment is proved in the prosody of Mandarin Chinese conversations in the present research, in which absolute entrainment is found over global units, and relative entrainment between the relative pitch registers of tones in the conversations of mixed gender pairs. The proposal of two-category entrainment in collaborative communication is beneficial to description and understanding of entrainment process in conversation.

Secondly, the cross linguistic comparisons of prosodic entrainment between Chinese and English are of significance in linguistic typology. From typological viewpoint, Chinese and English are different. It is worthy to do comparison of prosodic entrainment between the two in order to explore whether they have similarities or differences on pragmatic functions of prosody in different types of language. Thus, the present research helps people make deeper understanding of prosodic entrainment in different languages.

Practical significance of the present research comes from two aspects.

At first, strategies and instructions for successful communication can be found based on the results of this research. The prosodic entrainment involves speakers' mutual cooperation and coordination. People can take the prosodic parameters including the features of duration, F0 and intensity, which are analyzed in this study, as effective coordination means, and make appropriate adjustment in communication.

In addition, the results of this study are expected to bring certain benefits in speech synthesis. Making synthesized language as natural as that of human beings is one of the challenges in speech synthesis. Fine-grained adjustment of prosody in entrainment found in this research is of practical significance to improve the synthesized language in communication.

1.5 Structure of the Thesis

This work has 7 chapters.

Chapter 1 is an introduction of this thesis. Key terms are introduced at the beginning of this chapter. The motivations and significance of the present research are presented in this chapter.

Chapter 2 reviews relevant studies. At the beginning of this chapter, theories of entrainment including Communication Accommodation Theory (CAT), The Chameleon Effect, Perception-Behavior Link, and Interactive Alignment Model are introduced. Then, empirical researches on entrainment are reviewed. At the end of this chapter, differences between this study and the previous ones are emphasized.

Chapter 3 supplies detailed descriptions of the corpus and annotation in this research. It includes the experiment description, annotation process, data extraction, etc. In addition, turn identification in conversation is introduced in this chapter, because the analyses of entrainment at turn level need data over turns. The end of this chapter is about variables of this research, data extraction, and turn identification in Mandarin conversations.

Chapter 4 provides the analyses and discussion of entrainment at multiple levels. From the global to the local, prosodic entrainment is analyzed at three levels: the levels of conversation, turns and tone units. Synchronous entrainment between speakers is also analyzed at the levels of turn and tone units in order to find out similarity degree of two speakers in conversation. In addition, dynamic entrainment process is analyzed at these three levels in order to find out whether interlocutors become convergent at certain point of conversation or make constant entrainment till the end of conversation. The analysis of entrainment in the relative pitch registers of the corresponding tones produced by female and male subjects aims to find out whether there is entrainment over tones. Based on these analyses, at the end of this chapter, cross-level comparisons are made from the aspects of proximity, convergence and synchrony.

Chapter 5 provides the analyses of entrainment and social factors. The analyses include two parts: the analyses of entrainment and gender, and the analyses of entrainment and role. In the analyses of gender, two tests are made: the entrainment by gender groups and entrainment degree by gender groups. In the analyses of role, two tests are made: the role influence test and the role direction test.

Chapter 6 provides comparison of prosodic entrainment between Mandarin Chinese and Standard American English. Because the cross-linguistic comparison is made between the present research and the studies based on Columbia Games Corpus, this chapter provides the descriptions of Columbia Games Corpus in order to indicate the parallel of the two corpora and validity of the comparison. The cross-linguistic comparisons are made mainly from 3 aspects: prosodic entrainment at conversation level, turn level, and the relation between prosodic entrainment and gender. It is because the parallel studies from these 3 aspects in Mandarin and English are available.

Chapter 7 is the conclusion of the present research. This chapter supplies the major findings and limitations of this research. The research points for future studies are also mentioned at the end of this chapter.

Chapter 2

Relevant Studies

In this chapter, previous theoretical and empirical studies of entrainment are reviewed, and difference between the present study and the previous ones is emphasized at the end of this chapter.

2.1 Theoretical Research

Entrainment or adaptation in speech is ubiquitous in interaction as it facilitates, through the alignment of cognitive representations, comprehension and understanding between speakers. The theoretical research on entrainment mainly includes Communication Accommodation Theory, The Chameleon Effect, Perception-Behavior Link, and Interactive Alignment Model. All these theories provide influential and convincing explorations for alignment in conversation from the perspectives of sociolinguistics or psycholinguistics.

2.1.1 Communication Accommodation Theory (CAT)

In the theories of entrainment, Communication Accommodation Theory (CAT) is the most influential.

CAT founded by Giles (1973) states that speakers adjust their speech, vocal patterns and gestures to accommodate to their partners in conversation (Turner & West 2010). Various reasons for the facts that individuals emphasize or minimize the social differences between themselves and their interlocutors through verbal and nonverbal communication are supplied in this theory (Gallois *et al*. 2005).

CAT supplies a wide-ranging framework to predict and explain interlocutors' adjustments in creation, maintenance, or decrease of social distance in interaction (Giles & Ogay 2007). This theory explores the different ways in which people accommodate communication, motivations for doing adjustments, and the consequences.

CAT first appeared as Speech Accommodation Theory (SAT) in Giles (1973), which is a study of accent mobility. As a socio-psychological model exploring accent and bilingual shifts in interactions (Giles 1973; Giles, Taylor & Bourhis 1973), CAT becomes an interdisciplinary model of relational and identity processes in communicative interaction (Coupland & Jaworski 1997).

CAT is established on social psychology, especially from four main socio-psychology theories: similarity-attraction, social exchange, causal distribution and intergroup distinctiveness. The similarity-attraction theory points out that the more similar our attitudes and beliefs are to those of others, the more likely it is for them to be attracted to us; the social exchange process theory states that people tend to choose the action which bring greater rewards and less costs; the causal attribution process theory points out that people interpret others' behavior, and evaluate the individuals in terms of the motivations and intentions that people attribute as the cause of their behavior; the process of intergroup distinctiveness theory suggests that when people from different groups are in contact, they compare themselves on dimensions which are important to them, such as personal attributes, abilities, material possession and so on (Giles & Smith 1979). These theories supply the foundation to explain the convergence or divergence in interlocutors' speaking.

According to CAT, the benefits of adapting communication to others are to increase communication efficiency, accommodate the differences in language, ability, culture, etc., and gain social approval or desired level of social distance.

Two main accommodation processes described by this theory: convergence and divergence (Giles *et al*. 1991).

Convergence refers to the strategies through which individuals adapt to each other's communicative behaviors, in order to reduce these social differences. It is a process through which an individual shifts his or her speech patterns in interaction so that they more closely resemble the speech patterns of his interlocutor(S) (Giles & Smith 1979). People can converge through many features of communication such as their use of language, their "pronunciation, pause and utterance lengths, vocal intensities, non verbal behaviors, and intimacy of self disclosures" (Giles & Smith 1979).

Divergence refers to the instances in which individuals accentuate the speech and non-verbal differences between themselves and their interlocutors. This helps to sustain a positive image of one's in-group and hence to strengthen one's social identity. Divergence can thus be a way for members of different groups to maintain their cultural identity, a mean to contrast self images when the other person is considered a member of an undesirable group, and a way to indicate power or status differences (Turner &West 2010).

Some motives are supplied for convergence. An important one is the desire to gain approval from the other. A psychological reason is similarity attraction: The more similar we are to our conversational partner, the more he or she will like or respect us, and the more social rewards we can expect (Byrne 1971). Another motive for convergence is that converging into a common state can improve the effectiveness of communication, increase the predictability of the speaking partner, and hence make lower the uncertainty, interpersonal anxiety (Gudykunst 1995).

Some motives are supplied for divergence, too. One is the desire to emphasize distinctiveness from one's interlocutor. Social Identity Theory (e. g. Tajfel & Turner 1986) supplies the explanation: when speakers communicate with each other, an inter-individual interaction is entirely on the basis of their individual differences in temperament and personality and where their ethnicity, gender, age, etc.

Although the motives for convergence and divergence exist, speakers' converging are generally viewed more favorably than diverging, and are perceived as more efficient in their communication as well as more cooperative (Giles & Ogay 2007). From the perspective of perception, convergence is generally considered as the positive evaluation by receivers (Bourhis *et al.* 1975). For instance, increasing similarity in communicative behavior, such as the Speaking-rate increases in both sides of conversation is perceived attractiveness as well as their ability to gain addressees' compliance (Buller *et al.* 1992).

Therefore, accommodation most often takes the form of convergence, when a speaker chooses a language variety that seems to fit the style of the other speaker. Less frequently, accommodation may take the form of divergence, when a speaker signals social distance or disapproval by using a language variety that differs from the style of the other speaker.

2.1.2 The Chameleon Effect and Perception-Behavior Link

Different from CAT, which proposes speakers intentional and goal-oriented adjustment to converge, maintain, or diverge in interaction, Chartrand & Bargh (1999) put forward the Chameleon Effect in human's communication, that is, people communicate passively and unconsciously reflecting their interlocutors' social behavior like chameleons.

The Chameleon Effect refers to "non-conscious mimicry of the postures, mannerisms, facial expressions, and other behaviors of one's interaction partners, such that one's behavior passively and unintentionally changes to match that of others in one's current social environment" (Chartrand & Bargh 1999).

It is easy to discover in our daily life that one has taken on the accent, speech patterns, and even behavioral mannerisms of one's interaction partners. This process is always considered to be natural and unconscious. It has been proved early that a bi-directional relationship between non-conscious mimicry and liking, rapport, and affiliation of the speakers (Bandura 1977; Galef 1988; Heyes 1993; Chen & Bargh 1997; Chartrand & Bargh 1999). That is to say, affiliation can be conveyed by unconscious mimicry, and non-conscious mimicry creates affiliation. This kind of mimicry has been proved to play an important role in human evolution: initially, mimicry has survival value in helping people in communication; then mimicry has evolved to serve a social function; non-conscious behavioral mimicry produces affiliation, and serves to foster favorable relationship with others (Lakin *et al*. 2003).

Human beings automatically imitate different aspects of interaction patterns, including the speech patterns, facial expressions, emotions, moods, postures, gestures, mannerisms, or even idiosyncratic movements, etc. Studies in these fields are briefly listed below.

People mimic non-consciously the accent (Giles & Powesland 1975; Pardo 2006), rates of speech (Webb 1969, 1972; Levitan *et al*. 2012), and speech rhythms (Cappella & Panalp 1981). We also imitate the facial expressions of other people. Imitation of others' facial expressions can result in actually adopting the emotions and moods of others. For instance, when we see or hear others laugh, we are easy to laugh more than ourselves (Young & Frye 1966), or when we listen to happy or sad persons, we are easy to imitate their tone and take on their mood state (Neumann & Strack 2000).

Studies also prove the interpersonal coordination, which means "degree to which the behaviors in an interaction are nonrandom, patterned, or synchronized in both timing and form" (Bernieri & Rosenthal 1991). Interpersonal coordination can be further divided into interactional synchrony and behavior matching. Interactional synchrony means the rhythm of an interaction is smooth and synchronic (Bernieri *et al*. 1994); behavior matching refers to the tendency to mimic or mirror the behaviors of interactional partners (Bavelas *et al*. 1986).

Perception-behavior link is assumed to be the underlying mechanism for The Chameleon effect. Perception-behavior link means "the unintentional, non-conscious effects of social perception on social behavior" and more illustration about Perception-behavior link comes below (Chartrand *et al*. 2005):

> *Perception and behavior are inextricably intertwined such that people automatically behave as they perceive. The perception of observables may activate specific behavioral representations, trait constructs, or stereotypes. Mimicry is a manifestation of the perception-*

behavior link at its most fundamental level. It is no more than copying another's observables and requires only the ability to perceive the behavior in the other person and the ability to form the behavior oneself.

Dijksterhuis & Bargh (2001) provide the neurological evidence for perception-behavior link. They propose that in the process of thinking, neurological data have also accumulated for a link between the perception of others' behavior and one's own behavior; particularly, and they prove that perceiving someone else engaging in a behavior is neurologically similar to performing that behavior.

Because of the perception-behavior link, people entrain in a variety of ways, including speech, facial expressions, physical mannerisms, moods, emotions, etc. The present research focuses on the prosodic alignment in dialogues.

According to the theories of The Chameleon Effect and Perception-Behavior Link, in the real communication, if it is not an absolute duplication or perfect imitation between speakers, a linked perceptual-productive system might produce convergence. A central phenomenon produced by such approaches is an increase in similarity among linguistic components, which is termed convergence, accumulating common ground, or alignment (Pardo 2006).

2.1.3 Interactive Alignment Model

From psycho-linguistic aspect, Interactive Alignment Model lays the important foundation for the research on entrainment.

Interactive Alignment Model provides an account of psycho-linguistic mechanisms that interlocutors employ in dialogues. Pickering & Garrod (2004) propose this systematic account of dialogue, and assumes that "in dialogue, the linguistic representations employed by the interlocutors become aligned at many levels, as a result of a largely automatic process (p. 169)". This theory helps to generalize the process of production and comprehension in dialogue, one of most natural and basic forms in communication.

The interactive alignment includes mainly six points (Pickering & Garrod

2004 172):

(1) Alignment of situation model forms the basis of successful dialogue.

(2) The way that alignment of situation models is achieved is by a primitive and resource-free priming mechanism.

(3) The same priming mechanism produces alignment at other levels of representation, such as the lexical and syntactic.

(4) Interconnections between the levels mean that alignment at one level leads to alignment at other levels.

(5) Another primitive mechanism allows interlocutors to repair misaligned representations interactively.

(6) More sophisticated and potentially costly strategies that depend on modeling the interlocutor's mental state are only required when the primitive mechanisms fail to produce alignment.

Interactive Alignment Model explains how different levels of representation interact in a dialogue. Figure 2－1 shows how this model works (Pickering & Garrod 2004).

In Figure 2－1, A and B represent two interlocutors in a dialogue. This

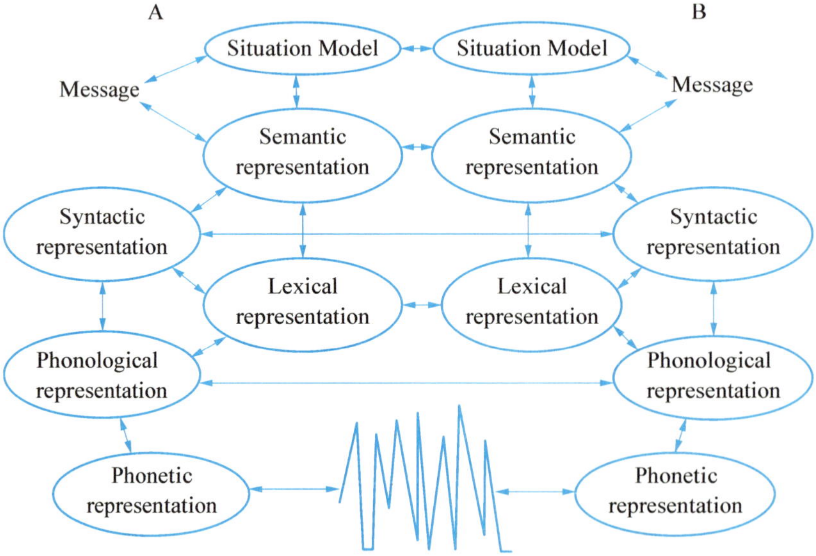

Figure 2－1　Interactive Alignment Model

schematic representation of the stages of comprehension and production processes is used to illustrate the overall architecture in dialogue. A situation model is located at the top, and other levels of linguistic representation are semantic, syntactic, lexical, phonological, and phonetic forms.

According to Pickering & Garrod (2004), alignment of situation model is the basis of successful dialogue. A situation model is a multi-dimensional representation of the situation under discussion (Johnson-Laird 1983). The key dimensions encoded in situation models are space, time, causality, intentionality, and reference to main individuals under discussion (Zwaan & Radvansky 1998). Based on some evidences for alignment of situation models (Garrod & Anderson 1987; Tanenhaus *et al.* 1995; Chambers *et al.* 2002), Pickering & Garrod (2004) assume that successful dialogue involves approximate alignment at the level of the situation model at least, and interlocutors develop aligned situation models.

In addition to the situation model, linguistic elements and structures indicate alignment at other levels. The successful dialogues are produced through the alignment at different levels of language representations.

Several studies supplied evidence for the lexical alignment in dialogue. Garrod & Anderson (1987) demonstrate the alignment of lexical processing in conversation. Studies show that interlocutors tend to develop the similar set of referring expressions to particular object (Clark & Wilkes-Gibbs 1986; Wilkes-Gibbs & Clark 1992; Brennan & Clark 1996).

A series of research provide evidence for the syntactic alignment in dialogue. Levelt & Kelter (1982) find that subjects tend to use consistent syntactic pattern in conversation. Bock (1986) finds that speakers tended to repeat syntactic form. Branigan *et al.* (2000) find that syntactic structure in dialogue is influenced mutually between two interlocutors. The further study of this group finds that syntactic alignment is not restricted between speaker-addressee (Branigan *et al.* 2007). A study of bilingual monologue and dialogue find that the integration of languages in sentence production relied on process of syntactic co-activation between languages and on the processes of alignment between dialogue partners (Kootstra *et al.* 2010).

Alignment is also found at the level of articulation. Fowler & Housum (1987) find that when speakers repeat expressions, articulation becomes reduced (the shortened expressions are the examples). Other studies also find the alignment in phonetic elements and prosodic expressions (Cummins 2009; Levitan & Hirschberge 2011; Levitan *et al*. 2012).

Alignment happens not only at a single level. There is interaction among the alignment from different levels, that is, alignment at one level leads to alignment at other levels. For instance, syntactic alignment is enhanced by lexical overlap, that is, syntactic alignment is considerably enhanced if the verb is repeated (Brannigan *et al*. 2000); syntactic alignment is enhanced by semantic overlap (Cleland *et al*. 2002). Cleland & Pickering (2003) find that the exact repetition at one level is not required, but if the relationship at one level is closer, the tendency to align at the other level is stronger. According to Pickering & Garrod (2004), speakers intend to align expressions at different levels simultaneously; when all the levels are entrained, speakers will repeat each others' expressions in the same way, for example, with the same intonation.

Interactive Alignment Model supplies an account for the alignment in dialogues. This model assumes that the linguistic representations used by speakers become aligned at levels, that the alignment at one level contributes to the alignment at other levels, and that the alignment at all the linguistic levels makes the state of speakers of conversation similar, which produces smooth and successful communication.

For the underlying mechanism of alignment, based on Interactive Alignment Model, Pickering & Garrod (2004) propose that alignment is unconscious, that is, interlocutors may be almost entirely unaware that alignment has taken place.

Is alignment intentional or unconscious in conversation? The theories viewed in this section seem to stand in two sides for this question. CAT proposes goal-oriented mechanism, while on the other side, The Chameleon Effect, Perception-Behavior Link, and Interactive Alignment Model support unmediated mechanism. However, some other scholars propose the coexistence of both, and interlocutors make balance between these two mechanisms in different communicative contexts. Branign, *et al.* (2010) point out that alignment in a particular context may have both unmediated and mediated components. Haywood *et al.* (2005) propose that unmediated alignment might occur alongside mediated alignment designed to enhance communicative effectiveness.

Although there are differences in the view of underlying mechanism for alignment in conversation, all these theories mentioned above have made influential contributions for the explanations of interlocutors' alignment, among which two points form solid foundation for the present research.

One point is the existence of entrainment in communication. Although the explanations come from different perspectives, agreement can be made on the existence of entrainment in communication among the theories mentioned above (CAT, The Chameleon Effect, Perception-Behavior Link, and Interactive Alignment Model). Based on this agreement, the present research aims to find out how prosodic entrainment is made in Mandarin conversation. The findings of this research are expected to confirm the existence of convergence in interaction from aspect of prosody, and to help people make deeper understanding of entrainment in communication.

The other is the multilevel exhibition of entrainment. The main claim Interactive Alignment Model has made is that interlocutors' alignment in conversation is realized at various levels of linguistic representations. According to this model, as one of linguistic representations, prosody is bound to exhibit alignment. Therefore, it is valid to do research on alignment at prosodic level. As one research in this kind, the present research focuses on interlocutors' alignment at this level, and aims to find out how people entrain by prosody in communication.

2.2 Empirical Research

The previous empirical researches are reviewed mainly from two aspects: the studies of entrainment over various language components, and pragmatic functions of entrainment.

2.2.1 Studies of Entrainment over Language Components

Motivated by the theories claiming entrainment's realization at various language representations, some studies have explored entrainment over different language components.

Lexical entrainment has been studied. There extensive evidence for alignment in word choice. Garrod & Anderson (1987) find that interlocutors use the same referring expressions, and they tend to interpret words in the same way when subjects did a cooperative maze game. Brennan & Clark (1996) find that directors and matchers prefer to use subordinate-level terms (eg., pennyloafer) rather than basic-level terms (eg., shoe) in card games, in which directors describe a set of cards depicting common objects to matchers so that they could reconstruct the directors' array. An explanation for lexical entrainment in this research is that interlocutors negotiate a given conceptualization or achieve conceptual pacts in referring an object. In the experiment following up, Metzing & Brennan (2003) show that when partners are changed and conceptual pact is broken by new referring expressions to refer to a previously discussed object, subjects experienced difficulty in locating the objects. Similarly, Horton & Gerrig (2005) find such partner-specific effects, and suggest interlocutors represent as a conjoined cue information about linguistic expressions and the person with whom the expressions is used, so that the presence of that particular interlocutor activates that expression.

Entrainment has been studied at syntactic level. Levelt & Kelter (1982) find alignment in syntactic structure between interlocutors in the study over telephone conversations. For instance, interlocutors tend to say *At 5 o'clock as the answer to At what time does your shop close? and tend to say 5 o'clock as the answer to What time does your shop close?* Garrod & Anderson (1987) find coordination in syntactic structure between partners in conversation in the study of the cooperative maze games. They find that participants tend to align on the same sentence structure, although there are various methods to describe their positions to each other. For example, one subject said: "I am two along, four up," and the partner tended to say, "I am one along, five up." When this player changed to say, "I am at B4", the partner tended to say, "I am at A5." The subjects tended to coordinate the sentence structure rather than specific words. Branigan *et al.* (2000) find that syntactic structure of a subject's utterance is influenced by that of a confederate's previous utterance in the study of card games. Reitter *et al.* (2010) find that interlocutors are more likely to use a given syntactic rule soon after their partners have used that rule in the study of the task-oriented conversations. Alignments in the syntactic representations are also found in bilinguals' conversation (Hartsuiker *et al.* 2004). Strong evidence for alignments in syntactic structure is found in other studies (Cleland & Pickering 2003; Haywood *et al.* 2005).

Entrainment has been studied at acoustic-prosodic level.

The earlier studies of prosodic entrainment are concerned with one or two aspects of prosody separately. Matarazzo & Wiens (1967) focus on adaptation (increasing or decreasing) in silence duration of an interviewer according to an interviewee's response time latency. Natale (1975) finds that subjects entrained to new intensity level when they were engaged in open-ended conversation from within-conversation intensity levels, and this entrainment increased over the course of a conversation. Street (1984) finds that interviewees converged towards their interviewers on response latency and speech-rate. Similarly, Giles *et al.* (1991) find that interlocutors tend to align on speech rate. Gregory *et al.* (1993) find by the measurement of pitch and intensity that similarity is greater in true conversations than in conversations simulated by splicing together utterances from speakers who do not actually interact. Ward & Litman (2007) find by the measurement of loudness and pitch through regression lines that students in tutorial dialogues converged to their tutor on max and mean amplitude and diverged on min pitch.

For instance, speakers are proved to converge in Speaking-rate (Giles *et al.* 1991), subvocal frequency or amplitude contour (Gregory 1990), vocal intensity (Natale 1975), etc. over longer speaking. Different from these studies, the present research has accomplished relatively comprehensive analyses of convergence in prosody, which involve main features of duration, fundamental frequency and intensity.

The recent researches involve relatively comprehensive and thorough aspects of prosody. Levitan & Hirschberg (2011) investigate four acoustic and prosodic dimensions (including 8 features from the duration, fundamental frequency, intensity, and voice quality) in the research on entrainment at multiple levels. In this research, they find the difference in speakers' coordination with each other in these dimensions over the conversation as a whole as well as on a turn-by-turn basis, and they find the coordination between interlocutors improve in the course of the conversation over certain prosodic features. De Looze *et al.* (2014) measure three prosodic parameters including pitch range, voice intensity and articulation rate. In this research, they propose an automatic system for the capture of dynamic manifestation in prosodic entrainment, and they find that prosodic accommodation changes dynamically over the course of a conversation and across conversations, and that these dynamics inform about the naturalness of the conversation flow, the speakers' degree of involvement and their affinity in the conversation.

Other language components are also involved in the studies of entrainment. Speech preceding backchannels are evidence of continued engagement by one's dialogue partner. Levitan *et al.* (2011) examine the backchannels in the Columbia Games Corpus and find that speaking partners tend to use similar sets of backchannels, and that the similarity increases over the course of a dialogue. Filled pauses such as *uh* or *um* seem ideal candidates for studying performances of language in communication because they are frequently used in spontaneous conversations, they are low information load, and they are subject to accommodation to the interlocutors (Beňuš, 2009). Beňuš *et al.* (2012) investigate immediately adjacent filled pauses produced by justices and lawyers during oral arguments of the Supreme Court. They find that lawyers' filled pauses are more similar to those of the justices who voted for them and to those of the justices who voted against them.

2.2.2 Studies of Entrainment and Its Pragmatic Functions

Some studies have explored the relationship between entrainment and its pragmatic functions.

Some studies have explored the relation between entrainment and task success. Reitter & Moor (2007) find that task success can be predicted by lexical and syntactic entrainment in just five minutes of an interaction in the Map Task Corpus. In their recent research, Reitter & Moor (2014) has accomplished deeper study of entrainment and task success. They develop two predictions from The Interactive Alignment Model, and use two methods to quantify the known structural priming effects in the full inventory of syntactic choices. In this research, they find a positive correlation of long-term adaptation and a quantifiable task success measure, and propose that lexical and syntactic repetition are reliable and computationally exploitable predictors of task success. Nenkova *et al*. (2008) find that there is significant correlation between the degree of entrainment on high-frequency words and affirmative cues words and game score in the Columbia Games Corpus, and that such entrainment is significantly correlated to dialogue naturalness and smooth interaction flow. Friedberg *et al*. (2012) find that the students who exhibited high level of alignment in the use of project-related words became more similar after the experiments, while those who exhibited low level tended to become less familiar. Levitan *et al*. (2012) have examined acoustic/prosodic entrainment in Columbia Games Corpus according to four objective measures of dialogue success: the mean latency between turns, the percentage of turns that are interruptions, the percentage of turns that are overlaps and the number of turns in a task. The results that latency is negatively correlated with entrainment and overlaps and the number of turns are positively correlated prove that entrainment is highly related to task success. Thomason *et al*. (2013) show that the students who exhibited higher degree of entrainment on pitch features gained higher scores in tests of a tutoring dialogue system.

Some studies are concerned with entrainment and interaction outcome. Niederhoffer & Pennebaker (2002) consider the relationship between Linguistic Style Matching (LSM), the degree to which participants in conversation match each other in the use of word categories representing a variety of psychological and linguistic dimensions, and interaction outcome.

They compare speakers' scores over 18 linguistic dimensions of language and find that in all cases, interlocutors exhibit significant LSM on both conversational level and a turn-by-turn level. Similarly, Taylor & Thomas (2008) have accomplished the research on Linguistic Style Matching (LSM) and Negotiation outcome. Correlational analyses over 18 linguistic categories in the negotiations between police negotiators and hostage takers show that successful negotiations are associated with higher aggregate levels of LSM than unsuccessful negotiations. Ireland *et al.* (2011) have investigated whether similarity in interlocutors' use of function words (LSM) predicts outcomes for romantic relationships. On the basis of the analyses in two experiments, they find that LSM appears to reflect implicit interpersonal processes central to romantic relationships. Levitan *et al.* (2012) has examined the relation between entrainment and social behaviors. Four parameters (including *gives encouragement*, *conversation awkward*, *trying to be liked*, and *like more*) are set as variables for social behaviors. Through the correlation analyses, they find that entrainment is correlated with the most social variables for female-male pairs, and these correlations are also the strongest. Lee *et al.* (2014) has done a research on prosodic entrainment in affective spontaneous spoken interactions of married couples. They quantify prosodic entrainment (one of aspects of interaction synchrony), especially over pitch and energy, in married couples' problem-solving interactions. A statistical testing in this research shows that higher values in entrainment over the features indicate highly positive affect, and these features are proposed to be effective predictors of session-level annotation on positive or negative affect.

Some studies are concerned with entrainment and social factors. The studies of entrainment and gender in dialogue are in relatively bigger number. Several theories of entrainment predict that females will entrain to a greater degree than males. The male dominance hypothesis (Bilous & Krauss 1988) asserts that differences in speech between males and females can be attributed to women's subordinate social status. Speech Accommodation Theory (Giles *et al.* 1987) claims that when a power imbalance exists between interlocutors, the less dominant or powerful speaker will converge more. Chartrand & Bargh

(1999) posits that the perception-behavior link is the mechanism behind entrainment, and thus, women should entrain more than men, regardless of the gender of their conversational partner, because women are known to have greater perceptual sensitivity to vocal characteristics. Namy, Nygaard & Sauerteig (2002) explain that female speakers are perceived to accommodate more in a shadowing task than male speakers in this way. Pardo (2006), on the other hand, finds that female pairs are less similar to each other than male pairs, and that functions outside the domain of perception appear to influence the degree of phonetic convergence. In English conversations, Levitan and her group finds (Levitan *et al.* 2012) that female-male pairs entrain on every prosodic feature examined; in addition, the degree of entrainment on Intensity mean and max is greatest for female-male pairs. Male pairs show the least evidence of entrainment, entraining only on Intensity mean, Intensity max, and syllables per second. All these results support the hypothesis that entrainment is less prevalent among males. Their degree of entrainment on these features is also lower than that displayed by female or mixed gender pairs. Female pairs entrain on all features except pitch mean, pitch max, and jitter.

In the study of entrainment and social dominance in dialogue, Worgan & Moore (2011) proposes that social dominance can be understood as an interaction affordance, revealing action potentials for each signaling participant, and can be detected as a feature of rapport not of the individual. This study finds that speakers adjust their speech to match the current dominant individual.

Some studies investigate the relation between entrainment and role in dialogue. Motivated by the hypothesis of *audience design* (Bell 1984), which means speakers might choose to use expressions that they believe will enhance communicative success, entrainment has been explored between speaker and addressee. Galati & Brenna (2010) have explored to what extent speakers adapt to their addressee. They find lexically identical expressions by the same speaker are more intelligible to another group of listeners when the expressions have been addresses to new addressees than when they had been addressed to old addressees, and they conclude that speakers' entrainment in spontaneous discourse is driven as least in part by addressees. Relative studies also involve the conversations with more than two participants. Branigan *et al.* (2007) have investigated whether the linguistic behavior of participants in a dialogue is affected by their role within that interaction by three experiments. This study finds that syntactic alignment is not limited to speaker addressee dyads, and that the prior participant role of the current speaker affected alignment, that is, prior addressees aligned more than prior side-participants.

2.3 Differences Between the Present Study and the Previous Ones

These theoretical and empirical studies in literature supply solid foundation and sufficient references for the present study. As an empirical study on entrainment, the present research not only revisits some dimensions and measurements which have been investigated in previous studies in order to make the analyses in the consistent frameworks, but also explores several new dimensions. The differences between this study and the previous ones are listed in this section.

Firstly, the research of prosodic entrainment is located in Mandarin conversation.

In previous studies of entrainment, the languages involved mainly are English (Natale 1975; Gregory & Hoyt 1982; Gregory & Dagan 1997; Levitan & Hirschberg 2011; De Looze *et al.* 2011; Levitan *et al.* 2012; Levitan 2013), and other languages involved are Dutch (Levelt & Kelter 1982), Swedish (Edlund *et al.* 2009), Japanese (De Looze *et al.* 2014), Arabic (Gregory *et al.* 1993), etc.

Different from the languages mentioned above, Chinese is a tone language, which has special tone and prosodic systems. The present research analyzes prosodic entrainment in Mandarin conversations at the levels of conversation, turn and tone units in Chapter 4. Here, the analyses over tone units are new measurements compared with the previous ones. Based on the analyses at these three levels, cross-level comparisons are made in order to find out the similarities and differences in prosodic entrainment from the global to the local. These cross-level comparisons are also new measurements.

Secondly, cross-linguistic comparison has been made between Mandarin and English.

In Chinese, the features of F0 play their roles in forming tones, intonation and expressing pragmatic meaning in communication. It is interesting to ask: What are the similarities or differences between Chinese and other types of languages in the use of prosody in entrainment?

In Chapter 6, the present research makes cross-linguistic comparisons of prosodic entrainment between Mandarin and English. The cross-linguistic comparisons are made over the parallel work of these two languages. In the researches of entrainment, some involve more than one language, but they are different cross-linguistic analyses. For example, the study of entrainment has been accomplished over the conversations of bilinguals (Sancier & Fowler 1997; Hartsuiker *et al.* 2004; Kooststra *et al.* 2010), or between native speakers and second language learners (Ferguson 1975; Bortfeld & Brennan 1997).

Thirdly, parameters investigated in this research are different from those in previous research.

The present research focuses on prosody in entrainment in Mandarin conversations. The present research follows the line of the previous studies, which are concerned with relatively comprehensive aspects of prosody, and aims to explore the performances of prosody thoroughly. But there are some differences in the choice of parameters in this research.

Seven variables are set in the analyses of Tongji Games Corpus in this study. These parameters come from three main aspect of prosody, including the feature of duration (Speaking-rate), the features of F0 (F0 min, F0 mean, F0 max), and the features of intensity (Intensity min, Intensity mean and Intensity max). Differently, some relative studies (Levitan & Hirschberg 2011, Levitan *et al.* 2012) set 8 variables in the analyses including four aspects prosodic parameters: the feature of duration (Speaking-rate), the features of F0 (F0 mean, F0 max), the features of intensity (Intensity mean, Intensity max) and the features of voice quality (jitter, shimmer, noise-to-harmonics ratio).

The most noticeable difference is the exclusion of the voice quality features from parameters in the present research. The main reason is that entrainment in the features of voice quality is found not prominent compared with other features (Levitan & Hirschberg 2011, Levitan *et al.* 2012). In addition, the parameters in the features of duration, F0 and intensity are increased. The reason for this increase is that duration, F0 and intensity are considered as the main 3 aspects of prosody. The present research focuses on these core features and aims to make a relatively comprehensive and thorough study.

Fourthly, new measurements have been made on the relationship between roles and entrainment.

Different from the analyses in relevant studies, which are accomplished between speakers and addressees according to the hypothesis of *audience design* (Bell 1984) or between speakers and side participants in group conversation, the present research has examine the entrainment between information givers and information followers. In Chapter 5, Role influence test is made to examine whether there is prosodic entrainment between information givers and information followers, based on which, Role direction test is made to find out the direction of entrainment between them, that is, whether information givers entrain to information followers, or followers entrain to givers.

Chapter 3

Corpus and Annotation

The present research explores prosodic entrainment in Chinese conversations. All the analyses of Chinese prosodic entrainment are conducted on the Tongji Games Corpus. The introduction of Tongji Games Corpus emphasizes the controls in experiments, including gender groups' control, roles control, and the control of tone units in carrier sentences.

Besides the introduction of the corpus, this chapter describes in detail the annotation work of this research including IPU segmentation, annotation in Praat, the calculation of weighted averages of IPUs, turn identification, etc.

Three main aspects of entrainment (proximity, convergence and synchrony) are introduced at the end of this chapter. Most of the analyses in Chapter 4, 5 and 6 are accomplished from these aspects.

3.1 Tongji Games Corpus

3.1.1 Subjects

This research aims to explore how prosody works in entrainment in Chinese conversations. The analyses of prosody in interaction are based on spontaneous conversations. Therefore, spontaneous speech was elicited from the subjects using computer games. The conversations in the games are recorded as the corpus for the present research.

According to Section 2.1, prosodic entrainment is related to the social status of the interlocutors. Because the age and background are not the variables of interest in the present research, these variables were controlled by the recruitment process. All the subjects are undergraduate students in grade two or three, so they are of similar age and background. Subjects are randomly selected from the students in Jiangsu Normal University with a National Mandarin Test Certificate Level 2, with a grade of A or above. The requirements in the subjects' proficiency is to increase the likelihood that the Mandarin spoken in the corpus is standard, and reduce the influence of Chinese dialects in prosody, because the people who are granted National Mandarin Test Certificate Level 2, with a grade of A or above, can speak Mandarin without the accent of dialects. The interlocutors in the games are strangers, that is, they never have communication before the games. Thus, there is not mutual influence in speaking between every pair in conversation before experiments. All the subjects formed 70 pairs, of which there are 23 female and female pairs, 30 female and male pairs, and 17 male and male pairs.

3.1.2 Facilities and Settings

The recording of the corpus was accomplished in a sound-proof booth in Jiangsu Normal University. During the experiments, the two interlocutors faced two computers, and played the games presented on the screens. There was a curtain between them, so neither could see the other's facial expressions or body movements in order to reduce the facial and gestures' aid in entrainment, thus the function of prosody became prominent. Every speaker wore a head microphone (Sennheiser, PC166), and their conversations were recorded by another computer with Cool Edit (Pro. 2.0). The parameters in Cool Edit were set as 44,100 Hz, 16, single track. It took 9 days for data recording from March 14 to 22 in 2013. In the course of games, nobody interrupted the subjects. They accomplished free conversations. The conversations stopped whenever subjects finished the task in the game.

Subjects were told to play games only. They did not know the research purpose.

3.1.3 Games

Two games were used to elicit spontaneous conversations in the experiments.

One is Picture Ordering Game, and the other is Picturing Classifying Game. The common feature of these two games is that there is cooperation between interlocutors in conversation. These cooperative games elicited the collaborative conversations, because in the present research it is assumed that entrainment in collaborative conversations is prominent.

In Picture Ordering Games, one subject played as the information giver, and the other subject played as the information follower. The information giver's screen displayed 18 cards in the correct order (Appendix A); the information follower's screen displayed the same 18 cards but in the incorrect order (Appendix B). The information giver instructed the information follower to put the 18 cards in correct order. 18 pictures were labeled by the numbers. The Picture Ordering Game started from the picture numbered as 1, continued to the picture numbered as 2, 3 ... and ended by the picture numbered as 18. When the task was completed, the same pair switched roles and accomplished the picture ordering game again, in which the previous information giver played as the information follower, and the previous follower as the giver.

In Picture Classifying Game, what is presented on the screens of computers for the two interlocutors are the same (the same 18 pictures in the same order, Appendix C, D). Each pair accomplished attributive classification over 18 pictures. Interlocutors had discussion, reached agreement on the common attributes they found for the pictures, and grouped the pictures with the common attributes together. Every picture was assigned to a category by the common attributes accepted by both of the interlocutors. The classification also started from the picture numbered as 1, continued to the picture numbered as 2, 3 ... and ended by the picture numbered as 18.

In both of the games (Picture Ordering Game and Picture Classifying Game), subjects took the same order in the operation of the pictures (ordering or classifying pictures): from the pictures numbered as 1, 2, 3 ... to the pictures numbered as 18. Therefore, all the conversations can be cut into parallel 18 sections, in which the object of operation is the same picture, although the operation of the pictures is in two kinds. The analyses over 18 sections are introduced in Chapter 4. In addition, the consistency in the operation order of the 18 pictures in two games made the comparisons over every picture in two games valid. The analyses are introduced in Chapter 7.

3.1.4 Gender Groups Control

Three gender groups were set in this study: female and female groups, male and male groups, female and male groups. All the subjects formed 70 pairs, of which there are 23 female and female pairs, 17 male and male pairs, and 30 female and male pairs. A series of analyses over prosodic entrainment and gender in Chapter 7 are based on the conversations produced by these gender groups.

3.1.5 Roles Control

Two types of roles are controlled in this research: unequal roles (information giver and information follower in Picture Ordering Games), and equal roles (the equal roles in the Picture Classifying Games). The effect of unequal roles on prosodic entrainment was analyzed in Chapter 7 by the comparisons with the effect of equal roles in the Role Effect Test. In addition, for the unequal roles, the entrainment direction was also analyzed to find out whether information givers entrain more to followers, or followers entrain more to givers.

3.1.6 Tone Units in Carrier Sentences

One of the analyses in the present research is to analyze the prosodic entrainment over tone units. In order to make the analyses over tone units valid, it is necessary to put the target tone units in carrier sentences, which supply the same environments for tone units and then make the comparisons over tone units valid. All the tone units in the present research are carried by bi-syllabic words, and both syllables carry Tone 1. The details of carrier sentences and bi-syllabic words are introduced in the following sections.

1. Carrier sentences

The carrier sentence is "下一个图标是××" (the next picture is ××). For the first and last of the 18 pictures, little modification is made for the carrier sentences, which still can supply similar environment to other carrier sentences. The carrier sentence for the first picture is "第一个图标是××" (the first picture is ××), and that for the last picture is "最后一个图标是××" (the last picture is ××).

Both subjects in conversation were asked to say the carrier sentences as the beginning of the operation of every picture for both the picture ordering and picture classifying games. After speaking the carrier sentences, the two interlocutors engaged in unstructured conversation in order to order or classify the picture. Since in both games, the operation of the pictures followed the same order from the picture 1 to the picture 18, the order of carrier sentences is the same. So the order of tone units is the same, which make the comparisons over corresponding tone units valid. The details are provided in Chapter 6.

2. Tone units

In the present research, tones units are restricted to the tones combination over bi-syllabic words. Why are the bi-syllabic words used? It is because in the formation of the Chinese words, about 80% are bi-syllabic (Liu & Liang 1990). That is, the tones of bi-syllabic words have the main proportion of Chinese tones (Kong 2001).

The present research restricted the tone combination in the bi-syllabic words to tone 1 plus tone 1. Why is the combination of tone1 used? The reason is to simplify the analyses of tones combinations in the present research. There are 4 tones in Mandarin, which produces 16 combinations of two tones, and a series of complicated tone sandhis. If the 18 target tone units carry different tones, it would be difficult to identify whether the significant differences found over these tones are caused by prosodic entrainment or the difference in tones combination. That is, it is difficult to control the interference caused by the difference in tones combination in the analyses of entrainment.

In the present research, tone units are designed in the carrier sentences, which supply same environment for the tone units and make the analyses over them valid. As shown in Appendix A to D, the target tone units carried by 18 bi-syllabic words are: shūbāo, fēijī, shātān, huādēng, wūguī, shānpō, sījī, xiānhuā, xīguā, shāfā, shānfēng, xiāngcūn, qīngwā, kāfēi, gōngjī, yīshēng, yāhuā, jūnguān. These words are designed as the names of pictures, and all the 18 pictures are labelled by sequence numbers from 1 to 18. In both Picture Ordering Games and Picture Classifying games, the operation of the pictures followed the same order from the picture numbered 1 to the picture numbered 18.

The exact matching of different tones combinations or tone sandhis could be the research points for the future studies. If the purpose is to make the prosodic entrainment over all combinations of tones and a series of tone sandhis in Mandarin conversation clear, there should be more fine-grained experiments.

3.1.7 Corpus Description

The corpus of the present research elicited by two games contains approximately 12 hours of spontaneous, task-oriented conversations between pairs of subjects. 70 pairs participated in the experiments, among which 17 pairs played the Picture Ordering game; 39 pairs played the Picture Classifying game, and 14 pairs played both. All the subjects produced 115 conversations (the pairs in Picture Ordering Game produced two conversations). The average duration of conversation is 6 minutes. The analyses of the present research were based on the conversations produced by the 70 pairs.

3.2 Annotation

The annotation work is the basis for the statistic analyses in the next step. The annotation work in the present research includes mainly 6 parts: IPU segmentation, labelling in Praat, modification of pitch, extraction of data, calculation of weighted averages, and turn identification.

3.2.1 IPU Segmentation

This section focuses on the IPU segmentation. The reasons for choosing

IPU as the minimal unit in analyses are introduced first. Then, how to set the threshold of pauses between IPUs is explained. Finally, a tool, SPPAS, used for automatic IPU segmentation in the present research is introduced.

1. IPU as the minimal unit

What is a minimal unit for the analyses of prosodic entrainment? It could be a whole conversation, the grammatical units, the turn unit or others. But these units are not suitable for the present research. The reasons are: (i) these units are too general. If the minimal unit is chosen as one conversation, or one turn in the present research, the prosodic performances over conversations or turns would be described, but the prosodic performances within turns would be ignored. Thus, the prosody in entrainment will not be depicted thoroughly; (ii) the present research focuses on the prosodic performances in entrainment instead of the grammatical factors in conversations, and choosing grammatical unit as the minimal analysis unit will make the investigation more complicated and will divert the researching focus.

IPU (Inter-Pausal Unit) is the stretch of a single speaker's speech bounded by pauses (for example 100 ms). It is a minimal unit frequently used in the analyses of conversations. Koiso *et al.* (1998) utilized Inter-Pausal Units (IPUs) as the minimal units in the research of intonation in the turn taking in Japanese. Casper (2003) also employed this unit in studying local speech melody in turn taking system in Dutch. Levitan & Hirschberg (2011), Levitan *et al.* (2012) annotated the conversations by IPUs (pause-free units of speech from a single speaker separated from one another by at least 50 ms) in the study of prosodic entrainment in English.

IPUs are adopted as the minimal units in present study for three reasons. Firstly, these units can be determined objectively. The precise duration of pauses made the boundary of IPUs clear. Secondly, one IPU is not larger than one turn. IPUs may occur within turns or at turn transitions. Thus, the prosodic features can be described thoroughly by cutting the corpus into small IPUs. Thirdly, these units eliminate syntactic interference, and make the role of intonation prominent. The identification of IPUs is made by the pauses rather than the grammatical positions in sentences.

2. Threshold of IPU segmentation

IPUs are set as the minimal units in analysis. IPU (Inter-Pausal Unit) is the stretch of a single speaker's speech bounded by pauses. Then an important question arises: how long is the threshold of pause between IPU for the present research? Casper (2003) set the threshold of pause in IPU as 100 ms in her research. Levitan & Hirschberg (2011), Levitan *et al.* (2012) set the threshold as 50 ms.

About setting the threshold of IPUs, the previous studies point out that the threshold can't be too big, because the longer pause in IPUs would cause the omission of the IPUs with shorter pauses, and the prosodic descriptions would be ignored; the threshold can't be too small, because it would be difficult to distinguish the real pause and the stop gap within segments, including plosives, affricatives, etc. So the threshold should be between these two extremes. It should be as small as possible, but it should be longer than the maximal stop gap of segments. Therefore, the threshold of IPUs is the maximal stop gap of segments in the corpus.

How do we find the maximal stop gap of segments in the corpus? Shih & Ao (1997) pointed out that in Chinese stop gaps of plosives were longer than those of affricatives, and that the stop gaps of plosives at the word initial position was longer than those at other positions of word. The study of Chen & Bao (2003) confirmed these findings. Therefore, the maximal stop gaps of segments could be found in the plosives, especially at the word initial position in Chinese conversations.

Thus, to find the threshold of IPUs is to find the maximal stop gap of plosives at the word initial position in Chinese conversations of this corpus. This method was carried out in several steps in the present research. The first step was to choose at random the recordings from 6 female and 6 male subjects. The second step was to find the stop gaps of plosives including [p^h], [p], [t^h], [t], [k^h], [k] at the word initial positions in these 12 recordings. The third step was to measure the durations of these stop gaps. The fourth step was to calculate the maximal stop gap.

The data in calculation is listed in the following tables.

Table 3-1 Durations (ms) of stop gap for $[p^h]$

Gender	Duration of stop gap in $[p^h]$													Average
male	60	55	65	22	35	60	78	64						
female	43	65	58	73										
average														56.5

Table 3-2 Durations (ms) of stop gap for [p]

Gender	Duration of stop gap in [p]														Average
male	68	70	57	61	69	81	51	65	66						
female	82	80	63	104	76	65	55	107	72	68	75	63	86	123	
average															74.2

Table 3-3 Durations (ms) of stop gap for $[t^h]$

Gender	Duration of stop gap in $[t^h]$																		Average
male	50	33	35	42	53	50	38	43	55	38	45	24	31	48	55	38	54	59	
	52	44	71	54	70	55	64	60	62	52	52	65	62	55	39	44	75	55	
	53	65	60	31	54	45	45	48	54	34	43	52	45	33	44	60	59		
female	57	55	64	38	62	55	57	42	60	44	61	65	59	65	78	85	64	44	
	62	77	54	49	75	48	54	56	48	97	46	45	57	60	85				
average																			53.7

Table 3-4 Durations (ms) of stop gap for [t]

Gender	Duration of stop gap in [t]													Average
male	42	34	62	99	84	82	62	88	63	40	55	55	109	
female	35	78	40	68	33	61	61	82	49	45	62			
average														53.7

Table 3 - 5　　Durations (ms) of stop gap for [k^h]

Gender	Duration of stop gap in [k^h]													Average
male	78	55												
female	45	50	76											
average														61

Table 3 - 6　　Durations (ms) of stop gap for [k]

Gender	Duration of stop gap in [k]													Average
male	89	41	69	63	35	54	107	68	50	44	55	54	70	
	32	36	65											
female	55	77	62	57	52	43	70	60	93	79	77			
average														61.4

From Table 3 - 1 to Table 3 - 6, the averages of stop gap's duration in [p^h], [p], [t^h], [t], [k^h], [k] are 56.5 ms, 74.2 ms, 53.7 ms, 62 ms, 61 ms, and 61.4 ms. The maximum is 74.2 ms, and the present research set the closest integer value as 80 ms. Therefore, the threshold of IPU segmentation in the present research is set as 80 ms.

According to the calculation above, the threshold for IPUs of the present research is 80 ms. However, one point should be mentioned. This threshold is an average according to the calculation above, which supplies reference to identify the boundaries of IPUs. In the corpus of this research, it is still possible to find out pauses shorter than 80 ms and stop gaps longer than 80 ms. Therefore, it is still necessary to check whether the pauses identified by SPPAS automatically are real pauses or parts of plosives. A check on IPUs' boundaries is one of tasks in the annotation work of the present study, which was accomplished by professional annotators.

3. IPU segmentation by SPPAS

IPU segmentation of the present study is accomplished in two steps. The first step is automatic labelling by SPPAS (Bigi & Hirst 2012). The second step is the check of IPUs' boundaries in Praat.

SPPAS is a tool to produce automatically annotations from a recorded speech sound and its transcription. The whole procedure is a succession of automatic steps. Result is a set of TextGrid files, which can be used in Praat for further annotation. It is open source software issued under the GNC Public License, and produced by Laboratoire Parole et Language of Aix-en-Provence in France.

IPU segmentation is one of SPPAS' functions, and the other 5 functions are Momel and INTSINT, Tokenization, Phonetization, Alignment, and Syllabification. The interface of IPU segmentation supplies the space to set the parameters for IPU segmentation. As Figure 2 shows, several parameters should be set before the running SPPAS, among which the most important one is the minimum silence of duration. Since the threshold of pauses for IPU segmentation of the present research was calculated to be 80 ms, the minimum silence of duration is set as 80. The interface of IPU segmentation is showed as follows in Figure 3 - 1.

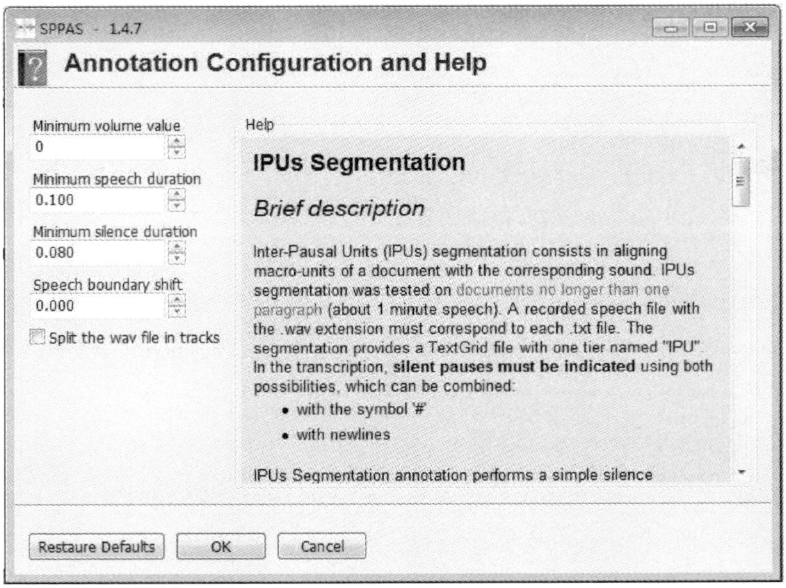

Figure 3 - 1 IPUs segmentation in SPPAS

It is necessary to mention the following points in using SPPAS: (i) only WAV MONO sound files can be annotated; (ii) no special characters are accepted in file names; (iii) the name for the sound files should be exactly same to the name for the transcription files.

After the automatic IPU segmentation, the following step is checking IPU boundaries in Praat. This task is accomplished by 6 professional annotators. It is introduced in detail in the following section with other annotation work.

3.2.2 Annotation in Praat

The annotation work in Praat of the present research includes 4 steps. The first step is a check on IPU boundaries. The second step is dealing with the spontaneous speech phenomena in conversation. The third step is dealing with the boundaries of initial plosives. After all these three steps, the boundaires of IPUs are fixed. Then, the last step is to input Mandarin characters within IPUs for the data extraction in the following task.

1. A check on IPU boundaries

The outputs of running SPPAS are Text-Grid files. These files can be opened by Praat. The segmented IPUs (the internal units between the pauses not less than 80 ms) were split automatically by the symbol "#".

As mentioned in last section, although the threshold is calculated to be 80 ms, it is still possible to find out pauses shorter than 80 ms or stop gaps longer than 80 ms. Therefore, it is still necessary to check whether the pauses identified by SPPAS automatically are real pauses or parts of plosives. The check of IPUs' boundaries is one of tasks in the annotation work of the present study.

The boundaries of IPUs are checked by professional annotators. The annotating group is comprised of two PhD students and four master students, who major in Phonetics and Phonology and are skillful in annotation work by Praat.

2. Dealing with the spontaneous speech phenomena

Spontaneous phenomena should be paid attention to in annotation work.

The present research analyzes spontaneous conversations. How are the spontaneous speech phenomena in conversations (including disfluencies, filled pauses, laugh, etc.) dealt with?

The present research excluded the laugh, cough, sneezing, etc, which contained no linguistic contents from IPUs, and they are not annotated in Praat. The filled pauses, repairing, restarting, backchannel, etc, which contained linguistic contents, were included in IPUs, and they were considered as valid speaking and were annotated in Praat.

3. Dealing with boundaries with initial plosives

Another work should be done in annotation is to deal with the boundaries with initial plosives. For all the conversations in Tongji Games Corpus, if plosives appear at the initial positions of IPUs, phrases, or conversations, how are the stop gaps distinguished from the pauses before the boundaries? Should the boundaries be put before the stop gaps of the plosives or after them?

The present research adopted the method of Shih & Ao (1997, pp. 387–388): "The closure portion of an utterance- or phrase-initial plosive, which coincides with silence, was always marked as having no duration of its own. The burst-aspiration duration was measured from the onset of the burst to the onset of the vowel."

This task has been accomplished by our annotation group, too.

4. Mandarin characters input

After the IPUs' boundaries are checked, text is labeled in the tier named syllable in Praat, which is orthographic tier. The speaking contents are put within IPUs by annotators. Chinese characters are put down within IPUs in Praat instead of syllables. The input of Mandarin characters has two advantages.

Firstly, it is efficient in the calculation of speaking-rate by Praat script. One character in Mandarin corresponds to one syllable. The number of characters equals the number of syllables in every IPU. In the computation of speaking-rate, the Praat script is run over the tier with Mandarin Chinese. The number of Chinese characters is identified automatically as the number of syllables, and calculations are made. More details are introduced in the section of data extraction.

Secondly, it makes clear exhibition of what the subjects said in conversation. The analyses of entrainment involved data from two sides in conversation. Matching the speaking of two interlocutors is necessary. The clear exhibition of what the subjects said is helpful in the matching of 18 sections, turns, and tone units in analyses.

Figure 3 - 2 is an example of annotation in Praat.

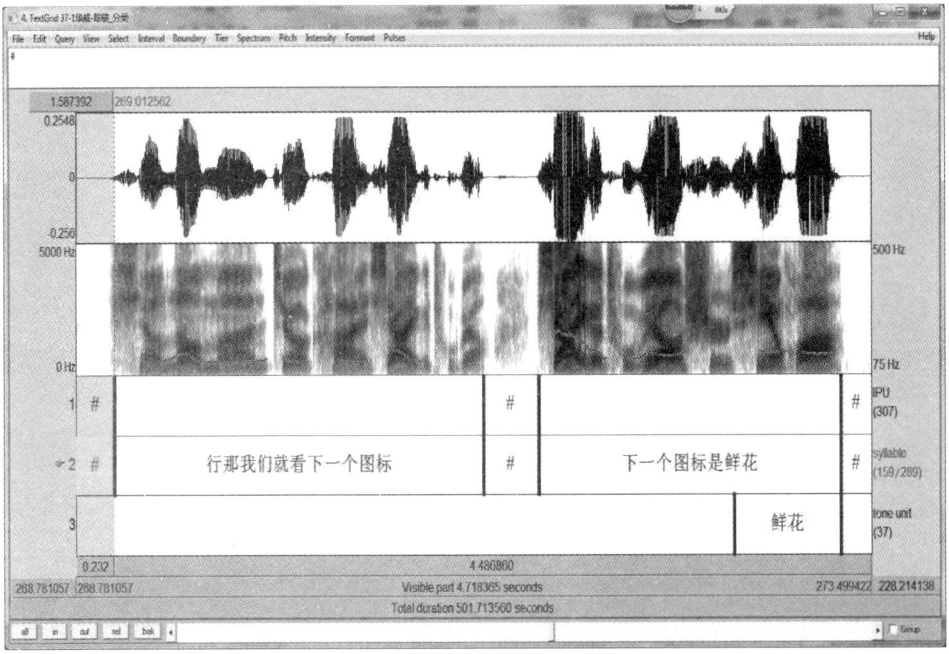

Figure 3 - 2 One example of annotation in Praat

In Figure 3, there is one example of annotation in Praat, which follows ToBI annotation conventions (Beckman & Hirschberg 1994). Three tiers are annotated in the data of the present research. The first tier is named IPU. In this tier, the IPUs were split by the symbol "#". The boundaries are identified automatically by SPPAS, and checked by annotation group. The second tier is named syllable. In this tier, all the Chinese characters were put within the IPU boundaries. The third tier is named tone unit. In this tier, the target tone units in carrier sentences are annotated.

3.2.3 F0 Modification

Although the corpus of the present research was recorded in sound proof booth, the detecting of F0 by Praat is not satisfactory. In Praat, the pitch floor and pitch ceiling are set by default to 75 and 600 Hz respectively. The F0 extraction under the default parameters contains pitch tracking errors.

For the pitch tracking errors, the manual modifications are used in some researches. Because the corpus of the present research is 12-hour spontaneous conversations, the manual modification would be a heavy load for annotation work. The present research adopted Daniel Hirst's two-pass method to solve this problem (Hirst 2011). In the first pass, default parameters are used, in which the pith floor is set at 50 Hz instead of Praat's default 75, because some male speakers go to 60 Hz in speaking, and pitch ceiling is set at 700 Hz instead of 600 Hz, because this ceiling is generally high enough to include even expressive female voices. In the second pass, the values of q_1 and q_3 are used, which refer to the fist and third quartiles of the F0 distribution. It is because the errors are likely to occur at the extreme values of distribution and the first and third quartiles of the distribution are much more robust estimates of the dispersion. Therefore, in the second pass, the new values are given to pitch floor and pitch ceiling, where pitch floor is given by the formula $0.75 * q_1$, and pitch ceiling is given by the formula $1.5 * q_3$.

The two-pass method is included in the Praat script (listed in Appendix 5) for extraction data of the present research. The main contents of two-pass method are listed as follows:

```
procedure automatic_min_max_pitch
q25=Get quantile... 0 0 0.25 Hertz
q75=Get quantile... 0 0 0.75 Hertz
min_pitch=0.75 * q25
max_pitch=1.5 * q75
```

By running the Praat script (listed in Appendix 5), the task of F0 modification was accomplished automatically with the extraction tasks together.

After all the annotation work, the extraction of data was accomplished. Data extraction is introduced in the following section.

3.2.4 Variables

The present research focuses on prosody in entrainment in Mandarin conversations. Seven variables are set in the analyses of Tongji Games Corpus in this study. These parameters come from 3 main aspects of prosody, including the feature of duration (Speaking-rate), the features of F0 (F0 min, F0 mean, F0 max), and the features of intensity (Intensity min, Intensity mean and Intensity max).

Speaking-rate equals the number of syllables per second in this study. Syllable counts are made automatically by Praat according to the orthographic transcriptions. Section 3.2.2 in this chapter provides detailed calculation of speaking-rate.

Fundamental frequency of a voice is used to measure how often the sound wave repeats itself. The present research adopts min, mean and max values of fundamental frequency, which are obtained automatically by Praat.

The features of intensity are used to describe the degree of energy in a sound wave. It is perceived as the volume of a sound. The present research adopts min, mean and max values of intensity, which are also obtained automatically by Praat.

3.2.5 Data Extraction

What kinds of data should be extracted in the present research? The answer is related to another question: what are the variables of this research? As illustrated in the review of previous research on prosodic entrainment in Section 2.3.4, most studies of prosodic entrainment focus mainly on 4 aspects of prosody: pitch, duration, intensity, and voice quality. The previous studies showed that the studies on adaptation over pitch, duration, and intensity are much more than those over voice quality. Considering the prominent roles of pitch, duration, and intensity play in entrainment (as reviewed in section 2.3.4), the present research set 7 variables from the 3 main aspects of prosody: minimal F0, mean F0, maximal F0, speaking-rate, minimal intensity, mean intensity, maximal intensity, of which the former 3 belong to the features of F0, Speaking-rate to duration, and the later three to intensity.

Therefore, data extraction was operated on these 7 variables over every IPU by Praat script (Appendix 5), written and modified by Professor Daniel Hirst.

3.2.6 Weighted Average of Larger Units than IPUs

Seven variables of every IPU were extracted by a Praat script. Data extraction is accomplished over the smallest analysis units – IPUs. However, some analyses of entrainment in the present research cover units larger than IPUs including turns, or conversations, which contain more than one IPU. The data extracted over IPUs cannot be used directly in these analyses.

When the analyses are made over larger units, which contain more than one IPU, the weighed averages are calculated over all the IPUs within these units. Thus, when the analysis is done for a whole conversation, the values of a variable cannot be the data directly extracted by Praat, but the average of all the IPUs within this conversation. Similarly, when the analysis is done for a turn, the values of a variable cannot be the data directly extracted by Praat, but the average of all the IPUs within this turn.

The averages mentioned here are weighted averages – weights being proportional to IPUs' durations. The averages calculated by proportional durations are the best representative averages for the large units. For the data extracted by Praat, the weighted averages of IPUs within the large unit were all computed before analyses.

Three kinds of larger units are analyzed in the present research.

One is a conversation. When analyses are done for one prosodic feature in one conversation, a weighted average of all the IPUs in this conversation is computed as the representative value of this conversation. The present research sets 7 parameters, so the values of 7 variables are not the data directly extracted by Praat, but the 7 weighted averages of all the IPUs within the conversation.

Another kind is a section in conversation. In Tongji Games Corpus, a conversation consists of 18 sections, each of which involves the operation of a single picture. In both of the games (Picture Ordering Game and Picture Classifying Game), subjects take the same order in ordering or classifying pictures from Picture 1 to Picture 18. Therefore, all the conversations can be cut into 18 sections, each of which focuses on the same picture. When the analysis is done for one prosodic feature over the sections in conversation, weighted averages of all the IPUs in the sections are computed as the representative value of the sections. The present research set 7 prosodic features as the variables, and the values of 7 variables are not the data directly extracted by Praat, but the 7 weighted averages of all the IPUs within the sections.

The third kind of unit is a turn. The present research did analysis of prosodic entrainment at the turn level. One turn contains at least one IPU. In present research, a weighted average of all the IPUs in the turn is computed as the representative value of this turn. Therefore, the values of 7 variables of every turn are not the data directly extracted by Praat, but the 7 weighted averages of all the IPUs within the turn.

One example of the calculating weighted averages is provided in one turn. Table 3 - 7 shows the calculation of weighted averages over all 5 IPUs within this turn.

Table 3 - 7　　One example of weighted averages in one turn

	file	duration	Speaking_ rate	F0_ min	F0_ mean	F0_ max	Int_ min	Int_ mean	Int_ max
turn2	IPU1	2 022	5. 44	175	234	313	10. 33	56. 60	64. 35
	IPU2	1 320	6. 06	193	232	277	12. 11	55. 70	64. 64
	IPU3	719	6. 95	206	234	312	26. 13	56. 33	63. 73
	IPU4	925	6. 49	213	233	291	9. 25	51. 34	58. 83
	IPU5	490	8. 16	175	224	258	38. 49	52. 78	58. 96
turn2	weighted average		6. 21	189. 83	232. 454	295. 6	15. 17	55. 12	62. 92

In summary, whether over the conversations, the sections, or the turns, the weighted average is calculated as the data in analyses of entrainment. In the following chapters, more statements about the weighted averages are made in the analyses.

3.2.7 Turn Identification

The present research did analyses of prosodic entrainment at turn level, so the turn identification is necessary.

Spontaneous speech is dynamic yet complex. The complexity mainly exists in the occurrence of spontaneous speech phenomena such as repairs, restarts, back-channels, overlapping, interruptions, etc. It is necessary to identify these conversational features as one turn or more than one turn. The present research adopted the methods of Caspers (2003) and Liu (2004) for judgment.

Figure 4 shows Caspers' (2003. p. 261) method, in which "hold" means that the same speaker continues after a pause of 100 ms or more, while "change" means that a turn change has happened, with or without an intervening pause.

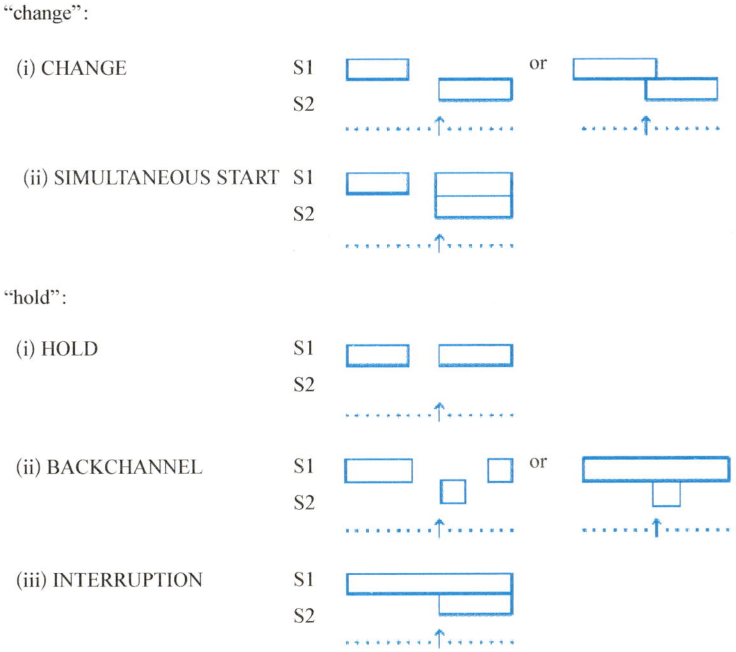

Figure 3 - 3 Schematic Representation of the Five Turn Transition Types

In Figure 3 - 3, the boxes following S1 depict stretches of speech uttered by Speaker 1. S2 indicates the speech by Speaker 2. The dotted line marks the time course, and the arrow indicates the relevant IPU boundary.

In addition, the present research also adopted Liu's (2004) method in turn identification: if the environments, where repairs, back-channels, overlaps, or interruptions exist, reach all the following three standards, they can be considered as one turn.

(1) The speakers' words are broken down by listeners' words.

(2) The roles of speaker and listeners are changed.

(3) Listeners' words supply new information.

Chapter 4

Entrainment at Multiple Levels

This chapter aims to answer research question: How is prosody used to entrain in Mandarin conversation? The question has been decomposed into the following two questions.

Is prosodic entrainment in Mandarin conversation global or local?

The relationship between global entrainment and local entrainment presents three possibilities. Two interlocutors in conversation probably entrain globally, but diverge at local positions; they may not be similar locally, but entrain locally; they entrain both globally and locally. The analyses in this chapter are to find out which possibility is the real situation. The global and local are relative. In order to make their relative relation clear, three levels are set in the analyses of entrainment from the global to the local: the levels of conversations, turns and tone units.

Is prosodic entrainment in Mandarin conversation convergent or constant as time goes on? Different from the static perspective in the question above, this question focuses on the dynamic entrainment process in conversation. There are two simple hypotheses for the entrainment process in conversation. One is that two interlocutors become more and more similar when time progresses till the end of conversation. Another is that distances of two interlocutors decreases to fixed distance, and the pair keep this fixed distance to the end of conversation. The analyses for convergence in this chapter are to find out which hypothesis is the real situation.

In this chapter, from the global to the local, prosodic entrainment is analyzed at three levels (the levels of conversations, turns and tone units).

The analyses at every level are mainly accomplished from three aspects: proximity, convergence and synchrony. It is necessary to explain these three aspects at the beginning of this chapter.

The terms of proximity, convergence and synchrony are adopted frequently in the studies of prosodic entrainment. They appear to be synonyms, but are defined differently in relevant literature (Edlund *et al.* 2009; Levitan & Hirschberg 2011; De Looze *et al.* 2014). Because clear distinction of these terms is made in Levitan & Hirschberg (2011), the present research adopts their definitions in this book, which are illustrated in Figure 4 - 1.

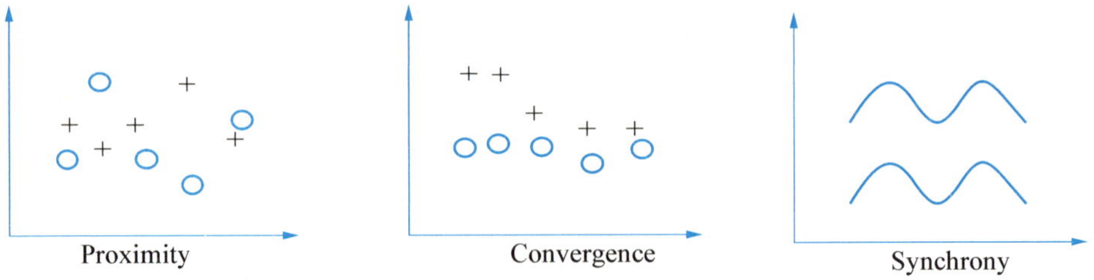

Figure 4 - 1 Three main aspects of entrainment

In Figure 4 - 1, the x-axis represents time, and the y-axis represents the value of a prosodic feature. The circles and crosses in the first two figures represent values from two different speakers partnered in a conversation.

Proximity refers to holistic approaching of prosodic features between two interlocutors over certain units in conversation.

Convergence refers to increase in similarity of prosodic features over the course of a conversation, reflecting an ongoing coordination process, and it is an increase in proximity over time.

Synchrony refers to a relative and synchronous coordination between two interlocutors.

The present research has tested prosodic entrainment mainly from these 3 aspects. At conversation level, entrainment proximity and convergence are examined in order to test the global performances of prosody in entrainment; at the turn level, entrainment proximity, convergence and synchrony are examined in order to test the relatively local performances of prosody in entrainment over turns; at the level of tone units, entrainment proximity, convergence, and synchrony are tested in order to test relatively local performances of prosody in entrainment over tone units. Cross-level comparisons are made at the end of this chapter from the same aspects and at different levels in order to present a holistic picture of entrainment from the global to local.

4.1 Entrainment at conversation level

Section 4.1 focuses on prosodic entrainment at conversation level. Three analyses are accomplished at this level: entrainment proximity, entrainment convergence, and the entrainment degree.

4.1.1 Proximity at Conversation Level

This analysis is to find out: Is there prosodic proximity in Mandarin conversations? The aim of this analysis is to test whether there is overall similarity of prosodic features from two interlocutors over a whole conversation. According to the definition of prosodic entrainment in Chapter 1, which says that speakers adapt their prosody to that of their interlocutors in conversation, and become similar in speaking for better, smooth and successful communication (Levitan & Hirschberg 2011; Levitan *et al.* 2012), it is hypothesized that there is prosodic proximity at the conversation level.

1. Paired T-tests between *disp* and *disnp*

In these analyses, the present research adopts paired T-tests over two sets of distances: *partner* distances and *non-partner* distances. This method is similar to that used in the previous studies (Levitan & Hirschberg 2011; Levitan *et al.* 2012) for proximity test at conversation level.

The *partner* distance is the distance of a prosodic feature between the speaker and his partner; *non-partner* distance is the mean of the distances of a prosodic feature between the speaker and other speakers, with whom he is not partnered in any conversations. In Picture Ordering Games, interlocutors' roles are different (the information giver or follower), so the non-partners in these games are restricted to those of the same gender and conversational role as their partners in dialogues. For each speaker in a conversation, a *partner* distance and *non-partner* distance are calculated. Thus, the hypothesis of this analysis is that the *partner* distance should be smaller than the *non-partner* distance, which can supply the evidence for entrainment at conversation level.

This method is explained by following formulas.

For each conversation, the present research defines *disp* as the *partner* distance between two partners (Speaker A, speaker B) on the prosodic feature f:

$$disp = | A_f - B_f | \qquad \text{(Formula 1)}$$

In Formula 1, *disp* represents the *partner* distance, A_f and B_f are weighted average (as what mentioned in Section 3. 2. 6) for the feature f over the whole conversation of the two partnered speakers A and B.

The present research define *disnp* as the *non-partner* distance on the feature f :

$$disnp = \frac{\sum_i | A_f - Xi_f |}{| X |} \qquad \text{(Formula 2)}$$

In Formula 2, *disnp* represents the *non-partner* distance, $X(i)$ are the set of speakers, which are selected randomly in the Tongji Games Corpus. These speakers have the same gender and role as the speaker's partner, and are not paired with the speaker in any conversations. The restriction to the speakers with the same gender and role as the speakers' partner is to decrease the influence of gender and role in the results. A_f and Xi_f are also the weighted mean (mentioned in Section 3. 2. 6) for the feature f over the whole conversation of the two non-paired speakers A and X. $| A_f - Xi_f |$ represents the distance between non partners, and is calculated automatically by the Computation Program 2 in Appendix G.

All the values put in the A_f, B_f and Xi_f in Formula 1 and 2 are the weighted averages of all the IPUs in the conversation, and the weights are proportion to IPUs' durations as mentioned in Section 3. 2. 6. The weighted averages are calculated by Computation Program 1. The contents of this program and an example of calculation are listed in Appendix F. By running the Computation Program 1, the values of A_f, B_f and Xi_f are calculated automatically.

Compared with *disp*, the calculation of *disnp* is more complicated. In the calculation of *disnp*, the most important part is the computation of $|A_f - Xi_f|$ by running Computation 2. Table 4 - 1 shows one example of this calculation.

Table 4 - 1 One example of calculating $|A_f - Xi_f|$ by Computation Program 2

	Speaking_rate	F0_min	F0_mean	F0_max	Int_min	Int_mean	Int_max
Target	3. 68	153. 37	205. 04	280. 53	30. 28	65. 71	72. 72
other1	4. 88	122. 89	148. 26	186. 37	21. 97	48. 84	56. 27
other2	4. 18	182. 00	229. 25	290. 03	10. 03	48. 07	55. 36
other3	5. 15	138. 68	163. 06	115. 90	22. 32	48. 08	54. 13
other4	5. 64	113. 61	136. 11	163. 23	23. 21	46. 67	53. 39
other5	4. 11	105. 41	125. 68	150. 22	21. 43	48. 85	55. 60
other6	6. 01	88. 51	110. 15	133. 80	25. 45	50. 25	57. 23
other7	4. 25	121. 48	154. 64	200. 01	16. 77	53. 44	61. 57
other8	4. 30	102. 54	121. 64	146. 92	23. 39	49. 53	57. 00
dis1	1. 21	30. 47	56. 78	94. 17	8. 31	16. 87	16. 45
dis2	0. 50	28. 63	24. 21	9. 50	20. 25	17. 64	17. 36
dis3	1. 47	14. 69	41. 98	164. 63	7. 96	17. 63	18. 59
dis4	1. 96	39. 76	68. 92	117. 30	7. 06	19. 03	19. 33
dis5	0. 43	47. 95	79. 36	130. 31	8. 85	16. 86	17. 12
dis6	2. 34	64. 86	94. 89	146. 73	4. 83	15. 46	15. 49
dis7	0. 58	31. 89	50. 40	80. 52	13. 50	12. 26	11. 15
dis8	0. 63	50. 83	83. 40	133. 61	6. 89	16. 18	15. 72

In Table 4-1, the values of A_f are listed in the Target line. The values of Xi_f. are listed in the lines from other 1 to other 8. The values of $|A_f - Xi_f|$ are calculated automatically by Computation Program 2 and listed in the lines from dis 1 to dis 8. These values are put in Formula 2, in which the value of i is 8. Then the values of *disnp* for this conversation are calculated.

Over all the 7 variables of the present research, the weighted averages and $|A_f - Xi_f|$ are calculated automatically by running Computation Program 1 and 2. These values are put into Formula 1 and 2 for all the 7 features. Thus, 7 sets of *disp* and *disnp* are calculated. The 7 paired T-tests are accomplished over 7 sets of *disp* and *disnp*.

In the corpus of the present research, there are 99 pairs of *disp* and *disnp*. Paired T-tests over these pairs for seven features are accomplished in SPSS 16. 0.

2. Results

The results of 7 paired T-tests over 99 pairs of *disp* and *disnp* for 7 variables are shown in Table 4-2.

Table 4-2 Paired T-tests between partner distances and non-partner distances

Feature	*t*	*df*	*p-value*	*Sig.*
Speaking-rate	−7. 994	98	0. 0	*
F0 min	0. 454	98	0. 650	/
F0 mean	0. 665	98	0. 507	/
F0 max	−3. 442	98	0. 001	*
Intensity min	−1. 156	98	0. 251	/
Intensity mean	−5. 054	98	0. 0	*
Intensity max	−5. 128	98	0. 0	*

In Table 4-2, an asterisk * indicates the significant difference, and the symbol/indicates no significant difference. According to this table, for all the 99 speakers, the distances of paired speakers are significantly smaller than those of non-paired speakers in terms of 4 prosodic features: Speaking-rate

($p=0.0<0.05$), F0 max ($p=0.001<0.05$), Intensity mean ($p=0.0<0.05$), and Intensity max ($p=0.0<0.05$). There are no significant difference between the two in term of F0 min ($p=0.650>0.05$), F0 mean ($p=0.507>0.05$), and Intensity min ($p=0.251>0.05$).

The results above indicate that speakers exhibit proximity at conversation level over the prosodic features of Speaking-rate, F0 max, Intensity mean, and Intensity max. Because Speaking-rate belongs to durational features, F0 max is one of the features of F0, and Intensity mean and Intensity Max are the features of Intensity, it is found that in Mandarin conversations, proximity in prosodic entrainment at conversation level is realized in the 3 main aspects of prosody: duration, F0 and intensity.

4.1.2 Convergence at Conversation Level

This analysis is to find out: Is there prosodic convergence in Mandarin conversations? While proximity at conversation level takes a static view of entrainment, the analysis of convergence at conversation level measures dynamic entrainment with time in order to see whether speakers increase similarity in prosody as conversations move forward. Therefore, in this analysis, the present research aims to test prosodic entrainment over the process of conversations.

1. Multiple tests

In the analyses of convergence, in order to trace the process of conversation, each conversation is cut into 18 sections, each of which focuses on the operation of one picture, and thus, these 18 sections represent the course of conversations. Distances over 18 sections between interlocutors represent the change in similarity in the course of conversations. As mentioned in section 3.1.3, in Tongji Games Corpus, for both of the games (Picture Ordering game and Picture Classifying game), subjects take the same order in the operation (ordering or classifying) of pictures from pictures 1 to picture 18. Thus, although in different games, all the conversations can be cut into 18 parallel sections, and each of them focuses on the same picture. For every picture in two games, the only difference is the operation of them, which means that this picture should be ordered or classified.

With the preparation mentioned above, the present research tried several methods in convergence analyses.

The first method is the same to that used in Levitan & Hirschberg's (2011) analyses of SAE, in which each conversation is divided into two parts (the first and second halves of conversation), and paired T-test is used in the comparison between these two parts. Similarly, the present research conducted a paired T-test over the distances between the first nine sections and the second nine, because 18 sections are divided in two halves, and each half includes 9 sections. However, no significant differences are found between the two halves in terms of 7 prosodic features. That is, no convergence is found by this method.

The second method the present research has tried is to compare the distance of the two interlocutors over the first section and the last (the 18th section) by paired T-test. However, no significant differences are found over 7 prosodic features, either. That is, no convergence is found by this method, either.

The third method the present research has tried is a method of descriptive statistics over two interlocutors' distances of all the 18 sections in order to trace the changes of the distances in conversations' progress. Data used in this method are listed below.

Data for this convergence analyses are calculated in the following steps:

The first step is to cut the conversations into 18 sections, each of which focuses on the operation of one picture. The convergence analyses are accomplished over 66 conversations (in 70 conversations, 4 are omitted because some parallel sections couldn't be found in two interlocutors' speaking in these 4 conversations).

The second step is to compute respectively the weighted averages of IPUs within all the 18 sections by Computation Program 1. As mentioned in Section 3. 2. 6, weighted averages of all the IPUs in the individual sections are computed as the representative value of the sections. Different from the calculation in proximity at conversation level, weighted averages come from all the IPUs within 18 sections, not the whole conversations. The present research has 7 prosodic parameters. So the values of 7 variables are not the data directly extracted by Praat, but the 7 weighted averages of all the IPUs within the sections.

The third step is to calculate the distances of the two speakers over the 18 sections, which represent the change in similarity in the course of conversations. Thus, for one conversation, there are 18 distances in the process of conversation.

The fourth step is to calculate averages for the distances over all the 66 conversations. For every section of one conversation, there is one distance between two interlocutors. For one specific section of 66 conversations, there are 66 distances between interlocutors. One average is made over these 66 distances for every section.

Finally, 18 averages are calculated over 66 conversations. The data are listed in Table 4 - 3.

Table 4 - 3 Averages of distances over 18 sections in 66 conversations

	Speaking_ rate	F0_ min	F0_ mean	F0_ max	Int_ min	Int_ mean	Int_ max
section 1	0. 90	42. 80	49. 40	65. 03	7. 63	4. 07	4. 36
section 2	0. 85	42. 04	49. 11	67. 13	8. 39	3. 75	4. 18
section 3	0. 79	43. 76	50. 89	68. 84	6. 82	3. 96	4. 09
section 4	0. 72	42. 51	50. 16	70. 80	7. 55	3. 80	4. 16
section 5	0. 71	43. 58	48. 24	62. 36	7. 72	3. 96	4. 45
section 6	0. 95	43. 51	48. 90	64. 56	7. 66	3. 99	4. 44
section 7	0. 72	40. 94	47. 88	66. 46	7. 65	3. 90	4. 46
section 8	0. 85	42. 46	50. 13	69. 67	7. 09	4. 05	4. 45
section 9	0. 82	42. 57	49. 19	66. 50	8. 24	4. 17	4. 57
section 10	0. 75	42. 57	49. 81	72. 16	8. 55	4. 15	4. 55
section 11	0. 84	44. 22	48. 48	61. 10	7. 40	4. 64	5. 02

(**continued**)

	Speaking_ rate	F0_ min	F0_ mean	F0_ max	Int_ min	Int_ mean	Int_ max
section 12	0.72	42.37	48.52	68.80	8.00	4.20	4.49
section 13	0.85	42.62	48.54	64.92	7.54	4.07	4.67
section 14	0.96	42.46	49.10	68.67	8.26	4.14	4.35
section 15	0.90	39.54	46.99	64.95	7.65	4.24	4.52
section 16	0.91	44.25	48.26	66.41	7.36	4.38	4.69
section 17	0.89	43.01	49.12	69.74	9.37	4.47	4.93
section 18	0.93	41.36	48.87	67.34	7.81	4.36	4.89

Table 4 - 3 shows the averages of two interlocutor's distances over 18 sections in 66 conversations for 7 variables. The measurement units for these variables are syllable per second for Speaking-rate, Hz for three features of F0, dB for three features of Intensity. Over these data, in terms of every prosodic feature, changes of the distances over 18 sections in conversations' progress are traced.

2. Results

In terms of every prosodic feature, changes of the distances over 18 sections in conversations' progress are traced. If the distances of two interlocutors become smaller in the process of conversations, convergence is found; if the distances of two interlocutors become bigger in the process of conversations, divergence is found. The following plots trace the changes of the distances over 18 sections in conversation.

The 18 distances over 18 sections in conversation are listed in Table 4 - 3. The average distances of 18 sections in terms of 7 prosodic features are put in the plots in order to illustrate clearly the process of mutual adjustment over the ongoing conversation. In these plots, x axis refers to the index of 18 sections, and they represents the conversations' progress; y axis refers to the average distances of 66 the conversations over the 18 sections.

Because 7 prosodic features are in three different measuring units (Syllable per second for Speaking-rate, Hz for three features of F0, dB for three features of Intensity), three figures are used to illustrate the changes in the distances over 7 prosodic features. Figure 4 - 2 is used for durational feature, Figure 4 - 3 for prosodic features of F0, and Figure 4 - 4 for prosodic features of intensity.

Eighteen distances over 18 sections in terms of Speaking-rate is shown in Figure 4 - 2.

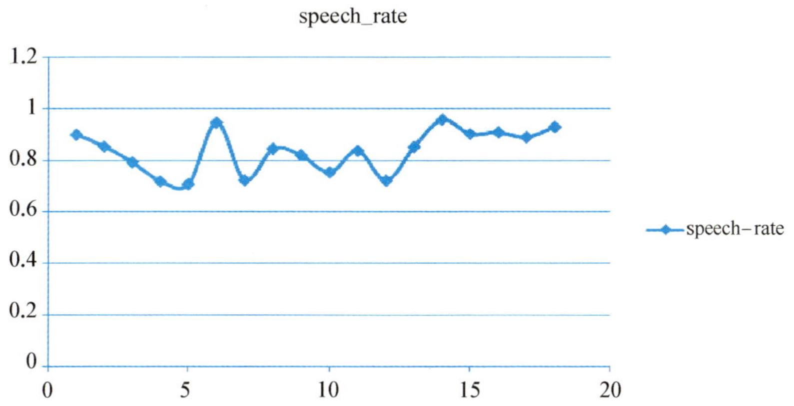

Figure 4 - 2 18 distances over 18 sections in terms of Speaking-rate

From Figure 4 - 2, it is found that the distances of two interlocutors over Speaking-rate decrease and increase alternately. That is, in terms of Speaking-rate, two interlocutors converge and diverge alternately in the process of conversations.

Eighteen distances over 18 sections in terms of 3 features of F0 (F0 min, F0 mean, and F0 max) are shown in Figure 4 - 3.

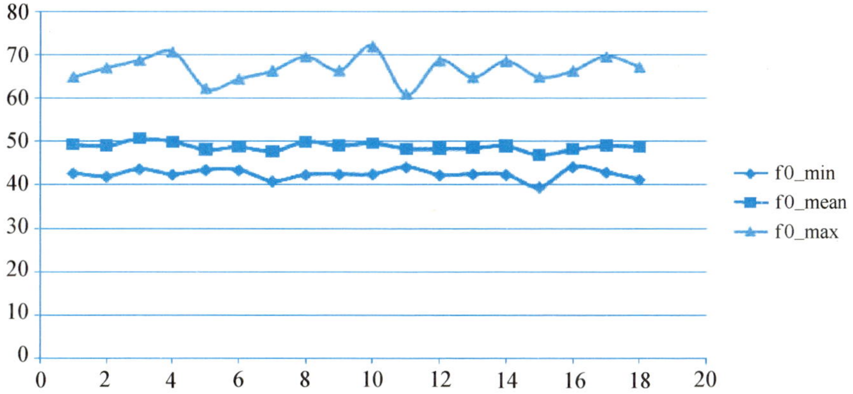

Figure 4 - 3 18 distances over 18 sections in terms of three features of F0

In Figure 4－3, it is found that the distances of two interlocutors over F0 min, F0 mean, and F0 max decrease and increase alternately, although the degree of increase and decrease are different. That is, in terms of the features of F0, two interlocutors converge and diverge alternately in the process of their conversations.

Eighteen 18 distances over 18 sections in terms of Intensity min, Intensity mean, and Intensity max are shown in Figure 4－4.

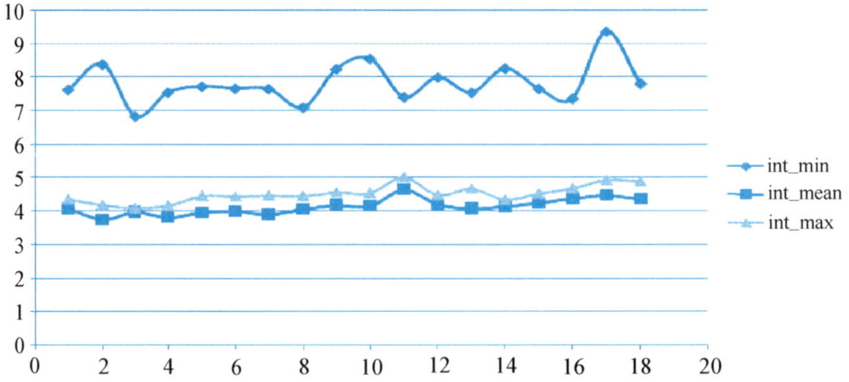

Figure 4－4　18 distances over 18 sections in terms of 3 features of Intensity

From Figure 4－4, it is found that the distances of two interlocutors over three features of Intensity decrease and increase alternately, although the degree of increase and decrease are different. That is, in terms of the features of intensity, two interlocutors converge and diverge alternately in the process of their conversations.

It is obvious that Figure 4－2, Figure 4－3 and Figure 4－4 show the similar pattern: the distances of all the prosodic features between two interlocutors become big and small alternately in the course of conversations. That the distance becomes bigger means there is divergence between the two interlocutors. That the distance becomes smaller means there is convergence between the two. That the distances become bigger and small alternatively means convergence and divergence appear alternately with the ongoing conversation.

From results above, the following can be found in the analyses of convergence at conversation level.

(1) In the process of Mandarin conversations, both convergence and divergence exist in prosodic entrainment.

(2) In the process of Mandarin conversations, convergence and divergence appear alternately.

4.1.3 Entrainment Degree at Conversation Level

This analysis is to find out: among the 4 prosodic features (Speaking-rate, F0 max, Intensity mean, and Intensity max) showing proximity simultaneously at conversation level, which features entrain more?

Four prosodic features are proved to show proximity simultaneously at conversation level in Section 4.1. That is, interlocutors exhibit significant adaption over 4 prosodic features at the same time and become similar to each other in Mandarin Chinese conversations. Then it is necessary to make further investigation into the difference in entrainment degree over these four features in order to find out over which features the adaptation in entrainment is the biggest or the least.

1. ANOVA tests

The method used in this analysis is ANOVA test, which are accomplished in three steps.

The first step is to select the conversations, which exhibit the proximity at conversation level over the 4 prosodic features at the same time. Among 70 conversations in Tongji Games Corpus, 31 conversations are chosen out to be the objects of analyses in this section.

The second step is to define a parameter - *sim*, in this analysis, which is calculated by Formula 3.

$$sim = 1 - \frac{disp}{disnp} \qquad \text{(Formula 3)}$$

In Formula 3, *sim* represents the adaptation degree of one prosodic feature. *disp* represents the *partner* distance as in Formula 1, and *disnp* represents the *non partner* distance as in Formula 2 in Section 4.1.1.

In this analysis, *non partner* distance is considered as the primitive distance of the two interlocutors, the distance without the mutual adaptation.

Thus, *disp*/*disnp*, in which *disp* is normalized by *disnp*, represents the ratio of the remained distance after adaption between interlocutors to the primitive distance. Then, *sim*, 1 − *disp*/*disnp*, represents a similarity ratio, the percentage of becoming similar. This similarity ratio or normalization in Formula 3 has an advantage to reduce the speakers' differences.

The third step is to do ANOVA tests, in which the dependent variable is *sim*, the independent variable is 4 prosodic features (Speaking-rate, F0 max, Intensity mean, Intensity max).

Among 70 conversations in the corpus, 31 conversations, which exhibit proximity at conversation level simultaneously over the 4 prosodic features, are chosen out to be the objects of the analysis in this section. The values of *sim* for 31 conversations are calculated out and listed in Table 4 - 4.

Table 4 - 4 The values of *sim* over 31 conversations

	Speaking_rate	F0_max	Int_mean	Int_max
1	0.76	0.33	0.76	0.78
2	0.78	0.20	0.78	0.81
3	0.97	0.52	0.85	0.92
4	0.93	0.50	0.59	0.70
5	0.66	0.33	0.80	0.98
6	0.31	0.95	0.77	0.98
7	0.58	0.93	0.76	0.99
8	0.07	0.69	0.09	0.10
9	0.47	0.55	0.73	0.39
10	0.48	0.55	0.70	0.60
11	0.97	0.84	0.50	0.50
12	0.61	0.88	0.59	0.55
13	0.74	0.56	0.60	0.49
14	0.70	0.05	0.24	0.26
15	0.55	0.50	0.61	0.60
16	0.29	0.36	0.17	0.04
17	0.56	0.20	0.76	0.60

(continued)

	Speaking_rate	F0_max	Int_mean	Int_max
18	0.87	0.42	0.07	0.14
19	0.39	0.54	0.94	0.58
20	0.33	0.54	0.84	0.58
21	0.62	0.59	0.85	0.51
22	0.09	0.43	0.77	0.94
23	0.27	0.36	0.70	0.93
24	0.44	0.16	0.19	0.03
25	0.29	0.15	0.32	0.25
26	0.57	0.27	0.45	0.38
27	0.20	0.11	0.51	0.64
28	0.78	0.39	0.86	0.89
29	0.64	0.50	0.43	0.61
30	0.86	0.93	0.62	0.61
31	0.73	0.05	0.59	0.56

Before doing the ANOVA tests over the values in Table 4－4, the distribution of these values is illustrated in Figure 4－5.

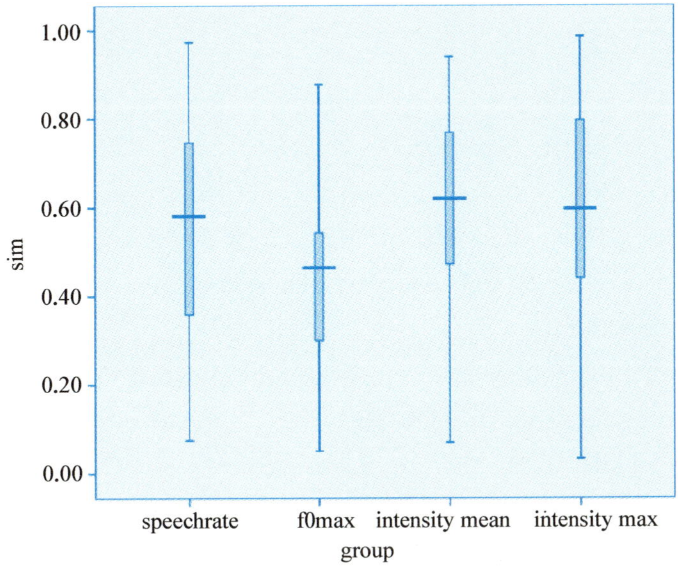

Figure 4－5　Data Distribution of ANOVA Tests for Entrainment Degree

In Figure 4 - 5, x axis refers to the four prosodic features, which show proximity at conversation level at the same time. y axis refers to the similarity ratio of these prosodic features. The distribution of the data for these prosodic features is illustrated in Figure 4 - 5.

2. Results

With the data from the 31 conversations, the ANOVA tests are used to find out whether the similarity ratio makes difference among the 4 prosodic features, which exhibit proximity at conversation level.

The result of ANOVA tests, in which the dependent variable is *sim*, the independent variable is 4 prosodic features (Speaking-rate, F0 max, Intensity mean, Intensity max) is illustrated in Table 4 - 5.

Table 4 - 5 **An ANOVA test of entrainment degree**

ANOVA

sim

	Sum of Squares	df	Mean Square	F	Sig.
Between Groups	.622	3	.207	3.396	.020
Within Groups	7.324	120	.061		
Total	7.946	123			

Table 4 - 5 shows that for 4 prosodic features, there are significant differences in similarity degree ($p = 0.020 < 0.05$). That is, the similarity ratios of the 4 prosodic features, which show proximity at conversation level at the same time, are significantly different. It is necessary to test further the difference between every two features. Therefore, the multiple comparisons are made in this section.

The results of the Post-hoc comparison are illustrated in Table 4 - 6.

The results in Table 4 - 6 show that similarity ratio of F0 max is significantly smaller than that of Speaking-rate ($p = 0.021 < 0.05$); the similarity ratio of F0 max is significantly smaller than that of Intensity mean ($p = 0.006 < 0.05$); the similarity ratio of F0 max also significantly smaller than that of Intensity max ($p = 0.011 < 0.05$). Therefore, the similarity ratio of F0 max is the smallest comparing with Speaking-rate, Intensity mean, and Intensity max. Meanwhile, there are no significant differences in similarity degree among other three prosodic features: Speaking-rate, Intensity mean, and Intensity max.

Table 4 - 6 **Post-hoc comparison of entrainment degree**

Multiple Comparison

sim

LSD

(I) Group	(J) Group	Mean Difference (I-J)	Std. Error	Sig.	95% Confidence Interval	
					Lower Bound	Upper Bound
Speech rate	F0 max	.147 22*	.062 75	.021	.023 0	.271 5
	Intensity mean	−.029 62	.062 75	.638	−.153 9	.094 6
	Intensity max	−.013 95	.062 75	.825	−.138 2	.110 3
F0 max	speechrate	−.147 22*	.062 75	.021	−.271 5	−.023 0
	Intensity mean	−.176 84*	.062 75	.006	−.301 1	−.052 6
	Intensity max	−.161 17*	.062 75	.011	−.285 4	−.036 9
Intensity mean	speechrate	.029 62	.062 75	.638	−.094 6	.153 9
	F0 max	.176 84*	.062 75	.006	.052 6	.301 1
	Intensity max	.015 68	.062 75	.803	−.108 6	.139 9
Intensity max	speechrate	.013 95	.062 75	.825	−.110 3	.138 2
	F0 max	.161 17*	.062 75	.011	.036 9	.285 4
	Intensity mean	−.015 68	.062 75	.803	−.139 9	.108 6

*. The mean difference is significant at the 0.05 level.

Based on the results above, the following are found:

For the 4 prosodic features exhibiting proximity at the conversation level at the same time (Speaking-rate, F0 max, Intensity mean, Intensity max), the similarity or adaptation degree of F0 max is the smallest; there are no difference in the adaption degree of the other 3 features.

4.1.4 Summary of the Results

Section 4.1 focuses on entrainment at conversation level. Three analyses of prosody in entrainment at conversation level are accomplished in this part: the proximity, convergence, and the entrainment degree.

In the analysis of proximity at conversation level, by paired T-tests on partner distances and non-partner distances over 7 variables, it is found that in Mandarin conversations the speakers exhibit proximity at conversation level over the prosodic features of Speaking-rate, F0 max, Intensity mean, and Intensity max. Therefore, the proximity in prosodic entrainment is found to be realized in the 3 main aspects of prosody: durational feature (Speaking-rate), the features of fundamental frequency (F0 max), and the features of intensity (Intensity mean and Intensity max).

In the analysis of convergence at conversation level, by a method of descriptive statistics over two interlocutors' distances in 18 sections, it is found that (i) in the process of Mandarin conversations, both convergence and divergence exist in prosodic entrainment; and that (ii) in the process of Mandarin conversations, convergence and divergence appear alternately.

In the analysis of entrainment degree at the conversation level, by ANOVA tests, in which the dependent variable is *sim* (the adaptation degree of the prosodic feature), the independent variable is 4 prosodic features (Speaking-rate, F0 max, Intensity mean, Intensity max), it is found that for the 4 prosodic features exhibiting proximity simultaneously in conversations (Speaking-rate, F0 max, Intensity mean, Intensity max), the similarity or adaptation degree of F0 max is the smallest; there are no difference in the similarity degree of the other 3 features. That is, in the realization of prosodic entrainment, F0 max exhibit the smallest adaptation degree, and other prosodic features exhibit entrainment in the similar degree.

4.2 Entrainment at Turn Level

The analyses of prosodic entrainment in previous section are accomplished over the whole conversation. This section focuses on the entrainment at turn level. Three analyses are accomplished in this part: proximity, convergence, and synchrony at turn level.

4.2.1 Proximity at Turn Level

This analysis is to find out: Is there proximity at turn level? The aim of this section is to test whether there is entrainment of prosodic features from two interlocutors over turns. According to the definition of prosodic entrainment in Chapter 1 that the two interlocutors become similar in speaking, it is hypothesized that there is prosodic proximity over turn units in Mandarin conversations.

1. Paired T-tests between *disa* and *disna*

The present research adopts paired T-tests, which are used by Levitan & Hirschberg's (2011) in similar analyses. Paired T-tests are conducted between the distance of *adjacent* IPUs at turn exchanges and the average distance of ten *non-adjacent* IPUs. The *adjacent* distance is the distance of a prosodic feature between the final IPU in turn $i-1$, uttered by speaker A, and the initial IPU in turn i, uttered by B (A's partner). The *non-adjacent* distance is the distance of a prosodic feature between the turn $(i-1)$'s final IPU spoken by A and the other ten randomly chosen IPUs uttered by B, which is not adjacent to the final IPU of turn $i-1$. If for a feature, adjacent IPUs are more similar than non-adjacent IPUs, it indicates that speakers entrain at turn level over that feature.

Two steps are involved in this method.

The first step is to define two parameters *disa, disna*, which are calculated by Formula 4 and 5 in this section.

$$disa = | IPU_t - IPU_p | \qquad \text{(Formula 4)}$$

In Formula 4, *disa* represents the distance of a prosodic feature over the adjacent IPUs at the turn transition places uttered by two speakers in one conversation. Figure 10 helps to indicate the location of adjacent IPUs.

In Figure 4 - 5, A and B refer to the two interlocutors. All the adjacent IPUs are circled at the turn exchange positions.

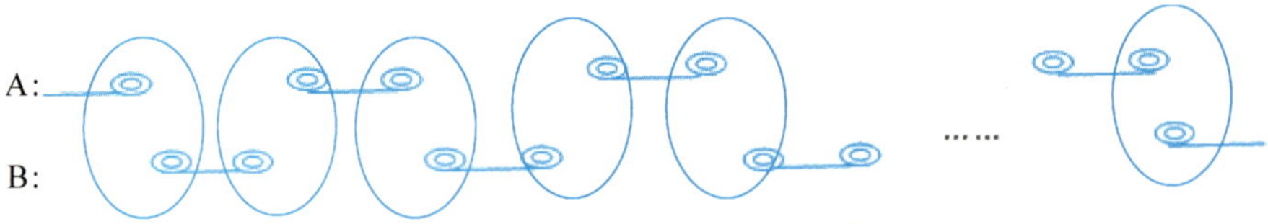

Figure 4-5 Adjacent IPUs at the turn transition places

In Formula 4, IPU_t refers to the target IPU, for instance, which is the final IPU of turn $i-1$ spoken by speaker A. IPU_p refers to the IPU, which is adjacent to the target IPU and is located at the initial position of turn i, uttered by speaker B (Speaker A's partner). $/IPU_t - IPU_p/$ represents the *adjacent* distance, which is the distance between the final IPU in turn $i-1$, and the initial IPU in turn i, uttered by A and B respectively.

$$disna = \frac{\sum_{i=1}^{10} |IPU_t - IPU_i|}{10} \qquad \text{(Formula 5)}$$

In Formula 5, *disna* represents the non *adjacent* distance of the IPUs uttered by two speakers in one conversation. IPU_t refers to the target IPU, which is the final IPU of turn $i-1$ spoken by speaker A. IPU_i is uttered by the target IPU speaker's conversational partner but is not adjacent to the target IPU. $|IPU_t - IPU_i|$ represents the *non-adjacent* distance, which is the distance between the target IPU and the other randomly chosen IPU, which is not adjacent to the target IPU, and uttered by B (A's speaking partner). $|IPU_t - IPU_i|$ is calculated automatically by the Computation Program 2 in Appendix G. *disna* is calculated by taking 10 *non-adjacent* distances, and getting the average of them.

After the definition of *disa* and *disna*, the next step is to do paired T-tests between *disa* and *disna*. One pair of *disa* and *disna* is calculated over one conversation. 70 pairs of *disa* and *disna* are computed over all the 70 conversations in Tongji Games Corpus. For one prosodic feature, one paired T-test is used for 70 pairs of *disa* and *disna*. For 7 variables of the present research, 7 paired T-tests are accomplished over all the 7 variables between *disa* and *disna*. The data in tests are listed in Appendix H.

2. Results

The results of the paired t-tests over 70 pairs of *disa* and *disna* are listed in the Table 4 - 7.

Table 4 - 7 Paired t-tests between adjacent and non-adjacent distances of IPUs

disa vs. *disna*	t	df	p	Sig.
Speaking-rate	−3.613	69	0.001	*
F0 min	−0.17	69	0.986	/
F0 mean	1.280	69	0.205	/
F0 max	0.813	69	0.419	/
Intensity min	0.747	69	0.458	/
Intensity mean	−3.716	69	0.0	*
Intensity max	−4.163	69	0.0	*

In Table 4 - 7, an asterisk * indicates the significant difference, and the symbol/indicates no significant difference. This table shows that the distance of the adjacent IPUs is significantly smaller than the distance of the non-adjacent IPUs over 3 variables: Speaking-rate ($p=0.001<0.05$), Intensity mean ($p=0.0<0.05$), and Intensity max ($p=0.0<0.05$), and there is not the significant difference between the two kinds of distances over other 4 variables.

The results that the distance of the adjacent IPUs is significantly smaller than the distance of the non-adjacent IPUs over 3 variables (Speaking-rate, Intensity mean, and Intensity max) show that these 3 prosodic features exhibit significant prosodic proximity at turn level. Comparing the results of prosodic proximity at conversation level in section 4.1, we can find that these 3 features (Speaking-rate, Intensity mean, Intensity max) show prosodic proximity at both conversation level and turn level. F0 max only shows prosodic proximity at conversation level, not at turn level.

4.2.2 Convergence at Turn Level

This analysis is to find out: Is there prosodic convergence at turn level?

As another view of entrainment at turn level, the aim of this analysis is to find out whether the prosodic similarity at turn level increases in the course of a conversation.

1. Correlation analyses of *disa* and time

The present research adopts Pearson's correlation analyses, which are used by Levitan & Hirschberg (2011) in similar analyses. Pearson's correlation analyses are conducted over the *adjacent* distances and time. *Adjacent* distance (*disa*) represents the distance of a prosodic feature over the adjacent IPUs at the turn transition places uttered by two speakers in one conversation (the definition is explained in detail by Formula 4 in The Section 4.2.1). If the correlation is positive, it means in the course of conversations, the *adjacent* distances of the adjacent IPUs at turn exchanges increase with the time; if the correlation is negative, it means in the course of conversations, the *adjacent* distances of the adjacent IPUs at turn exchanges decrease with time. If convergence at turn level happens, the *adjacent* distance of the adjacent IPUs at turn exchanges decrease with time. Therefore, the negative correlation is what is hypothesized.

Adjacent distances are calculated over the adjacent IPUs at the turn exchanges position. There are two possible plans to locate the adjacent IPUs.

In Plan 1, all the adjacent IPUs are located at the turn transition places, shown in the circles, at the beginning and end of turns uttered by two speakers respectively in Figure 4 - 6.

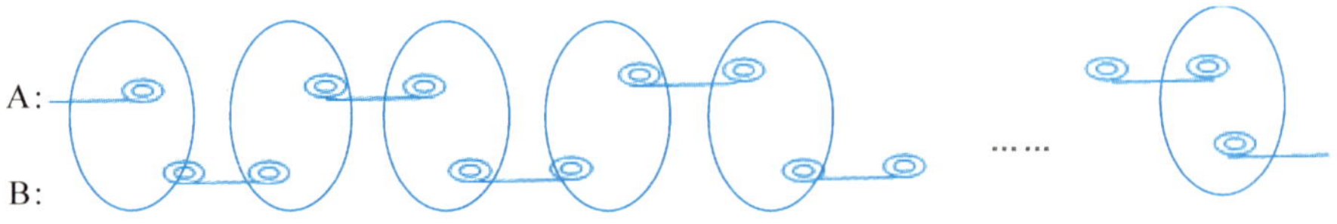

Figure 4 - 6 Plan 1: Two sets of adjacent IPUs for every two turns

In Figure 4 - 6, A and B represent two interlocutors. All the adjacent IPUs are circled at the turn exchange positions. For every turn, there are two sets of adjacent IPUs. They match at the beginning and ending positions of every turn. The pairs are shown in the circles.

An advantage of plan 1 is that it covers all the possible adjacent IPUs. However, there is a big disadvantage in this plan. If the turn contains more than one IPU, it is possible to do the matches according to plan 1; but if the turn contains only one IPU, it is not possible to do the matches of IPUs shown in Figure 11 at both the beginning and ending positions.

In Plan 2, one set of adjacent IPUs are chosen, which are shown in the circles in Figure 4 - 7.

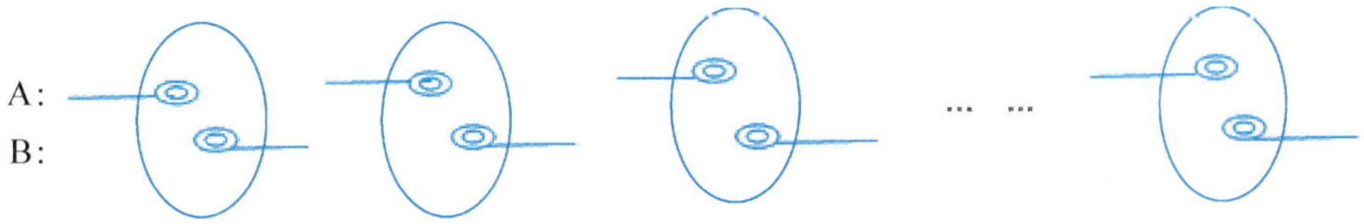

Figure 4 - 7 Plan 2: One set of adjacent IPUs for every two turns

As Figure 4 - 7 shows, in plan 2, one set of adjacent IPUs are circled for every two turns at the ending position of the former turn and the beginning position of the latter turn. Plan 2 works well no matter how many IPUs are included in turns. Therefore, the present research adopts the plan 2 in the measurement of synchrony in entrainment.

In Pearson's correlation analyses between *disa* and time, *disa* is clearly defined, but how is the value of time decided? Since what is extracted directly by Praat script is not the beginning or ending time of the IPUs but their durations, and it is more complex to extract the time of each pair of IPUs than its duration, the present research use turn indexes to represent the time indexes in Pearson's correlation analysis, because turn indexes are easy to define, and represent well the course of conversations (for example, the increase of time indexes represents the progress of conversations).

To reduce the degree of computation for convergence at turn level, the present research computed the correlations over 30 conversations of the total 70 conversations. Every 10 conversations are selected randomly from the conversations produced by each of three groups (female-female, male-male, or mixed gender groups).

2. Results

For 7 prosodic features, seven sets of Pearson's correlation analyses are conducted over *adjacent* distances and turn indexes over 30 conversations. The results of are listed in Table 4 - 8.

Table 4 - 8　　Pearson's correlation analyses between *disa* and turn indexes

	r	p	Sig.
Speaking-rate	0.128	0.000	*
F0 min	−0.193	0.000	*
F0 mean	−0.218	0.000	*
F0 max	−0.238	0.000	*
Intensity min	−0.086	0.001	*
Intensity mean	0.028	0.295	/
Intensity max	0.022	0.418	/

In Table 4 - 8, an asterisk * indicates the significant difference, and the symbol/indicates no significant difference. According to this table, it is found that although the correlations are not strong, they are significantly negative for 4 prosodic features: F0 min ($r=-0.193$, $p=0.00<0.05$), F0 mean ($r=-0.218$, $p=0.00<0.05$), F0 max ($r=-0.238$, $p=0.00<0.05$), Intensity min ($r=-0.086$, $p=0.00<0.05$). These results indicate that in the course of conversations, the *adjacent* distances of the adjacent IPUs at turn exchanges decrease when the time increases in conversation over these 4 features. The features show significantly negative correlations, which provide evidence for the turn-level convergence.

Speaking-rate shows significantly positive correlation ($r=0.128$, $p=0.00<0.05$), which shows the turn-level divergence. All the features of F0 examined in the present research show turn-level convergence. Among the features of intensity, only Intensity min shows the turn-level convergence. Other two features of intensity have not significant correlations.

4.2.3 Synchrony at Turn Level

This analysis is to find out: Is there prosodic synchrony at turn level?

Synchrony is another way of measuring entrainment at turn level. Synchrony refers to a turn-by-turn relative and synchronous coordination between partners. It is hypothesized that there are dynamics of turn-by-turn synchronous matching between interlocutors. The aim of this section is to find out how the prosodic features exhibit synchrony at turn level.

1. Correlation analyses of adjacent IPUs

Adopting the method used in Levitan & Hirschberg's work (2011), the present research has conducted Pearson's correlation analyses between the adjacent IPUs from two speakers at the turn transition places.

Similar to the method in the analysis of proximity at turn level, one set of adjacent IPUs are chosen in this analysis, which is shown in Figure 4 - 8.

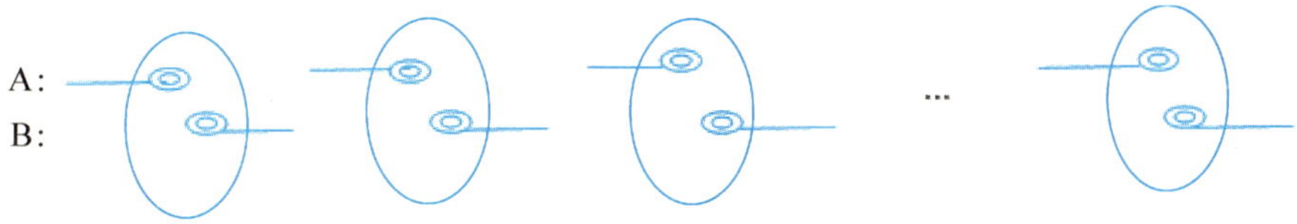

Figure 4 - 8 Adjacent IPUs for every two turns for synchrony

If the correlation is positive, it means when the prosodic features of one IPU increase, its adjacent IPU at the turn exchanges increase synchronically, and if the former decrease, the latter decrease synchronically, too. That is, with the progress of conversations, the prosodic features over the adjacent IPUs at turn exchanges change similarly. If the correlation is negative, it means with the progress of conversations, the adjacent IPUs at turn exchanges make divergence, and do not show synchrony. Positive correlations are what are hypothesized in the analysis of synchrony.

In order to reduce the degree of computation, 30 conversations are used for the analysis of synchrony at turn level. They are randomly chosen from all 70 conversations in Tongji Games Corpus. The analysis of convergence at turn level used the same conversations. Every 10 conversations are selected randomly from the conversations produced by each of three groups (female-female, male-male, or mixed gender groups).

2. Results

The Pearson's correlation analyses over the last IPUs at the former turns and the first IPUs at the following turns of the 30 conversations are accomplished in terms of the 7 prosodic features. The results are listed in Table 4 - 9.

Table 4 - 9 Pearson's correlation analyses of adjacent IPUs

	r	p	Sig.
Speaking-rate	−0.048	0.073	/
F0 min	0.625	0.000	*
F0 mean	0.661	0.000	*
F0 max	0.610	0.000	*
Intensity min	0.311	0.000	*
Intensity mean	0.628	0.000	*
Intensity max	0.551	0.000	*

In Table 4 - 9, an asterisk * indicates the significant difference, and the symbol/indicates no significant difference. This table shows that 6 features examined in the adjacent IPUs from two interlocutors in conversation indicate significant positive relations: F0 min ($r=0.625$, $p=0.00<0.05$), F0 mean ($r=0.661$, $p=0.00<0.05$), F0 max ($r=0.610$, $p=0.00<0.05$), Intensity min ($r=0.311$, $p=0.00<0.05$), Intensity mean ($r=0.628$, $p=0.00<0.05$), Intensity max ($r=0.551$, $p=0.00<0.05$). No significantly positive correlation is found over Speaking-rate ($r=-0.048$, $p=0.073>0.05$).

These results show that in terms of F0 min, F0 mean, F0 max, Intensity min, Intensity mean and Intensity max, when the values of these prosodic features in the last IPU of the former turns become bigger, the values of the features at the initial IPU of the following adjacent turns also become bigger; and the former become smaller, the latter smaller synchronically. This is the exhibition of synchrony at the turn-level.

Six features (F0 min, F0 mean, F0 max, Intensity min, Intensity mean, and Intensity max) show significant synchrony at turn level. Synchrony is possible even without proximity. Speaking-rate shows no synchrony at turn level.

4.2.4 Summary of Results

Section 4. 2 focuses on the analyses of entrainment at turn level. Three analyses are accomplished in this part: the proximity, convergence, and synchrony at turn level.

In the analysis of proximity at turn level, by the paired T-tests of the distances between adjacent IPUs at turn exchanges and non-adjacent IPUs, it is found that the distances of the adjacent IPUs are significantly smaller than that of the non-adjacent IPUs over 3 variables (Speaking-rate, Intensity mean, and Intensity max), which shows that these 3 prosodic features exhibit significant prosodic proximity at turn level.

In the analysis of convergence at turn level, by Pearson's Correlation Analysis between distances of the adjacent IPUs from two speakers and turn index (representing time), it is found that at turn level, the 3 features of fundamental frequency show significantly negative correlations in the analyses, which prove the turn-level convergence. In all the features of Intensity, only Intensity min shows significantly negative correlation. Other two features of Intensity do not. Speaking-rate shows a significantly positive correlation, which proves the turn-level divergence over this feature. Therefore, a conclusion can be made that the features of F0 show better prosodic convergence than the feature of duration and intensity, although they does not entrain at conversation level.

In the analyses of synchrony at turn level, by Pearson's Correlation analyses between the adjacent IPUs from different speakers at the turn transition places, it is found that except Speaking-rate, other 6 features (F0 min, F0 mean, F0 max, Intensity min, Intensity mean, Intensity max) show significant synchrony at turn level. Speaking-rate shows no synchrony at turn level. Through the comparisons with the results of proximity at both conversation and turn level, it is found that synchrony is possible even without proximity.

4.3 Entrainment over Tone Units

This section focuses on the analyses of entrainment over tone units, which include four parts: proximity, convergence and synchrony over tone units and entrainment over tones.

Two points should be mentioned in these analyses.

Firstly, all the tone units are extracted from carrier sentences. In these analyses, the carrier sentences are the same, except the positions of target tone units (as in Section 3.1.6). The carrier sentences guarantee the same environment to the target tone units and make the comparisons over tone units valid.

Secondly, all the tone units in the present research are carried by bi-syllabic words, and both syllables carry tone 1.

The reason why bi-syllabic words are used is that according to the formation of the Chinese words, about 80% are bi-syllabic (Liu & Liang 1990). That is to say, the tones of bi-syllabic words have the greatest proportion in Chinese tones (Kong 2001). Therefore, bi-syllabic words carry the main use of tones in Chinese.

The reason why both syllables in each word carry tone 1 is to simplify the analyses of tones combinations in the present research. There are 4 tones in Mandarin, which produces 16 combinations of two tones and several tone sandhis. As one of the studies of prosodic entrainment, the present research measured prosodic alignment over the units in different size including conversation units, turn units and tone units. It is because that entrainment is assumed to be more prominent over larger speaking units in the present research. The matching within tone units with different tones combinations or tone sandhis could be studied in the future.

More details of carrier sentences and bi-syllabic words therein are introduced in the Chapter 3.

4.3.1 Proximity over Tone Units

This analysis is to find out: Is there proximity over tone units? The aim of this analysis is to investigate whether there is holistic approaching in prosody over the whole tone units, and how prosodic parameters play roles in the entrainment over tone units.

Prosodic proximity is analyzed at conversation level and at turn level in section 4.1 and section 4.2. Based on these results, the present research assumes that the prosodic entrainment is an accumulative process from relatively local level to global level. Therefore, in the analysis of proximity over tone units, it is hypothesized that there is prosodic proximity over tone units.

1. Paired T-tests between *disc* and *disnc*

Similar to the methods used in the analyses of proximity at both conversation and turn levels, the method adopted in this analysis over tone units is also paired T-test: using paired T-tests over two sets of distances: *corresponding distances* and *non-corresponding distances*.

A *corresponding distance* is a distance of a prosodic feature between the target tone unit in one's speaking and the corresponding tone unit in his partner's speaking, which hold the same tone and refer to the same picture as the target tone unit; a *non-corresponding distance* is the mean of the distances between the target tone unit and non-corresponding tone units in conversation, which hold the same tones but refer to different pictures. Both *corresponding distances* and *non -corresponding distances* are restricted to the same conversation in order to control for the influence of different speakers.

It is hypothesized that if there is prosodic proximity over tone units, the *corresponding distance* should be smaller than the *non-corresponding distance*.

This method is explained by following Formula 6 and 7.

In Formula 6, *disc* represents the *corresponding distance*. TU_t refers to the target tone unit, which is randomly chosen from speaker A. TU_c refers to corresponding unit, which is uttered by the target IU_t speaker's conversational partner and refers to the same picture as the target IU_t. For each conversation, the present research defined *corresponding distance* (*disc*) as the distance of a prosodic feature between the target tone unit (TU_t) in one speaker's speaking and its corresponding tone unit in his interlocutor's speaking, which hold the same tones and refer to the same picture (TU_c).

$$disc = | TU_t - TU_c | \qquad \text{(Formula 6)}$$

The present research defined *non-corresponding distance* as shown in Formula 7.

$$disnc = \frac{\sum_{i=1}^{8} | TU_t - TU_i |}{8} \qquad \text{(Formula 7)}$$

In Formula 7, *disnc* represents the *non-corresponding distance*. TU_t refers to the target tone unit, which is randomly chosen from speaker A. TU_i is uttered by the target IU_t speaker's conversational partner and refers to the different pictures. $| TU_t - TU_i |$ represents a distance between the target TU and the other randomly chosen TU. As the description of the corpus in Chapter 3, 18 tone units are set in the 18 carrier sentences. If one of the 18 tone units is chosen as the target, there would be other 17 tone units left. To reduce the degree of computation, this test randomly chose 8 from the 17. And *disnc* in Formula 7 represents the mean of the distances between the target TU and other 8 randomly chosen TU in the same conversation. The calculation of *disnc* is accomplished automatically by the Computation program 2 in Appendix G.

For each conversation, the *corresponding distance* and *non-corresponding distance* are calculated by Formula 6 and 7. Thus, for one prosodic feature, one pair of distances is computed. For 7 prosodic features, 7 pairs of distances are computed.

In order to reduce the degree of computation, every 10 conversations are selected randomly from the conversations produced by each of three groups (female-female, male-male, or mixed gender groups). For one prosodic parameter, there are 30 pairs of distances; for 7 prosodic parameters, there are 210 ($30\times7=210$) pairs of *disc* and *disnc*, which are listed in Appendix I.

2. Results

These values are put into the paired T-test by SPSS 16.0. The results are listed in Table 4 - 10.

Table 4 - 10 Paired T-test of corresponding distances and non-corresponding distances

disc vs. *disnc*	*t*	d*f*	*p*	Sig.
Speaking-rate	−4.613	29	0.000	*
F0 min	−0.639	29	0.528	/
F0 mean	−0.840	29	0.408	/
F0 max	−2.349	29	0.026	*
Intensity min	−3.567	29	0.001	*
Intensity mean	−3.513	29	0.001	*
Intensity max	−5.672	29	0.000	*

In Table 4 - 10, an asterisk * indicates the significant difference, and the symbol/indicates no significant difference. This table shows that the corresponding distance is significantly smaller than the non-corresponding distance over 5 variables: Speaking-rate ($p=0.000<0.05$), F0 max ($p=0.026<0.05$), Intensity min ($p=0.001<0.05$), Intensity mean ($p=0.001<0.05$), and Intensity max ($p=0.000<0.05$), and there are not the significant difference between the two kinds of distances over other 2 variables of fundamental frequency (for F0 mean, $p=0.528>0.05$, F0 max, $p=0.408>0.05$).

Based on the results above, it is found that the corresponding distance is significantly smaller than the non-corresponding distance over 5 variables (Speaking-rate, F0 max, Intensity min, Intensity mean, and Intensity max). This indicates that these 5 prosodic features exhibit significant prosodic proximity over tone units.

4.3.2 Convergence over Tone Units

This analysis is to find out: Is there prosodic convergence over tone units in Mandarin conversations? In this section, the present research aims to analyze prosodic entrainment over tone units with the progress of conversations. That is, the purpose of this analysis is to investigate whether speakers increase similarity over tone units as conversations progress.

1. Correlation analyses of *disc* and time

In the analysis of prosodic entrainment over tone units in the course of conversations, tone units are the 18 bi-syllabic words in the carrier sentences (the reason is stated in the beginning of this section).

Similar to the method used in the analysis of convergence at turn level, the method used in the analysis of convergence over tone units is also Pearson's correlation analysis. This analysis is accomplished over distance of corresponding tone units, *corresponding distance* (*disc*) and time index. As mentioned in section 4. 3. 1, *disc* is defined as the distance of a prosodic feature between a target tone unit (TU_t) in one's speaking and its corresponding tone unit in his partner's speaking (TU_c). These two units hold the same tones and refer to the same picture in conversation. *disc* is calculated by Formula 6.

Time index is used to represent time in this Pearson's correlation analysis, which is similar to the analysis of convergence at turn level. The reason for using time index is that what is extracted directly by Praat script is not the beginning or ending time of the turn units, and it is complex to extract the real time of each pair of tone units. Time index is easy to define. Time index of every picture equals the number of every picture where a tone unit is located. Therefore, time index represents well the course of conversation. The increase of time indexes represents the progress of the conversation.

In this section, Pearson's correlation analysis is accomplished over the distance of corresponding units and time index. If the correlation is positive, it means in the course of conversations (the increase of the time index), the distance between the corresponding tone units increases with the progress of conversations; if the correlation is negative, it means in the course of conversations, the distance between the corresponding tone units decreases with the progress of conversations. The latter result is what is hypothesized in this analysis.

For each conversation, the 18 *disc* over 18 tone units are calculated by Formula 6. Every 10 conversations are selected randomly from the conversations produced by each of three groups (female-female, male-male, or mixed gender groups). For every prosodic parameter, there are 540 ($30 \times 18 = 540$) corresponding distances. All the values for 7 prosodic parameters are put into the Pearson's correlation analysis by SPSS 16. 0. The results are listed in the following section.

2. Results

The results of Pearson's correlation analysis between *disc* and time indexes are listed in Table 4 - 11.

Table 4 - 11 Pearson's correlation analysis between *disc* and time indexes

	r	p	Sig.
Speaking-rate	−0. 044	0. 335	/
F0 min	−0. 030	0. 511	/
F0 mean	−0. 013	0. 770	/
F0 max	−0. 015	0. 735	/
Intensity min	−0. 012	0. 792	/
Intensity mean	−0. 047	0. 304	/
Intensity max	−0. 033	0. 461	/

In Table 4 - 11, the symbol/indicates no significant difference. According to this table, it is found that the correlations are negative, but they are not significant for any prosodic parameter. The correlations are negative, which means with the ongoing of conversations, the distances over tone units decrease with the increase of time indexes, but the correlations are not significant in this test.

According to the results above, one conclusion can be made that we can't find the convergence over the tone units with progress of the conversation. That is, we do not find the prosodic features over the tone units become more similar in the process of conversation.

4.3.3 Synchrony over Tone Units

The analysis in this section is to find out: Is there prosodic synchrony over tone units? Similar to the synchronical analysis at turn level (in Section 4.2), this section aims to capture the synchronous matching of tone-unit by tone-unit between two interlocutors in one conversation, which refers to relative and synchronous coordination between partners over tone units.

1. Correlation analyses of corresponding tone units

The analysis of prosodic synchrony over tone units is accomplished between all the pairs of corresponding bi-syllabic words, which are the same name of the same picture, but produced by two interlocutors in speaking. These corresponding words are extracted from the carrier sentences.

Similar to the method used in the test of synchrony at turn level, the method used in the analysis of convergence over tone units is also Pearson's correlation analysis. This analysis is accomplished over the pairs of bi-syllabic words set in the carrier sentences.

If the correlation is positive, it means with the ongoing of conversations, the prosodic features over pairs of tone units change synchronically. That is, when the prosodic features of one tone unit increase, those of its corresponding tone unit (the other of the pair) increase synchronically, and if the former decrease, the latter decrease. If the correlation is negative, it means with the ongoing of conversations, the prosodic features exhibit divergence over the pairs of tone units. That is, no matter the prosodic features of one tone unit increase or decrease, those of its corresponding tone unit (the other of the pair) do not increase or decrease synchronically. The first result is what is hypothesized in this analysis.

For each conversation, there are 18 pairs of bi-syllabic tone units. In order to reduce the amount of computation, 30 conversations are randomly chosen from 70 in the corpus for this analysis. For every prosodic parameter, there are 540 ($30 \times 18 = 540$) pairs of tone units in this test.

2. Results

All the values for 7 prosodic parameters are put into the Pearson's correlation analyses by SPSS 16. 0. The results are listed in Table 4 - 12.

Table 4 - 12 Pearson's correlation analyses between the pairs of tone units

	r	*p*	Sig.
Speaking-rate	0. 426	0. 000	*
F0 min	0. 491	0. 000	*
F0 mean	0. 557	0. 000	*
F0 max	0. 525	0. 000	*
Intensity min	0. 364	0. 000	*
Intensity mean	0. 689	0. 000	*
Intensity max	0. 673	0. 000	*

In Table 4 - 12, an asterisk * indicates the significant difference. This table shows that pairs of tone units from different speakers show significant positive relation over all the 7 features examined in the present research ($p = 0.000 < 0.05$). These results indicate that prosodic features show synchrony over tone units.

With the Pearson's correlation analysis of prosodic synchrony over tone units accomplished between all the pairs of bi-syllabic words designed in the carrier sentences, it is found in this analysis that all the 7 features examined in the present research show significant synchrony over tone units.

4. 3. 4 Entrainment of Tones

The analysis in this section is to find out: Is there entrainment over tones? This section aims to capture the entrainment of tones.

In the present research, the analysis of entrainment over tones focuses on the relative pitch registers of the corresponding tones produced by female and male pairs.

Here are the reasons for making this focus. The analysis in this section emphasizes the entrainment over the tones produced by female and male subjects. The main reason for this emphasis is that the test of coordination between female and male pairs, which own different pitch ranges by nature in producing tones, is much more difficult yet valuable than that between the pairs with the same gender, which own the same pitch range in the analyses of entrainment. The major difficulty in analysis is how to make tones within different pitch ranges comparable. The method adapted in this analysis is to use the relative pitch registers of tones for individual subjects.

Therefore, the analysis of entrainment over tones in this section aims to find out whether there is entrainment in the relative pitch registers of the corresponding tones produced by female and males. It is hypothesized that there is such relative entrainment in the relative pitch registers of tones.

1. Correlation analyses of tones' pitch registers

This section aims to find out whether there is entrainment between the relative pitch registers of the corresponding tones units produced by female and male subjects. Pearson's correlation analyses are adopted to find out their relationship. It is hypothesized that there is relative entrainment over the relative pitch registers of tones produced by mixed gender pairs. That is, if the relative pitch registers of male speakers become higher, those of their female pairs also go higher, and if that of male speakers become lower, those of their female pairs also go lower.

According to the corpus description in Chapter Three (Section 3. 1. 6), in order to simplify the analyses of tone combinations, the present research has made control of two-tone1 combinations carried by bi-syllabic words in the carrier sentences. In this section, the analysis of entrainment over tones is accomplished over these two-tone1 combinations.

The analysis of entrainment between the relative pitch registers of the corresponding tones produced by female and male subjects is accomplished in the following three steps.

The first step is to find the corresponding tone units produced by female and male subjects in the corpus of the present research. In order to reduce the computation burden, 10 conversations are randomly chosen from all the 30 conversations produced by mixed gender pairs in the corpus. As mentioned above, the two-tone1 combinations are carried by 18 bi-syllabic words in the carrier sentences in each conversation. There should be 180 ($18 \times 10 = 180$) two-tone1 combinations in the chosen conversations for the female or male subjects respectively. Because some of the carrier sentences are missed in the spontaneous conversations, 161 corresponding two-tone1 units are found out in the 10 chosen conversations respectively for female or male subjects.

The second step is to calculate the values representing the relative pitch registers of all the two-tone1 combinations. Because all the tones in this analysis are the two-tone1 combinations, the mean of pitch values over these tone units are used to represent the positions that the pitch registers occupy within the pitch range of the subject. Besides, the absolute mean of pitch value should be normalized by the pitch range of the speaker.

The method of Five Point Scale (FPS Chao 1930) is adopted in the normalization. In this method, pitch mean is converted to the five-point-scale value by the formula: $T = [(\lg x - \lg min)/(\lg max - \lg min)] \times 5$ (Shi 1986), in which x is the mean of pitch values of a two-tone1 unit, min is the minimal pitch value within the pitch range of the speaker, and max is the maximal pitch value.

For one speaker, the five-point-scale value of the pitch mean over the tone unit within his pitch range is adopted to represent the pitch register that this tone unit occupies. Therefore, the comparisons of the female and male pith registers are accomplished in the comparisons of their corresponding five-point-scale values. 161 five-point-scale values are respectively calculated for 161 target tone units produced by female speakers and their male pairs.

The third step is to do Pearson's correlation analyses. This section aims to find out whether there is entrainment between the relative pitch registers of the corresponding tones units produced by female and male subjects. Pearson's correlation analyses are adopted to find out their relationship. As mentioned in the second step, the comparisons of the female and male pith registers are accomplished in the comparisons of their corresponding five-point-scale values. Pearson's correlation analyses are accomplished between the 161 five-point-scale values of female speakers and 161 values of their male pairs.

Data in this analysis are listed in Appendix J.

2. Results

The results of Pearson's correlation analyses by SPSS 16.0 are listed in Table 4 - 13.

Table 4 - 13　　Pearson's correlation analyses between female and male pitch registers

Correlations

		dmale	dfemale
dmale	Pearson Correlation	1	.501**
	Sig. (2-tailed)		.000
	N	161	161
dfemale	Pearson Correlation	.501**	1
	Sig. (2-tailed)	.000	
	N	161	161

**. Correlation is significant at the 0.01 level (2-tailed).

In Table 4 - 13, dmale refers to five-point-scale values of the pitch mean over the tone unit of a male speaker, and dfemale to the similar value of the female partner. The table 4 - 13 shows that there is significantly positive correlation between dmale and dfemale ($r=0.501$, $p=0.000$).

These results indicate that there is significantly positive correlation between the relative pitch registers of the corresponding tone units produced by female and male pairs, although they are in different pitch range in speaking. Therefore, the hypothesis that there is relative entrainment between the relative pitch registers of tones in the conversations of mixed gender pairs is proved. Based on these results, the approach of relative pitch registers of mixed gender pairs in collaborative conversations is proposed.

In collaborative converstions, for the mixed gender pairs, the approach of the relative pitch registers of tones is reasonable, while the approach of their absolute pitch registers sounds weird, because two speakers with gender differences stay within different pitch ranges in speaking.

How do mixed gender pairs exhibit collaboration in the production of tones? The analysis in this section shows that there is relative entrainment between the relative pitch registers of tones in the conversations of mixed gender pairs. That is, they exhibit significant relative entrainment instead of absolute entrainment in the production of tones to show collaboration.

4.3.5 Summary of Results

This section focuses on the analysis of entrainment over tone units. Four analyses over tone units are accomplished in this part: the proximity, convergence, and synchrony over tone units, and entrainment over tones.

In the analysis of proximity over tone units, by the paired T-test of the distance between *corresponding* tone units with the average of eight *non-corresponding* tone units, it is found that the corresponding distance is significantly smaller than the non-corresponding distance over 5 variables (Speaking-rate, F0 max, Intensity min, Intensity mean, and Intensity max), which indicates that these 5 prosodic features exhibit significant prosodic proximity over tone units.

In the analysis of convergence over tone units, by Pearson's correlation analyses between these distances of corresponding tone units and time (represented by tone unit index), we can't find the convergence over the tone units with the ongoing of the conversation. That is, the prosodic features over the tone units do not become more similar in the process of conversation.

In the analysis of synchrony over tone units, by Pearson's correlation analyses between the corresponding tone units, it is found that all the 7 features examined in the present research show significant synchrony over tone units.

In the analysis of entrainment over tones, by Pearson's correlation analysis of the relative pitch registers between female and male pairs, it is found that mixed gender pairs exhibit significant relative entrainment instead of absolute entrainment in the production of tones to show collaboration.

4.4 Cross-level Comparison

The analyses of prosodic entrainment in Mandarin conversations have been accomplished at multiple levels and in multiple dimensions. The comparison of the results from these levels and dimensions should bring valuable findings.

In detail, the analyses of prosodic entrainment are accomplished at three levels (conversation, turn, and tone units), and from three main aspects of entrainment (proximity, convergence and synchrony) at each level, it is necessary to make cross-level comparison of the results from the same aspects.

4.4.1 Comparison of Proximity

Comparison is made from the aspect of proximity.

In the analysis of proximity at the conversation level, by paired T-tests on partner distances and non-partner distances over 7 variables, it is found that in Mandarin conversations, the speakers exhibit proximity at the conversation level over the prosodic features of Speaking-rate, F0 max, Intensity mean, and Intensity max. The proximity in prosodic entrainment is found to be realized in the 3 main aspects of prosody: duration, pitch, intensity: durational feature (Speaking-rate), the features of pitch (F0 max), and the features of intensity (Intensity mean and Intensity max).

In the analysis of proximity at the turn level, by the paired T-test of the distances between adjacent IPUs at turn exchanges and non-adjacent IPUs, it is found that the distances of the adjacent IPUs are significantly smaller than those of the non-adjacent IPUs over 3 variables (Speaking-rate, Intensity mean, and Intensity max), which indicates that these 3 prosodic features exhibit significant prosodic proximity at turn level.

In the analysis of proximity over tone units, by the paired T-test of the distances between corresponding tone units with the averages of eight non-corresponding tone units, it is found that the corresponding distances are significantly smaller than the non-corresponding distances over 5 variables

(Speaking-rate, F0 max, Intensity min, Intensity mean, and Intensity max), which indicates that these five prosodic features exhibit significant prosodic proximity over tone units.

Differences and similarities in proximity at different levels are obvious when all the results of proximity are put in a table for comparison. All the results of proximity above are put in the Table 4 - 14, in which "√" represents that the prosodic feature shows proximity.

Table 4 - 14 Cross-level comparison of proximity

	Conversation level	Turn level	Tone unit level
Speaking-rate	√	√	√
F0 min			
F0 mean			
F0 max	√		√
Intensity min			√
Intensity mean	√	√	√
Intensity max	√	√	√

From Table 4 - 14, it is found that Speaking-rate, Intensity mean and Intensity max show proximity at all these 3 levels. F0 max only shows prosodic proximity at the conversation and tone unit levels. Intensity min shows proximity only at the tone unit level.

Through cross-level comparison of proximity, it is found that the feature of duration and most features of intensity show proximity at all the levels.

4.4.2 Comparisons of Convergence

Comparison is made from the aspect of convergence.

In the analysis of convergence at conversation level, for MC, in the Tongji Games Corpus, each conversation consists of 18 sections, each of which involves the placement or description of a single picture in both games. We compared partner differences over the first nine sections with those in the second nine. We also compared partner differences in the first section with those in the last. The analysis in this section is over 66 conversations (four were omitted from the 70 conversations because they were missing speech from one of the interlocutors for one or more of the 18 sections). No significant differences were found. We therefore cannot conclude that MC speakers globally converge on any of the features we examined.

By the descriptive method to trace the two interlocutors' distances over all the 18 sections, it is found that (i) in the process of Mandarin conversations, both convergence and divergence exist in prosodic entrainment; and that (ii) in the process of Mandarin conversations, convergence and divergence appear alternately.

In the analysis of convergence at the turn level, by Pearson's correlation analyses between distances of the adjacent IPUs from two speakers and turn index (representing time), the results show that at turn level, the 3 features of F0 show significantly negative correlation, which is evidence of turn-level convergence. Among the features of intensity, only Intensity min shows significantly negative correlation, which indicates evident convergence at the turn level. Other two features of intensity have not significant correlation. Speaking-rate shows significantly positive correlation, which shows the turn-level divergence. Therefore, it is found that the features of F0 show better prosodic convergence than the feature of duration and intensity, although they do not entrain on global level.

In the analysis of convergence over tone units, by Pearson's correlation analyses between the distances of corresponding tone units and time (represented by tone unit index), we can't find the convergence over the tone units with the ongoing of the conversation. That is, we do not find the prosodic features over the tone units become more similar in the process of conversation.

Differences and similarities in convergence at different levels are obvious when all the results of convergence are put in a table for comparison. All the results of convergence above are put in the Table 4 - 15, "√" represents that the prosodic feature shows convergence.

Table 4 - 15 **Cross-level comparison of convergence**

	Conversation level	Turn level	Tone unit level
Speaking-rate			
F0 min		√	
F0 mean		√	
F0 max		√	
Intensity min		√	
Intensity mean			
Intensity max			

Table 4 - 15 shows that we can't find convergence at both levels of the conversation and tone unit. At turn level, convergence is found over 3 features of F0 and Intensity min.

Through cross-level comparison of convergence, it is found that (i) it is more difficult to capture convergence in conversation than proximity and synchrony; (ii) convergence is found at turn level, and at this level, the features of F0 show better prosodic convergence than the feature of duration and intensity.

4.4.3 Comparison of Synchrony

Comparison is made from the aspect of synchrony.

At the beginning of this chapter, synchrony is defined as a relative and synchronous coordination between partners. That is, synchrony is a conception which can be realized over relatively local units. In the present research, synchrony is tested at two levels: turn and tone units.

In the analysis of synchrony at turn level, by Pearson's correlation analyses between the adjacent IPUs from different speakers at the turn transition places, it is found that except Speaking-rate, other 6 features (F0 min, F0 mean, F0 max, Intensity min, Intensity mean, Intensity max) show significant synchrony at turn level. Speaking-rate shows no synchrony at turn level.

In the analysis of synchrony over tone units, by Pearson's correlation analyses between the corresponding tone units, it is found that all the 7 features examined in the present research show significant synchrony over tone units.

Differences and similarities in proximity at different levels are obvious when all the results of synchrony are put in a table for comparison. All the results of proximity above are put in the Table 4 - 16, in which "√" represents that the prosodic feature shows proximity.

Table 4 - 16 **Cross-level comparison of synchrony**

Feature	Turn level	Tone unit level
Speaking-rate		√
F0 min	√	√
F0 mean	√	√
F0 max	√	√
Intensity min	√	√
Intensity mean	√	√
Intensity max	√	√

Table 4 - 16 shows that almost all the features examined show synchrony at turn and tone unit levels.

Compared with the results in Table 4 - 13 and Table 4 - 14, what should be emphasized that all features of F0 show evident synchrony, while they show little proximity and convergence at the same levels.

Therefore, through cross-level comparisons of synchrony, it is found that (i) almost all the features examined show synchrony at the relatively local levels (turn and tone unit levels), and that (ii) synchrony is possible even without proximity and convergence at the local levels, which means that over certain features, speakers entrain over local units, irrespective of their global similarity.

4.5 Discussions

How is prosody used to entrain in Mandarin conversation? In this chapter, the present research has decomposed this research question into another two questions.

The first is: *Is prosodic entrainment in Mandarin conversation global or local?* From the global to the local, the present research set three hierachical levels (the levels of conversation, turn, and tone unit) in conversation. At these levels, the analyses mainly from the aspects of proximity, convergence and synchrony are conducted. Based on these analyses, the cross-level comparisons of these three aspects are accomplished in order to show the relationship between global and local entrainment in conversation. Based on the results of these analyses, two points are found.

(i) Entrainment in Mandarin conversation is proved to exist in 3 main aspects of prosody.

The analyses in the present research provide considerable evidences for the existence of entrainment in 3 main aspects of prosody: the features of duration, F0 and intensity. 7 variables, Speaking-rate (the feature of duration), F0 min, F0 mean, F0 max (the features of F0) and Intensity min, Intensity mean, Intensity max (the features of intensity) are set as parameters in the present research, over which entrainment in conversation has been proved. In addition, different prosodic features exhibit prominent entrainment at different levels.

This conclusion supports the viewpoint that prosody plays roles in keeping effective interaction. Current research on prosody in spoken interaction covers emotional prosody, prosody in cooperation or affiliation, attitudinal intonation, etc.

Prosody is used in interaction to express emotions. The processing of multimodal emotional cues is involved in interpersonal communication. These cues include particularly facial expressions (visual modality) and emotional speech prosody (auditory modality) and their interaction during information processing (Scherer 2003; Hirschberg 2004; Wichmann *et al*. 2009).

Speech prosody is used also show cooperation or competition, agreement or disagreement, affiliation or disaffiliation in interaction. French & Local (1968) have examined the differences between turn-competitive and non-competitive interruptions, and find that pitch and loudness are raised in competitive interruptions, and that when the raised pitch and loudness are identified in an interruption, the interlocutor modifies the prosody of speech, showing a willingness to give up the floor, or hold the floor by further raising pitch and loudness. Brazil (1985) points out three significant keys in speech prosody: high, mid and low, which set up constraints across speaker turns. He proposes a principle of pitch concord between two interlocutors in compliant conversations: high termination expected high key; mid termination expected mid key; low termination permitted high, mid and low key; the matching of relative register or key in prosody is perceived as supportive. Couper-Kuhlen (1996) finds that the verbal and prosodic imitation in a relative register matching had a supportive function, and the absolute register matching indicates negative comment; the exact copy in prosody was perceived as mimicry and was considered to be mocking the current speaker. Wichmann (2000) finds that the backchannels with a rising tone or echoing the current speakers' prosody can be heard as supportive and collaborative response to encourage interlocutor's continuation; however, the backchannels with falling tone or distinctive performance in prosody make different effect to end the current speaker's topic and turn. Therefore, Wichmann (2000) assumes that "the most important way in which intonation contributes to conversational interaction is not in features of pitch direction but of pitch range".

Prosody also can express attitudes in interaction. In communication, intonation works with other linguistic patterns to express attitudes. Knowles (1987: 205 - 206) states that "it is extremely unlikely that there are any attitudes which are conveyed uniquely by intonation ... It is possible that intonation patterns that are regarded as attitudinally marked use the intonation system in an unexpected way, and possibly in conjunction with other linguistic patterns". Wichmann (2000) points out the implied or inferred meanings are the key to many cases of perceived "tone of voice" or attitude; some intonationally conveyed attitudes, however, in particular negative ones, are the result of some kind of mismatch, when it is "possible to assign to a particular intonation pattern, or some aspect of intonational behavior, or a 'normal' or 'expected' meaning which then has the potential to be exploited in an unexpected way, generating an inference on the part of the receiver".

The currently contribution to our understanding of attitudinal meaning in intonation is the study of "affiliating and disaffiliating" behavior. The investigation of intonation of cooperative behavior, and uncooperative behavior is beneficial because it can explain participants' response. Brown, Currie & Kenworthy (1980) have investigated the low endpoint of a terminal contour (falling tone) to be an important finality signal and not-low terminals are associated with a range of affective meanings including deference, politeness, vulnerability. Müller (1996) points out the cooperative backchannel responses are in time and in tune with the current talk, then it is also clear that the backchannel responses are not in time or not in tune.

Recently, more and more attention is paid to attitudinal function of prosody because of the need in development of human-machine dialogue systems. The related research is helpful to make machines produce voices that sound cooperative, friendly, or polite, along with the aim to recognize when human customers are irate, frustrated or just plain exasperated (Ang *et al.* 2002).

Because emotional prosody and attitudinal prosody are frequently considered to be synonymous, or overlapping, the distinction between them is unclear (Tench 1997). Crystal (1995) points out that an important function of intonation is attitudinal, but he puts it under the heading of emotion: "Intonation's most obvious role is to express attitudinal meaning - sarcasm, surprise, reserve, impatience, shock, anger, interest, and thousands of other semantic nuances." Couper-Kuhlen (1986: 185 - 187) made a more detailed distinction between emotion and attitude, emotion representing a speaker state (happy, sad, ...) and attitude representing a kind of behavior (condescending, friendly, ...), and a good contrast between emotional prosody and attitudinal prosody was also put forward: while emotions could be felt whether or not another person was present, attitude could not be present independently of interaction, that is, one could be happy on his own, but could not be condescending on his own (Leech 1983: 106). Wichmann (2000) points out that "expressive" intonation refers to the prosodic features conveying pure emotion and emotion arising from beliefs, knowledge and opinion, and that "attitudinal" intonation, on the other hand reflected a certain speaker behavior.

Entrainment in conversation is both attitudinal and emotional, because it can be considered as cooperation, agreement, or support in communication. However, entrainment emphasizes adjustment and alignment between two interlocutors in cooperation. Therefore, the research of entrainment pays more attention to the coordination or adjustment between two parties in interaction, while the studies of emotional and attitudinal prosody mentioned above pay more attention to a single part. It is from this different perspective that prosody is proved to play crucial roles in interaction.

(ii) For the prosodic features measured in the present research, local entrainment is more evident than global entrainment, and different prosodic features exhibit entrainment at different levels: at both global and local levels, features of intensity exhibit prominent entrainment; entrainment over the durational feature is more prominent at relatively global level; entrainment over the features of F0 is more prominent at relatively local level.

The results of cross-level comparisons above supply evidences for this finding. At first, more prosodic features exhibit entrainment at relatively local level than at global level. In terms of proximity, 5 features show entrainment over tone units, and 4 features at conversation level; in terms of synchrony, 7 features show entrainment over tone units, 6 features at turn level. Secondly, the features of fundamental frequency show more prominent entrainment at relatively local level, irrespective of their global similarity.

In terms of the relationship between global entrainment and local entrainment, the present research makes three hypotheses: two interlocutors in conversation probably entrain globally, but diverge at local positions; they may not be similar globally, but entrain locally; they entrain both globally and locally.

According to the analyses of entrainment at multiple levels, all these hypotheses are proved to exist in conversation for different prosodic features.

Features of intensity exhibit prominent entrainment at both global and local levels. In detail, Intensity mean and Intensity max show significant proximity at the levels of conversation, turn and tone units. Features of intensity show synchrony at the levels of both turn and tone units. The finding that the features of intensity show entrainment at both global and local levels is consistent with that of the research on English (Levitan & Hirschberg 2011; Levitan *et al*. 2012).

The hypothesis of both global and local entrainment is proved in the analyses of the Intensity features. For these features, entrainment can be considered as a dynamic and accumulative process of continuous matching from the local units to the local ones. The possible reason is that two interlocutors are the most sensitive to the change in the production and perception of intensity in conversation, that the features of intensity are preferred tools in the adaptation of prosody.

Features of duration exhibit more prominent entrainment at relatively global levels. In detail, speaking-rate shows holistic similarity over the whole units of conversation, turn, and tone units (Significant entrainment is found in the analyses of proximity at these levels). However, no such consistent entrainment is found locally. The synchrony of Speaking-rate is found over tone units, but is not found at turn level.

The hypothesis that two interlocutors in conversation probably entrain globally, but diverge at local positions is proved in the analyses of the durational features. The possible reason is that the change in Speaking-rate costs longer time and covers larger scales than that in the features of intensity. So it is not easy to make or perceive the adaptations in speaking-rate over minor units, and the realization of prosodic entrainment is more prominent at the more global level.

The features of F0 exhibit more prominent entrainment at relatively local levels. In detail, more features of F0 show entrainment in synchrony at levels of the turn and tone unit, and less show entrainment at conversation level. The finding is consistent with that of the research on English (Levitan & Hirschberg 2011; Levitan *et al*. 2012).

The hypothesis that two interlocutors in conversation are not similar globally, but entrain locally is proved in the analyses of the F0 features.

Although there is prominent entrainment at local level over the features of F0, why does the local entrainment not accumulate to the global level? One of the possible reasons is that the features of F0 play multiple roles in conversations, including lexical tones, intonation, all kinds of pragmatic function, etc. These multiple roles share the effect of local entrainment over F0 features, and can't make it accumulative to be prominent at global level. This assumption needs to be tested in the future research.

Therefore, all the three hypotheses, which are made for the relationship between global entrainment and local entrainment at the beginning of this chapter, proved to exist in Mandarin conversation for different prosodic features. The features of Intensity exhibit both global and local entrainment, the features of fundamental frequency exhibit more prominent entrainment at local level than at global level, and the feature of duration exhibit more prominent entrainment at global level than at local level.

Another decomposed research question in this chapter is: *Is prosodic entrainment in Mandarin conversation convergent or constant as conversation goes on?* The analyses of dynamic entrainment during the course of conversation have been accomplished at the three hierarchical levels (the levels of conversation, turn, and tone units). One point is found.

(iii) With the progress of conversation, increased similarity between two interlocutors is found at turn level, but no increased similarity is found at conversation level or over tone units.

The present research has accomplished the analyses of convergence at three levels. Two simple hypotheses for the entrainment process in conversation are made in Chapter 4. One is that two interlocutors become more and more similar when time progresses till the end of conversation. Another is that distances of two interlocutors decreases to fixed distance, and the pair keep this fixed distance to the end of conversation.

The analyses in this chapter indicate that with the progress of conversation, convergence at the turn level is found, but no convergence is found at conversation level or over tone units. The comparison of convergence at three levels show that it is more difficult to capture convergence in conversation than proximity and synchrony, and that convergence is found at turn level. Only one of the two hypotheses for the entrainment process in conversation is proved at one level (turn level).

To capture entrainment dynamic manifestation is not an easy task. The difficulties exist mainly in two sides.

One is that spontaneous conversations involve various factors, and the adaptation of two interlocutors changes with the situation where they are. Any psychological, social, behavioral, or other factors probably trigger the interlocutors' states in conversation. It is difficult to find a fixed model to capture these changes.

Another difficulty is that the adaptation between partners is not time-aligned. Speakers do not accommodate to each other immediately due to the inherent temporally reactive nature of conversational speech (De Looze *et al.* 2014: 15).

The difficulty in model the entrainment process causes the inconsistency in relevant researches, in which different models of convergence in conversation are proposed.

Levitan & Hirschberg (2011) predict a linear entrainment process. There are gradual coordination and more entrainment over the course of English conversations.

De Looze *et al.* (2014) assume that speech accommodation can actually manifest as both a linear and dynamic phenomenon, because the fact that prosodic accommodation has been shown to increase continuously as well as to vary over the course of the conversation.

The present research predicts a wave entrainment process. Both convergence and divergence exist in Mandarin conversation, and they appear alternately. However, this wave model is proposed based on descriptive statistics. Therefore, this prediction needs to be tested by different research methods.

Therefore, it is necessary to do more exploration on the model of prosodic entrainment process in conversation in the future studies.

(iv) Mixed gender pairs exhibit significant relative entrainment instead of absolute entrainment in the production of tones to show collaboration.

Whether there is entrainment in the relative pitch registers of the corresponding tones produced by female and male pairs is analyzed in this chapter. Pearson's correlation analyses are adopted in this analysis. For one speaker, the five-point-scale value of the pitch mean over the tone unit within his pitch range is adopted to represent the pitch register that this tone unit occupies. Pearson's correlation analyses are accomplished between the 161 five-point-scale values of female speakers and 161 values of their male pairs.

Through this analysis, it is found that there is significantly positive correlation between the relative pitch registers of the corresponding tone units produced by female and male subjects, although they are in different pitch ranges in speaking. Therefore, the hypothesis that there is relative entrainment between the relative pitch registers of tones in the conversations of mixed gender pairs is proved.

In collaborative conversations, for the mixed gender pairs, the approach of the relative pitch registers of tones is reasonable, while the approach of their absolute pitch registers sounds weird, because two speakers with gender differences stay within different pitch ranges in speaking.

How do mixed gender pairs exhibit collaboration in the production of tones? The analysis in this section shows that there is relative entrainment between the relative pitch registers of tones in the conversations of mixed gender pairs. That is, they exhibit significant relative entrainment instead of absolute entrainment in the production of tones to show collaboration.

Section 4.3 is about the analyses of entrainment over tone units, which can be divided into two parts. In the former three sub-sections, absolute entrainment over tone units is proved, and 7 prosodic features from the 3 main aspects of prosody (duration, fundamental frequency, and intensity) are comprehensively investigated. In the last sub-sections, relative entrainment over tone units is proved, and this part focuses on pitch registers of tones. The former part follows the line in the analyses of the entrainment from the global to the local, in which the method used is consistent with that in more global units (the units of conversation and turn). The latter part highlight relative pitch registers of Mandarin tones. Therefore, two parts in this section are mutual complementary, and form comprehensive analyses of entrainment over tone units.

At the end of this chapter, it is necessary to have discussion on the research methods used the analyses of absolute entrainment in this chapter, which have reference value for the future researches.

Two methods should be mentioned. One is the method for measurement of entrainment, and the other is the method for the identification of entrainment.

Firstly, let's talk about the method used for measurement of entrainment. Measurement of entrainment is difficult. For one thing, entrainment involves the performances of two interlocutors, and there are several possible directions in entrainment between pairs (A, B), including A to B (A→B), B to A (A←B), and both A and B approaching to an intermediate state (A→←B) (Kristiansen 2008). For the other, the values of entrainment can not be extracted directly by Praat. They should be calculated over the values of prosodic features directly extracted by Praat.

The present research follows the way of the measurement in previous studies, and adopts distances between two interlocutors to present entrainment. In detail, distances of prosodic performances between two interlocutors are calculated for the measurement of entrainment only with a negative correlation between them. That is, when interlocutors' distance becomes smaller, entrainment becomes bigger. Thus, no matter in which direction interlocutors entrain, it is valid that distances of interlocutors' represent entrainment degree. The method that adopting distances between two interlocutors to present entrainment forms the base for other methods used in the analyses of prosodic entrainment in the present research.

Secondly, let's talk about the method used for the identification of entrainment. How to identify entrainment in conversation is also a difficult task. Methods used to test whether two interlocutors become similar or not are not easy to find. If distance between two interlocutors is smaller than a baseline, it can be concluded that this pair entrain in conversation. The difficulty is to find out the valid baseline in comparison.

The present research adopts the notion of Levitan and her group (Levitan & Hirschberg 2011, Levitan *et al.* 2012) that the comparisons between partner distances and non-partner distances are used to identify entrainment in conversation. In detail, if the partner distances between A and B are smaller than non-partner distances between A and C, entrainment can be identified in the conversations of this pair. Here, A and B are two interlocutors in conversation, C is the speaker with the same gender and role to B and never talks with A. Here, the non-partner distance is taken as the baseline in comparison.

The present research makes sufficient use of this method. Besides the comparisons between partner distances and non-partner distances in the analyses of proximity at conversation level, in the analyses of proximity at turn level, comparisons between adjacent IPUs at turn exchanges and non-adjacent IPUs are used. In the analyses of proximity over turn units, comparisons between corresponding distances and non-corresponding distances are used. Although the units in comparisons are different in size, the key point that the irrelevant third party is borrowed in comparisons of two parties is the same.

Another benefit from the adoption of these partner and non-partner distances is the exclusion of pitch normalization between female and male speakers. The pitch of a voice depends on the length of the speaker's vocal tract. In general, female pitches range from about 75 to 500 Hz, and male pitches range from about 50 to 300. Therefore, the female usually have high-pitched voices than the male. In order to make valid comparisons between female and male speakers, their raw pitches are usually scaled to the same range. However, this kind of pitch normalization is excluded in the present research. In the series of Paired T-tests, for example, partner and non-partner distances are compared. The non-paired partners are restricted to those who have the same gender and role with the partners of the target speakers, and never talk to the target speakers. This restriction makes the use of raw F0 values valid in the analyses.

Other baselines might be valid. The difficulty is to find out them.

For example, the distance of two interlocutors' primary states before they have conversation could be a baseline. Here, the primary states refer to the states of the individual speakers of the pair in conversation before they talk to each other. In general, in the design of experiments entrainment, interlocutors are strangers and never talk to each other before the experiments in order to reduce the mutual influence of the pair in experiments. If the distance of the pair in conversation is smaller than their primary distance before conversation, it can be concluded that this pair entrain. Thus, it is necessary to record the primary states of two interlocutors before their conversation. This should be an essential part in experiment design. It is necessary to test the validity of this baseline in future studies. More valid baselines are expected to be found in the future research.

Chapter 5

Entrainment from Social Aspect

In the previous chapter, prosodic entrainment at multiple levels is analyzed. This chapter focuses on the analyses of entrainment and social factors.

Entrainment in conversation is related closely to social factors. The individual differences of the interlocutors decide the direction and state of entrainment in conversation.

The present research made gender control and role control in experiments as mentioned in Section 3. 1. 4 and Section 3. 1. 5. The analyses in this chapter include two parts, one of which is about entrainment and gender, and the other is entrainment and role.

5. 1 Entrainment and Gender

The analyses of entrainment and gender include two parts: proximity and the entrainment degree of pairs with different gender combination. In the present research, there are three kinds of gender combination in conversation (female-female groups, female-male groups, male-male groups).

5. 1. 1 Proximity of Pairs with Different Gender Combination

This analysis is to find out: Are there any differences in proximity among different gender groups?

The analyses of proximity in this section are set at the conversation level. In the previous chapter (Chapter 4), proximity has been analyzed at three levels (the levels of conversation, turn, and tone units). In order to make the factor of gender prominent, and simplify the analyses, the analyses of proximity among pairs with different gender combination in this section are accomplished only at the conversation level.

As mentioned in Chapter 1 and 2, relevant studies have proved the difference in prosodic entrainment among the pairs with different gender combinations. Therefore, it is hypothesized that there are differences in prosodic proximity among different gender groups in Mandarin conversations.

1. Paired T-tests over different gender groups

Paired T-tests are accomplished between the *partner* distances and *non-partner* distances in this analysis. This similar method has been adopted in Section 4.1 for the analyses of proximity at conversation level. What is different here in this section is that the paired T-tests are accomplished over female-female groups, female-male groups, and male-male groups respectively, but there is no necessity to make distinctions in gender groups in the analyses in Section 4.1.

For each speaker in a conversation, a *partner* distance and *non-partner* distance are calculated. The *partner* distance is the distance of a prosodic feature between the speaker and his partner; *non-partner* distance is the mean of the distances of a prosodic feature between the speaker and other speakers, with whom he is not partnered in any conversations. The non-partners are restricted to those of the same gender and conversational role (the information giver or follower). It is hypothesized that *partner* distance is smaller than the *non-partner* distance in this analysis. That is, if there is prosodic proximity, the *partner* distance should be smaller than the *non-partner* distance, which can supply the evidence for entrainment at conversation level. More details of this method are illustrated in Formula 1 and Formula 2 in Section 4.1.

The paired T-tests are accomplished over the pairs with three kinds of gender combination (female-female groups, female-male groups, male-male groups). 39 female subjects participated in the female-female conversations; 20 male subjects participated in the male-male conversations; 40 subjects (20 female subjects and 20 male subjects) participated in the mixed-gender conversations.

For female-female groups, 39 pairs of *partner* distances and *non-partner* distances are calculated for one variable (one prosodic feature), and are put in a paired T-test. There are 7 variables in the present research, so 7 series of paired T-tests are accomplished over all the prosodic features examined.

For male-male groups, 20 pairs of *partner* distances and *non-partner* distances are calculated for one variable (one prosodic feature), and are put in a paired T-test. There are 7 variables in the present research, so 7 series of paired T-tests are accomplished over all the prosodic features examined.

For female-male groups, 40 pairs of *partner* distances and *non-partner* distances are calculated for one variable (one prosodic feature), and are put in a paired T-test. There are 7 variables in the present research, so 7 series of paired T-tests are accomplished over all the prosodic features examined.

2. Results

Since the paired T-tests are accomplished over 3 gender groups respectively, the results of analyses are listed separately.

For female-female group, the results of paired T-tests are listed in Table 5-1.

Table 5-1 Paired T-tests of female-female groups

Feature	*t*	*df*	*p-value*	Sig.
Speaking-rate	−5.792	38	0.0	*
F0 min	−1.283	38	0.207	/
F0 mean	−0.523	38	0.604	/
F0 max	−0.241	38	0.811	/
Intensity min	−1.726	38	0.092	/
Intensity mean	−4.765	38	0.0	*
Intensity max	−5.075	38	0.0	*

In Table 5-1, an asterisk * indicates the significant difference, and the symbol/indicates no significant difference. This table shows that in female-female conversations, speakers show significant entrainment over 3 prosodic features: Speaking-rate ($p=0.0<0.05$), Intensity min ($p=0.0<0.05$), and Intensity max ($p=0.0<0.05$).

For male-male group, the results of paired T-tests are listed in Table 5 - 2.

Table 5 - 2 Paired T-tests of male-male group

Feature	*t*	d*f*	*p-value*	Sig.
Speaking-rate	−6.804	19	0.0	*
Pitch min	0.453	19	0.656	/
Pitch mean	0.228	19	0.822	/
Pitch max	0.595	19	0.559	/
Intensity min	−1.869	19	0.077	/
Intensity mean	0.176	19	0.862	/
Intensity max	0.099	19	0.922	/

In Table 5 - 2, an asterisk * indicates the significant difference, and the symbol/indicates no significant difference. Table 24 shows that in male-male conversations, speakers show significant entrainment over 1 prosodic feature: Speaking-rate ($p=0.0<0.05$).

For female-male group, the results of paired T-tests are listed in Table 5 - 3.

Table 5 - 3 Paired T-test of female-male group

Feature	*t*	d*f*	*p-value*	Sig.
Speaking-rate	−3.024	39	0.004	*
Pitch min	1.032	39	0.309	/
Pitch mean	0.972	39	0.337	/
Pitch max	−4.281	39	0.000	*
Intensity min	0.684	39	0.498	/
Intensity mean	−3.379	39	0.002	*
Intensity max	−3.225	39	0.003	*

In Table 5 - 3, an asterisk * indicates the significant difference, and the symbol/indicates no significant difference. Table 5 - 3 shows that in female-male conversations, speakers show significant entrainment over 4 prosodic features: Speaking-rate ($p=0.004<0.05$), F0 max ($p=0.0<0.05$), Intensity mean ($p=0.002<0.05$), and Intensity max ($p=0.003<0.05$).

The results of paired T-tests over the pairs with 3 kinds of gender combination show that in female-female conversations, speakers show significant entrainment over 3 prosodic features: Speaking-rate, Intensity min, and Intensity max; in male-male conversations, speakers show significant entrainment over 1 prosodic feature: Speaking-rate; in female-male conversations, speakers show significant entrainment over 4 prosodic features: Speaking-rate, F0 max, Intensity mean, and Intensity max.

Then it is found that more features are entrained in female-male conversations. The number of prosodic features entrained in mix gender group's conversations is the most, and the number of the prosodic features in male-male group's conversations is the least.

In conversations of the pairs with the same gender (female-female and male-male conversations), the features of duration and intensity are entrained; in mixed gender group's conversations, including the feature of duration, features of F0 are also entrained.

5.1.2 Entrainment Degree of the Pairs with Different Gender Combination

In addition to the number of features speakers entrained over, the present research also analyzes the degree of entrainment in the pairs with different gender combination.

The research question in this section is: Is there any difference in entrainment degree in the pairs of different gender combination?

From the results above in Section 5.1.1, over Speaking-rate, Intensity mean and Intensity max, pairs in female-female, female-male and male-male conversations exhibit entrainment. It is necessary to explore further what is the difference of entrainment degrees over three gender combinations for anyone feature of the three.

1. ANOVA tests

ANOVA tests are adopted in the analyses of entrainment degree, in which adaptation degrees are considered as dependent variables, and 3 gender combinations are independent variables. Similar method is used in Section 4.1.3 for the analysis of entrainment degree at conversation level. The similarity is that these two series of ANOVA tests have similar dependent variables, the adaptation degree, *sim*, and what is different here in this section is that the independent variable of the ANOVA tests is 3 gender combinations, while that of the ANOVA tests in Section 4.1.3 is 4 prosodic features which show entrainment simultaneously in conversation.

In this analysis, *sim* represents the adaptation degree of the prosodic feature *f*. *disp* represents the *partner* distance as in Formula 1, and *disnp* represents the *non partner* distance as in Formula 2. More details are shown in Formula 3 in Section 4.1.3.

In this analysis, *non partner* distance is considered as the baseline in the distance of the two interlocutors, the distance without the mutual adaptation. Thus, *disp/disnp*, *disp* normalized by *disnp*, represents the ratio of the remained distance after adaption between interlocutors to the primitive distance. Then, *sim*, 1 − *disp/disnp*, represents a similarity ratio, the percentage of becoming similar. This similarity ratio or normalization in Formula 3 has an advantage to control for speaker' differences.

For Speaking-rate, Intensity mean, and Intensity max, over which all the pairs with 3 gender combinations exhibit entrainment, ANOVA tests are conducted over female-female, female-male, and male-male groups.

39 female subjects participated in the female-female conversations; 20 male subjects participated in the male-male conversations; 40 subjects (20 female, 20 male) participated in the mixed-gender conversations. *Sim* is calculated by Formula 3 over the values of *disp* and *disnp* from these conversations.

39 *sim* come from 39 female-female conversations; 20 *sim* come from 20 male-male conversations; 40 *sim* come from female-male conversations. ANOVA tests are accomplished over 3 prosodic features, taking *sim* as the dependent variable and 3 gender groups the independent variables.

2. Results

For Speaking-rate, Intensity mean, and Intensity max, over which all pairs with 3 gender combinations exhibit entrainment, ANOVA tests are conducted over the female-female, female-male, and male-male groups, and the results of these tests are listed respectively below.

The results of ANOVA test in terms of Speaking-rate over 3 gender combinations are listed in Table 5 - 4.

Table 5 - 4 An ANOVA test in terms of Speaking-rate over 3 gender combinations

ANOVA

	Sum of Squares	*df*	Mean Square	*F*	Sig.
Between Groups	2.056	2	1.028	4.508	.013
Within Groups	21.886	96	.228		
Total	23.942	98			

Table 5 - 4 shows that over Speaking-rate, *sim* has significant difference in the pairs with 3 gender combinations ($p=0.013<0.05$, $F=4.508$). That is, in terms of Speaking-rate, entrainment degree is significantly different over the pairs with three gender combinations. It is necessary to test further the difference between every two gender combinations. Therefore, the multiple comparisons are made below.

The results of post-doc comparison are listed in Table 5 - 5.

Table 5 - 5 Post hoc comparison of ANOVA test in terms of Speaking-rate

Multiple Comparison

LSD

(I) Group	(J) Group	Mean Difference (I-J)	Std. Error	Sig.	95% Confidence Interval	
					Lower Bound	Upper Bound
ff	fm	.236 22*	.107 45	.030	.022 9	.449 5
	mm	−.124 86	.131 32	.344	−.385 5	.135 8
fm	ff	−.236 22*	.107 45	.030	−.449 5	−.022 9
	mm	−.361 08*	.130 76	.007	−.620 6	−.101 5

(continued)

(I) Group	(J) Group	Mean Difference (I-J)	Std. Error	Sig.	95% Confidence Interval	
					Lower Bound	Upper Bound
mm	ff	.124 86	.131 32	.344	−.135 8	.385 5
	fm	.361 08*	.130 76	.007	.101 5	.620 6

*. The mean difference is significant at the 0.05 level.

Table 5 - 5 shows that over Speaking-rate, *sim* is the smallest in female-male conversations within 3 gender combinations, because *sim* in the female-male group is significantly smaller than that in the female-female group ($p=0.030<0.05$) and *sim* in the female-male group is significant smaller than that in the male-male group ($p=0.007<0.05$). *Sim* is not significantly different between the female-female group and the male-male group. That is to say, in terms of Speaking-rate, the entrainment degree over the female-male group is the smallest, and there is no significant difference between female-male group and the male-male group.

The results of ANOVA test in terms of Intensity Mean in the pairs with 3 gender combinations are listed in Table 5 - 6.

Table 5 - 6 An ANOVA test in terms of Intensity mean over 3 gender combinations

ANOVA

	Sum of Squares	d*f*	Mean Square	*F*	Sig.
Between Groups	2.204	2	1.102	3.131	.048
Within Groups	33.791	96	.352		
Total	35.996	98			

Table 5 - 6 shows that over Intensity mean, *sim* is significantly different in the pairs with 3 gender combinations ($p=0.048<0.05$, $F=3.131$). That is, in terms of Intensity min, entrainment degree is significantly different over the pairs with three gender combinations. It is necessary to test further the difference between every two gender combinations. Therefore, the multiple comparisons are made below.

The results of post-hoc comparison are listed in Table 5 - 7.

Table 5 - 7 Post hoc comparison of ANOVA test in terms of Intensity mean

Multiple Comparison

LSD

(I) group	(J) group	Mean Difference (I-J)	Std. Error	Sig.	95% Confidence Interval	
					Lower Bound	Upper Bound
ff	fm	.120 49	.133 51	.369	−.144 5	.385 5
	mm	.407 64*	.163 17	.014	.083 7	.731 5
fm	ff	−.120 49	.133 51	.369	−.385 5	.144 5
	mm	.287 15	.162 48	.080	−.035 4	.609 7
mm	ff	−.407 64*	.163 17	.014	−.731 5	−.083 7
	fm	−.287 15	.162 48	.080	−.609 7	.035 4

*. The mean difference is significant at the 0.05 level.

Table 5 - 7 shows that over Intensity mean, *sim* is the smallest in male-male conversations within 3 gender groups, because *sim* in the male-male group is significantly smaller than in the female-female group ($p=0.014<0.05$), and *sim* in the male-male group tends to be smaller than in the female-male group ($p=0.080<0.01$). *Sim* in the male-male group is not significantly different from that in female-female groups or female-male groups. That is to say, in terms of Intensity mean, the entrainment degree over male-male group tends to be the smallest, and there is no significant difference between the female-female group and the female-male group.

The results of ANOVA test in terms of Intensity max in the pairs with 3 gender combinations are listed in Table 5 - 8.

Table 5 - 8 An ANOVA test in terms of Intensity max over 3 gender combinations

ANOVA

	Sum of Squares	*df*	Mean Square	*F*	Sig.
Between Groups	2.446	2	1.223	3.729	.028
Within Groups	31.484	96	.328		
Total	33.930	98			

Table 5 - 8 shows that over Intensity max, *sim* is significantly different in the pairs with 3 gender combinations ($p=0.028<0.05$, $F=3.729$). That is, in terms of Intensity max, entrainment degree is significantly different over the pairs with three gender combinations. It is necessary to test further the difference between every two gender combinations. Therefore, the multiple comparisons are made below.

The results of post-hoc comparisons are listed in Table 5 - 9.

Table 5 - 9 Post hoc comparison of ANOVA test in terms of Intensity max

Multiple Comparison

LSD

(I) group	(J) group	Mean Difference (I-J)	Std. Error	Sig.	95% Confidence Interval	
					Lower Bound	Upper Bound
ff	fm	.183 79	.128 87	.157	−.072 0	.439 6
	mm	.426 89*	.157 50	.008	.114 3	.739 5
fm	ff	−.183 79	.128 87	.157	−.439 6	.072 0
	mm	.243 10	.156 83	.124	−.068 2	.554 4
mm	ff	−.426 89*	.157 50	.008	−.739 5	−.114 3
	fm	−.243 10	.156 83	.124	−.554 4	.068 2

*. The mean difference is significant at the 0.05 level.

Table 5 - 9 shows that over Intensity max, *sim* tends to be the smallest in male-male conversations among the 3 gender groups, because *sim* in the male-male group is significantly smaller than that in the female-female group ($p=0.008<0.05$), and *sim* in the male-male group is smaller than that in the female-male group, although the result is not significant ($p=0.124>0.05$). *Sim* in the male-male group is not significantly different from that in the female-female group or the female-male group. That is to say, in terms of Intensity max, the entrainment degree in the male-male group tends to be the smallest, and there is no significant difference between the female-female group and female-male group.

According to the results of a series of ANOVA tests over Speaking-rate, Intensity mean, and Intensity max, it is found that in terms of Speaking-rate, the entrainment degree over female-male group is the smallest, and there is no significant difference over the female-male group and the male-male group; in terms of Intensity mean, the entrainment degree of the male-male group tends to be the smallest, and there is no significant difference between the female-female group and the female-male group; in terms of Intensity max, the entrainment degree of male-male group tends to be the smallest, and there is no significant difference between the female-female group and the female-male group.

Therefore, based on the results above, it is found that male-male pairs tend to entrain least in MC conversations.

5.1.3 Summary of the Results

A summary of the research on entrainment and gender was made.

It is found that mixed gender pairs entrain over the most number of features, and male pairs on the least in both languages.

It is also found that 3 gender groups show significant difference in entrainment degree, and male-male pairs tend to entrain least. Entrainment of mixed gender pairs is most prevalent but not necessarily strongest.

Therefore, it can be concluded that in both number of features entrained and degree of entrainment: males entrain the least.

5.2 Entrainment and Role

According to the description of corpus in Chapter 3, the speakers' roles are controlled in conversations through the design of two kinds of games.

In Picture Ordering Games, two interlocutors in the conversation take different roles (unequal roles): information giver and information follower, in which information givers instructs followers to make correct order of the pictures, while in Picture Classifying Games, two interlocutors have free discussion and make classification of all the pictures into certain categories, in which pairs take the equal roles in discussion, and there is not the same role distinctions to those in Picture Ordering Games.

Besides, in order to reduce the interference caused by different speakers, the present research makes the control that the same pairs play both games. Thus, the interference from the different pairs of speakers is controlled for in the analysis. The details of role control are introduced in Section 3. 1. 5. This control of roles in the two games makes the analyses of entrainment and role valid.

The analyses of entrainment and role are accomplished by two steps. The first step is the Role Influence Test, which aims to test whether the unequal roles affect the degree of entrainment or not. If the unequal roles prove to affect the degree of entrainment in the test of first step, it is necessary to test where the differences in the degree of entrainment come from. Then the second step is accomplished, which is called Role Direction Test. This test aims to test the direction of entrainment between two roles in conversations. In detail, in the present research, this test aims to find out whether givers entrain more to followers or followers entrain more to givers?

5. 2. 1 Role Influence Test

This analysis is to find out: Does the unequal roles affect the degree of entrainment?

The unequal roles in this section are restricted to the information giver and information follower. According to the literature viewed in Chapter 2, entrainment in conversation is proved to be related closely to social factors, and the individual differences of the interlocutors decide the direction and state of entrainment in conversation. Therefore, it is hypothesized that the unequal roles affect the degree of entrainment in conversation.

1. Paired T-tests between *odis* and *cdis*

In order to find out whether the unequal roles affect the degree of entrainment or not, the present research compares the entrainment degree of the pairs with unequal roles and that of the pairs with equal roles, which are controlled in Picture Ordering Games and Picture Classifying Games. So research question in this section is converted to find whether the entrainment degree is different between Picture Ordering Games and Picture Classifying Games or not.

It is hypothesized that the unequal roles affect the degree of entrainment.

In order to analyze the role influence in the Picture Ordering Games and Picture Classifying Games, paired T-test is used in comparing entrainment degree between these two games. As mentioned above, the present research has made the control that the same pairs play both games, so the interference from the different pairs of speakers is controlled for in this analysis. Thus, the paired T-tests over the same interlocutors are valid to find out the difference of entrainment degree between two games.

The entrainment degree in Picture Ordering Games, *odis*, refers to the distance of prosodic features over the whole conversation between two speakers in Picture Ordering Games. The entrainment degree in Picture Classifying Games, *cdis*, refers to the distance of prosodic features over the whole conversation between two speakers in Picture Classifying Games. Paired T-tests are accomplished between *odis* and *cdis*.

According to the description of corpus in Chapter 3, 14 pairs of subjects participated in both the Picture Ordering Games and Picture Classifying Games.

In terms of *odis*, the distance of prosodic features over the whole conversation between two speakers in the Picture Ordering Games conversations, the average distance from two conversations is calculated as its value, because every pair of subjects plays the Picture Ordering Game twice by switching the roles from information giver to information follower in Picture Ordering Games. Thus, 14 *odis* are computed for one prosodic parameter over 28 conversations in Picture Ordering Games by getting their averages.

In terms of *cdis*, the distance of prosodic features over the whole conversation between two speakers in Picture Classifying Games conversations, one value of *cdis* comes from one conversation, because every pair plays classifying game once. 14 pairs participated in 14 conversations, so 14 *cdis* are computed over 14 conversations for one prosodic parameter.

One paired T-test is accomplished between 14 *odis* and 14 *cdis* for one prosodic parameter. 7 paired T-tests are accomplished for 7 prosodic parameters.

The data used in paired T-tests are listed in the following Table 5 - 10 and Table 5 - 11.

Table 5 - 10 The values of *odis* in Picture Ordering Games

	Speaking_ rate	F0_ min	F0_ mean	F0_ max	Int_ min	Int_ mean	Int_ max
1	1.36	24.56	19.43	31.92	6.54	7.70	7.83
2	0.33	19.38	31.72	32.16	14.02	9.78	9.07
3	0.10	13.06	8.50	15.25	1.55	7.16	8.84
4	1.09	12.82	26.33	56.78	5.17	3.85	3.83
5	1.09	78.38	104.50	152.71	8.60	0.59	0.19
6	0.59	27.76	45.63	57.65	2.64	7.31	8.26
7	0.98	29.28	28.73	37.18	3.24	4.48	4.34
8	1.18	21.78	21.20	22.51	6.79	4.19	4.82
9	0.19	13.80	14.38	21.62	2.39	2.95	3.16
10	1.09	2.97	13.71	32.23	3.69	4.01	4.31
11	0.70	6.08	1.64	5.93	2.04	3.71	3.73
12	0.87	7.23	6.14	15.05	1.48	1.47	1.26
13	0.85	26.81	25.72	23.99	2.88	6.79	7.13
14	0.46	16.57	14.00	30.11	2.68	2.63	3.24

Table 5 - 11 The values of *cdis* in Picture Classifying Games

	Speaking_ rate	F0_ min	F0_ mean	F0_ max	Int_ min	Int_ mean	Int_ max
1	1.66	19.49	25.55	38.02	11.45	6.05	5.64
2	0.30	11.65	27.60	33.57	11.92	11.02	10.45
3	0.34	0.71	1.89	4.12	3.74	3.08	3.80
4	0.51	5.08	18.68	44.65	9.07	4.78	3.62

(continued)

	Speaking_ rate	F0_ min	F0_ mean	F0_ max	Int_ min	Int_ mean	Int_ max
5	1. 26	72. 52	105. 69	150. 37	13. 43	1. 55	1. 77
6	0. 15	26. 78	49. 28	64. 88	3. 03	8. 79	9. 70
7	0. 29	21. 09	22. 59	28. 09	0. 54	2. 65	3. 33
8	0. 55	15. 70	18. 67	21. 59	7. 14	2. 19	1. 89
9	0. 78	15. 13	13. 22	20. 45	1. 26	2. 18	2. 21
10	0. 54	4. 54	10. 07	28. 00	4. 31	3. 31	3. 71
11	0. 15	1. 01	0. 95	1. 70	1. 95	1. 32	1. 55
12	0. 40	11. 54	6. 96	6. 47	3. 25	2. 87	3. 37
13	0. 05	24. 31	20. 15	12. 65	5. 12	9. 19	9. 13
14	0. 29	18. 81	6. 40	21. 38	0. 56	2. 46	2. 97

2. Results

The results in paired T-tests of entrainment degree for the same interlocutors between two games are listed in Table 5 - 12.

Table 5 - 12 Paired T-tests in entrainment degree between two games

Feature	*t*	d*f*	*p-value*	Sig.	*meano*	*meanc*
Speaking-rate	2. 225	13	0. 044	*	0. 778 2	0. 519 4
F0 min	2. 887	13	0. 013	*	21. 464 6	17. 739 9
F0 mean	2. 119	13	0. 054	/	25. 830 4	23. 407 8
F0 max	2. 506	13	0. 026	*	38. 221 3	33. 995 9
Intensity min	−1. 391	13	0. 187	/	4. 551 7	5. 483 1
Intensity mean	0. 746	13	0. 469	/	4. 758 7	4. 388 8
Intensity max	0. 875	13	0. 397	/	5. 000 7	4. 509 4

In Table 5 - 12, an asterisk * indicates the significant difference, and the symbol/indicates no significant difference. According to this table, the entrainment degree between the Picture Ordering Games and Picture Classifying Games are significantly different over 3 prosodic parameters:

Speaking-rate ($p=0.044<0.05$), F0 min ($p=0.013<0.05$) and F0 max ($p=0.026<0.05$). The entrainment degree between two games is significantly different over F0 mean ($p=0.054<0.1$) at confidence level 0. 1.

These results indicate that the degree of entrainment is significantly different between Picture Ordering Games and Picture Classifying Games over three prosodic parameters: Speaking-rate, F0min, and F0max, and the feature of F0 mean tends to be different between the two games.

In addition, the mean entrainment degree in picture ordering game (indicated by *meano* in Table 5 - 11) is bigger than the mean entrainment degree in picture classifying game (indicated by *meanc* in Table 5 - 12) over almost every prosodic feature tested over the feature of duration and F0. It is the same for the features of intensity, although the differences are not significant.

These indicate that the entrainment degree in the picture ordering game is larger than the entrainment degree in the picture classifying game over almost every prosodic feature tested.

The results above prove that the unequal roles (information giver or follower) affect the entrainment degree in conversation over the prosodic features of duration and F0, and the entrainment in the picture ordering games is stronger than that in the picture classifying games. That is, there is more entrainment in the conversations with unequal roles than in those with equal roles.

5. 2. 2 Role Direction Test

It is proved in the Section 5. 2. 1 that the unequal roles (information giver or follower) affect the entrainment degree in conversation over the prosodic features of duration and F0. Questions can be asked further: what is the entrainment direction? Do information givers entrain more to followers, or do followers entrain more to givers?

1. Paired T-tests between $|Ag-A0|$ and $|Af-A0|$

As mentioned at the beginning of this section (Section 5. 2), the Role Direction Test is the second step in the analyses of entrainment and role. In the first step, the Role Influence Test, it is found that the degree of entrainment is significantly different between Picture Ordering Games and Picture Classifying Games over the features of duration and F0. Then it is necessary to analyze where the differences in the degree of entrainment come from.

As mentioned above, some subjects are chosen to participate in both Picture Ordering Games and Picture Classifying Games. In Picture Ordering Games, two interlocutors (A and B) have different roles as information giver and information follower. When they finished the first game, they switched the roles in another ordering game. That is, two interlocutors participated in two ordering games, in which they switched the roles between information giver and information follower. In picture classifying, two speakers have the same roles in discussion. Thus, every subject has 3 speaking states.

For instance, a subject in a pair (A & B) has 3 speaking states.

Ag: A plays as an information giver in the first picture ordering game with B.

Af: A plays as an information follower in the second picture ordering game with B.

A0: A plays in an equal role with B in a picture classifying game.

Bg: B plays as an information follower in the first picture ordering game with A.

Bf: B plays as an information giver in the second picture ordering game with A.

B0: B plays in an equal role with A in a picture classifying game.

The same pair plays two kinds of games: the Picture Classifying Games and Picture Ordering Games. Taking one side of the interlocutors as an example, A0 is A's speaking state with equal roles; Ag is A's speaking state when A is an information giver; Af is A's speaking state when A is an information follower. The difference between Ag and Af is the change in speaking state caused by the change in A's roles from the information giver to the information follower, while the partner is still B. What is changed in B in

Picture Ordering Games is also the state of speaking from the information follower to the information giver. Therefore, as the other side of the pair, the partner of A, B also has 3 similar speaking states.

The differences in the entrainment degree between two kinds of games found in the Section 5.1 are assumed to be caused by the difference in the roles. In the present research, among the 3 speaking states of A, A0 is considered as a reference state, because this speaking state is produced under the equal role with the partner. The deviation between Ag and A0 is caused only by A's role of a giver, and the deviation between Af and A0 is caused only by A's role of a follower. Therefore, |Af—A0| is the deviation caused by the role of giver; |Af—A0| is the deviation caused by the role of follower. The key point to make such comparisons valid is that in this analysis the partner of A is not changed, and what is changed is only the role of A. And all of this attributes to the experiment design of the present research that several pairs of subjects participated in both games.

A paired T-test between |Ag—A0| and |Af—A0| is adopted in this section in order to find out which role causes bigger deviation. If |Ag—A0| is bigger than |Af—A0|, the deviation caused by the role of giver is bigger than that caused by the role of follower. That is, the giver makes larger deviation in entrainment than the follower does in conversation, so the giver entrains more to the follower. If |Ag—A0| is smaller than /Af—A0/, the deviation caused by the role of giver is smaller than that caused by the role of follower. That is, the follower makes a larger derivation in entrainment than the giver does in conversation, so the follower entrains more to the giver.

One point should be mentioned in the use of this method. The post-conversation influence is not considered in this analysis. Fourteen pairs participated in both the Picture Ordering Games and Picture Classifying Games. Every two interlocutors of them participated in two ordering games, in which they switched the roles between information giver and information follower, and a picture classifying game, in which two speakers in the pair have the same roles in discussion. One pair of these subjects actually produced three conversations. Thus, a question is raised: is there post-conversation influence among these conversations? That is, is the entrainment state in the followed conversations influenced by the previous ones?

In the present research, the post-conversation influence of these three conversations produced by every pair of the 14 is not considered, because the requirements of these games are different. After the first picture ordering game, the roles of two interlocutors are changed in the second picture ordering game, and the content of picture classifying game is quite different from the previous two. Thus, the requirements of the games are always different. Therefore, the post-conversation influence is excluded in these analyses.

According to the corpus description in Chapter 3, 14 pairs (28) subjects participated in both the Picture Ordering Games and Picture Classifying Games. Then 28 subjects made 28 conversations. One subject (A) has 3 speaking states, Ag, Af and A0 from the Picture Ordering Games and Picture Classifying Games. For 28 subjects, there are 28 groups of Ag, Af and A0.

The role influence test in Section 5.1 is the precondition of the Role Direction Test in Section 5.2. That is, those features which show role influence could be tested further for the role direction. According to the results of role influence test, different entrainment degree is found between unequal roles (the role of information giver and follower) and equal roles (the role of picture classifier) over the features of duration and F0. So as the further test of Role Influence Test, in the Role Direction Test, paired T-tests are accomplished over the features of duration and F0 including Speaking-rate, F0 min, F0 mean, and F0 max.

The values of |Ag_A0| and |Af_A0| used in paired T-test are listed in the following Table 5 - 13.

Table 5 - 13 The values of |Ag_A0| and |Af_A0|

	|Ag_A0|				|Af_A0|			
	Speaking_rate	F0_min	F0_mean	F0_max	Speaking_rate	F0_min	F0_mean	F0_max
1	0.34	5.40	1.01	11.92	0.18	19.03	10.64	4.00
2	0.98	1.93	20.62	33.59	0.12	1.55	1.23	5.46

(continued)

	|Ag_A0|				|Af_A0|			
	Speaking_ rate	F0_ min	F0_ mean	F0_ max	Speaking _ rate	F0_ min	F0_ mean	F0_ max
3	0. 36	2. 90	3. 30	1. 31	0. 14	6. 42	1. 86	9. 68
4	0. 16	5. 27	0. 88	8. 18	0. 00	0. 87	5. 91	13. 74
5	0. 29	2. 90	2. 62	8. 67	0. 07	10. 90	3. 06	3. 26
6	0. 08	5. 66	12. 74	26. 45	0. 07	6. 66	6. 16	1. 36
7	0. 23	7. 66	17. 63	27. 87	0. 60	22. 36	4. 84	6. 97
8	0. 24	4. 46	1. 84	2. 52	0. 09	15. 40	5. 32	0. 83
9	1. 16	2. 91	0. 93	0. 32	0. 13	8. 47	5. 85	2. 23
10	0. 49	7. 20	2. 80	18. 33	0. 67	10. 08	0. 27	11. 74
11	0. 72	1. 77	1. 69	2. 82	0. 22	3. 96	0. 89	0. 02
12	0. 26	5. 85	9. 95	16. 97	0. 20	1. 70	18. 06	34. 23
13	1. 30	3. 31	3. 68	6. 80	0. 20	9. 66	0. 69	13. 59
14	1. 56	2. 24	3. 79	11. 89	0. 70	1. 18	5. 50	13. 07
15	0. 68	1. 94	4. 37	4. 95	0. 02	0. 24	1. 01	1. 48
16	0. 83	6. 23	8. 45	10. 47	0. 87	7. 62	2. 00	2. 20
17	0. 03	1. 91	7. 56	8. 39	0. 67	6. 50	2. 47	2. 95
18	1. 35	7. 36	5. 48	4. 95	1. 03	3. 73	2. 24	1. 83
19	0. 81	5. 37	7. 03	11. 39	0. 13	8. 50	3. 41	2. 02
20	0. 09	1. 42	3. 53	6. 37	0. 07	0. 26	0. 37	1. 42
21	0. 03	3. 20	0. 51	1. 34	0. 46	3. 68	0. 83	2. 82
22	0. 57	3. 25	0. 84	4. 99	0. 33	2. 04	1. 90	0. 71
23	0. 75	5. 57	14. 72	24. 58	0. 83	6. 81	8. 23	5. 04
24	0. 41	2. 22	12. 23	25. 72	0. 47	1. 53	9. 07	21. 07
25	0. 26	1. 53	5. 77	10. 86	0. 20	5. 38	4. 19	3. 33
26	1. 20	1. 72	1. 44	0. 94	0. 86	0. 18	2. 62	9. 43
27	0. 04	1. 98	7. 46	26. 30	0. 03	0. 21	2. 66	2. 19
28	0. 09	0. 47	13. 40	35. 19	0. 31	2. 23	4. 48	3. 46

2. Results

In Table 5 - 13, for the features of duration and F0, 28 groups of |Ag−A0| and |Af−A0| are listed. The paired T-tests are accomplished between these groups.

The results of paired T-tests between |Ag−A0| and |Af−A0| are listed in Table 5 - 14.

Table 5 - 14 Paired T-tests between |Ag−A0| and |Af−A0|

Feature	*t*	d*f*	*p-value*	Sig.	|Ag−A0|	|Af−A0|
Speaking-rate	2.481	27	0.02	*	0.547 2	0.344 8
F0 min	−2.437	27	0.8	/	3.702 0	5.969 8
F0 mean	1.912	27	0.067	/	6.295 7	4.134 7
F0 max	2.790	27	0.01	*	12.645 7	6.433 9

In Table 5 - 14, an asterisk * indicates the significant difference, and the symbol/indicates no significant difference. According to this table, the |Ag−A0| is significantly and consistently bigger than |Af−A0| over speaking rate and F0 max ($p=0.02$, $0.01<0.05$). In addition, |Ag−A0| is significantly bigger than |Af−A0| over F0 max ($p=0.067<0.1$) at confidence level 0.1. These show that Ag makes the significantly bigger deviation than Af. That is, when A plays as the information giver, deviation in entrainment is bigger than that when A plays as the information follower.

The results in Table 5 - 13 indicate that givers make larger adjustments towards their followers, and followers make smaller adjustments towards their givers. When a giver makes larger adjustment and a follower makes smaller adjustment, the giver entrains more to the follower.

Based on the results above, it is found that there is more entrainment when speakers are givers than when they are followers. Information givers entrain more than followers in conversation.

In conversation, givers entrain more to followers. And the entrainment from givers to followers is prominent over Speaking-rate and F0 max which are the main features that show global entrainment as well.

5.2.3 Summary of the Results

A summary was made for the analyses of entrainment and role.

This section includes two tests: Role Influence Test and Role Direction Test.

Through the Role Influence Test, it is found that the unequal roles (information giver or follower) affect the entrainment degree in conversation over the prosodic features of duration and F0, and there is more entrainment in the conversations with unequal roles than in those with equal roles.

Through the Role Direction Test, it is found that there is more entrainment when speakers are givers than when they are followers. Information givers entrain more than followers in conversation.

In conversations, givers entrain more to followers. And the entrainment from givers to followers is prominent in Speaking-rate and F0 max.

5.3 Discussion

Chapter 5 is about entrainment and social factors. Since the gender and role have been controlled in the experiments, the present research focuses on the analysis of entrainment and gender, and that of entrainment and role.

Two points are found in the analyses of entrainment and gender.

1) Mixed gender pairs entrain over the most number of features, and male pairs on the least in both languages.

2) It is also found that 3 gender groups show significant difference in entrainment degree, and male-male pairs tend to entrain least. Entrainment of mixed gender pairs is most prevalent but not necessarily strongest.

Therefore, all these results indicate that in both number of features entrained and degree of entrainment: males entrain the least.

The results from the analyses of entrainment and gender in this section show that theories of dominance and perception are partially supported. In relevant studies of entrainment and gender differences, the related theories are dominance and perception. In terms of dominance, Bilous & Krauss (1988) make the male dominance hypothesis, and point out differences in speech between men and women have to do with men's dominant position in society. In addition, according to CAT (Giles *et al*. 1987), it is proposed that when there is an imbalance of power between speakers, the less dominant speaker will entrain more. In terms of perception, perception behavior link (Chartrand & Bargh 1999) states that perceiving something makes people more likely to mimic it and females are known to be more sensitive to perceived differences in speech. Based on these theories, predictions are made: in mixed gender pairs' conversations, females should entrain more, and there should be more entrainment in female-female pairs' conversations than male-male pairs' conversations. The result that the most prosodic features are involved in mixed gender pairs' entrainment, and in both number of features entrained and degree of entrainment, males entrain the least support partially the theories of dominance and perception.

Two points are found in the analyses of entrainment and role.

1) The unequal roles (information giver or follower) affect the entrainment degree in conversation over the prosodic features of duration and F0, and there is more entrainment in the conversations with unequal roles than in those with equal roles.

2) There is more entrainment when speakers are givers than when they are followers. Information givers entrain more than followers in conversation. In conversation, givers entrain more to followers. And the entrainment from givers to followers is prominent in Speaking-rate and F0 max.

These results supply evidence for the fact that there is directive distinction in entrainment between two interlocutors. That is, the entrainment degree of a pair in conversation is unbalanced. We can feel the entrainment direction in our daily life. For instance, in Child-directed speech or motherese (Fernald *et al*. 1989), which is a term used to describe speakers' accommodation when having conversations with children. It is observed that adults entrain more to children in their conversations. For another example, in foreign talk or foreigness (Ferguson 1975; Zuengler 1991; Smith 2007), which is used when talking with non-native speakers, we observe that native speakers entrain more to the foreigners.

The analyses of prosodic entrainment and role (information givers and information followers) in the present research support the existence of directive distinction in entrainment between two interlocutors as the previous studies in literature. Motivated by the hypothesis of *audience design* (Bell 1984), which means the audience-oriented entrainment, studies have been accomplished to find out to how and what extent speakers adapt to their addressees (Branigan *et al*. 2007; Galati & Brenna 2010). Kristiansen (2008) proposes that there are three possible directions in entrainment between two interlocutors (A, B) in conversation. One is A to B (A→B), the other one is B to A (A←B), and the third one is that both A and B approach to an intermediate state (A→←B).

There exists unbalanced entrainment between two interlocutors in conversation. It is necessary to do research on the production and perception of the unbalanced entrainment in conversation.

Different from the analyses in previous studies, the present research has examined the entrainment between information givers and information followers. In this chapter, Role influence test is made to examine whether there is prosodic entrainment between information givers and information followers, based on which, Role direction test is made to find out the direction of entrainment between them, that is, whether information givers entrain to information followers, or followers entrain to givers. It is found by the present research that more entrainment is made from givers to followers.

The present research analyzes the gender and role in entrainment. These two factors are controlled in the experiments. Actually, the entrainment in conversation is closely related to the social factors: the status, age, gender, role, region, ethnicity, environment, etc. The various responses to individual's interaction with the environment are assessed with reference to the individual himself; this assessment produces the perception of affordances which exist as a mix of an individual's abilities, their background, and even the environmental features.

The present research analyzes the gender and role in entrainment. These two factors are controlled in the experiments.

Besides gender and role, more social factors should be involved in the study of prosodic entrainment.

The emphasis and difficulty in research on the various social factors in entrainment is how to appropriately control these factors in experiments. In order to make some factors prominent, it is necessary to control for other factors. It is usually not easy to control several social factors in one experiment. Efforts should be made to produce well balanced experimental design in order to control some social factors in one experiment or a series of experiments. Much future work could be done in this direction.

At the end of this chapter, it is necessary to have discussion on the methods used in this chapter.

The method of comparing partner distances and non-partner distances, which is discussed at end of the previous chapter, is also used in the analyses of proximity over the pairs with different gender combination.

The notion of using partner distances and non-partner distances is used further in the analyses of entrainment degree over different gender groups (Section 5.1.2), *sim*, $1 - disp/disnp$, represents a similarity ratio, the percentage of becoming similar. In this formula, *disp* represents the *partner* distance, *disnp* represents the *non partner* distance, which is considered as the baseline in the distance of the two interlocutors, the distance without the mutual adaptation, and *disp/disnp*, *disp* normalized by *disnp*, represents the ratio of the remained distance after adaption between interlocutors to the primitive distance. This similarity ratio or normalization has an advantage to control for speaker' differences. This kind of method makes the use of raw F0 values valid in the analyses.

What should be mentioned is the method used in Role Direction Test.

In this test, a subject in a pair (A & B) has 3 speaking states (A0, Ag, and Af). Taking one side of the interlocutors as an example, A0 is A's speaking state with equal roles; Ag is A's speaking state when A is an information giver; Af is A's speaking state when A is an information follower. The difference between Ag and Af is the change in speaking state caused by the change in A's roles from the information giver to the information follower.

Because several pairs of the subjects are asked to play two kinds of games, the interference from the speakers is reduced. In the present research, A0 is considered as a reference state, because this speaking state is produced under the equal role with the partner. The deviation between Ag and A0 is caused only by A's role of a giver, and the deviation between Af and A0 is caused only by A's role of a follower. Therefore, $|Ag-A0|$ is the deviation caused by the role of giver; $|Af-A0|$ is the deviation caused by the role of follower. The key point to make such comparisons valid is that in this analysis the partner of A is not changed, and what is changed is only the role of A. And all of this attributes to the experiment design of the present research that several pairs of subjects participated in both games.

However, there are limitations in the use of this method.

Firstly, the number of subjects who participated in both games should be enlarged. In the present research, 14 pairs of subjects participated in both the Picture Ordering Games and Picture Classifying Games. Then 28 subjects made 28 conversations. One subject (A) has 3 speaking states, Ag, Af and A0 in the Picture Ordering Games and Picture Classifying Games. For 28 subjects, there are 28 groups of Ag, Af and A0. Therefore, there 28 groups of $|Af-A0|$ and $|Af-A0|$ in the paired T-tests. 28 values are not the big samples in statistics. The number should be larger. That is, there should be more subjects who participate in both games in the future experiments.

Secondly, quantitative analyses are needed to test post-conversation influence between the conversations produced by each pair in this analysis. As mentioned in the Section 5.2.2, the post-conversation influence of the three conversations produced by every pair of the 14 is not considered in this analysis, because the requirements of these games are different. In detail, after the first picture ordering game, the roles of two interlocutors are changed in the second picture ordering game, and the content of picture classifying game is quite different from the previous two. However, we can't deny the existence of the post-conversation influence between conversations. Quantitative analyses are needed to test it in the future studies.

Chapter 6

Comparison of Prosodic Entrainment with English

In Chapter 5 and 6, the prosodic entrainment in Mandarin conversation has been analyzed at multiple levels and from the aspect of social factors. These results are compared with those in previous research on English in this chapter.

The study of prosodic entrainment in Mandarin Chinese is accomplished over Tongji Games Corpus in the present research. Relatively comprehensive studies of prosodic entrainment in English have been completed by Professor Julia Hirschberg's group (Levitan & Hirschberg 2011; Levitan, *et al*. 2012; Xia *et al*. 2014). Therefore, the main cross-linguistic comparison of prosodic entrainment between Mandarin Chinese and English is accomplished from the common aspects in these studies, from which the parallel work is available in these two languages. In addition, some comments are also made on entrainment over tone units in Mandarin Chinese, which are different from prosodic entrainment in English.

6.1 Two Corpora

Cross-linguistic comparison is made between the studies of Tongji Games Corpus and Columbia Games Corpus. It is necessary to make introductions of these two corpora. Since details can be found in Chapter 3 for Tongji Games Corpus, this section focuses on the introduction of Columbia Games Corpus.

Most researches on prosodic entrainment done by Professor Julia Hirschberg's group are based on Columbia Games Corpus. The present research on prosodic entrainment in Mandarin is based on Tongji Games Corpus. The similarities of these two corpora make the cross-linguistic comparisons valid between two languages.

In previous research on prosodic entrainment, a research group led by Professor Julia Hirschberg in Columbia University has accomplished a large scale of studies. They find considerable evidence for prosodic entrainment in English by their Columbia Games Corpus. In their research, prosodic entrainment is studied in various dimensions: such as measuring acoustic-prosodic entrainment at global and local levels (Levitan & Hirschberg 2011), investigating prosodic entrainment in terms of social behavior (Levitan *et al*. 2012), studying temporal accommodation in turn-taking (Benus, Gravano & Hirschberg 2011), and so on. Over the Columbia Games Corpus, besides the research on prosodic entrainment, this group also did research on entrainment of speech preceding backchannels (Levitan *et al*. 2011), and of turn-taking and affirmative cue words in task-oriented dialogue (Gravano 2009).

The present research aims to explore prosodic entrainment in Mandarin Chinese conversations, and at same time to make feasible comparison of prosodic entrainment between Chinese and English on several possible aspects. With the similar research design, analysis methods, the direct and convincing comparisons are made between Tongji Games Corpus and Columbia Games Corpus. The work based on the Columbia Games Corpus supplies direct reference to the present research. Therefore, it is necessary to make an introduction of Columbia Games Corpus in order to show the validity of the comparisons between the two corpora. The following is about detailed introduction of Columbia Games Corpus.

6.1.1 Columbia Games Corpus

Columbia Games Corpus is a corpus of spontaneous, task-oriented speech between pairs of strangers. The corpus comprises twelve dyadic conversations elicited from thirteen native speakers of Standard American English (SAE) (Six female, seven male). Each pair of subjects played a set of computer games that required them to cooperate in order to achieve a mutual goal. Subjects accomplished experiments in a sound-proof booth on laptops with a curtain between them. Neither could see the other's screen. There are two games in this corpus: Cards Games and Object Games. In the Cards games, one speaker (the information giver) described the cards she saw on her screen, and her partner (the follower) attempted to match them to the cards on his screen. In the Objects games, one speaker (the giver) described the location of an object on her screen, and her partner (the follower) attempted to place the corresponding object in exactly the same location on his own screen. For each game, participants received points based on how exact a match was; they later were paid for each point. Each of the twelve sessions consists of two Cards Games and one Objects Game. The corpus consists of approximately nine hours of recorded dialogues. It has been orthographically transcribed and annotated with prosodic and turn-taking labels.

6.1.2 The Relation Between Two Corpora

Comparisons of Tongji Games Corpus and Columbia Games Corpus are made in this section. Despite of several differences, similarities they own form the base for validity comparison.

Although the contents of the games are different, subjects in both corpora are required to produce cooperative speaking by achieving a mutual goal in the games. Picture Ordering Games and Picture Classifying Games are the main contents in Tongji Games Corpus, and Cards Games and Object Games are the main contents in Columbia Games Corpus. Despite of different game contents, cooperative conversations are elicited by these games, which form the base for the researches on prosodic entrainment. In addition, other design of experiments in both corpora (for example, strange subjects, curtain between the interlocutors, etc.) aims to make prosodic function prominent in entrainment.

Although different sets of variables are set in these corpora, comparisons are possible over the common parameters. 7 variables in the analyses of Tongji Games Corpus (Speaking-rate, F0 min, F0 mean, F0 max, Intensity min,

Intensity mean, Intensity max), which come from the 3 main aspects of prosody (duration, fundamental frequency and intensity); 8 variables in the analyses of Columbia Games Corpus (Speaking-rate, F0 mean, F0 max, Intensity mean, Intensity max, jitter, shimmer, noise-to-harmonics ratio), which come from the 4 aspects of prosody (duration, fundamental frequency, intensity, and voice quality). In spite of the difference in the number of variables, the comparison still covers the 3 main aspects of prosody in durational feature (Speaking-rate), F0 features (F0 mean, F0 max), and intensity features (Intensity mean, Intensity max). Cross-linguistic comparisons of prosodic entrainment are accomplished from these aspects.

Other differences are concerned with the new dimensions the present research aims to explore. They are the differences in language type and variable controls in experiments. The target language in Tongji Games Corpus is Mandarin Chinese, and that in Columbia Corpus is Standard American English. In terms of variable control, the present research has accomplished analyses of prosodic entrainment over tone units. The control of target tone units in carrier sentences is made in Tongji Games Corpus. In addition, as a new dimension of research on prosodic entrainment and social factors, the present research does analyses of role and prosodic entrainment. Equal roles and unequal roles are controlled in the experiments in the two games in Tongji Games Corpus. There are not such controls in Columbia Games Corpus.

6.2 Comparison Between Mandarin and English

Cross-linguistic comparison is based on the parallel work in Tongji Games Corpus and Columbia Games Corpus, which includes the analyses of entrainment at conversation and turn level, and analyses of entrainment and gender.

6.2.1 Comparison at Conversation Level

Comparison at conversation level is accomplished from the aspects of proximity and convergence in two languages.

1. Comparison of proximity

The results of prosodic proximity at conversation level are compared between Mandarin Chinese (MC) conversations in Tongji Games Corpus and Standard American English (SAE) in Columbia Games Corpus. The results of MC come from the analyses in Section 4.1, and the results of SAE come from the research of Levitan & Hirschberg (2011).

As mentioned above, in spite of the difference in the number of variables in two corpora, the comparisons still covers the 3 main aspects of prosody in durational feature (Speaking-rate), F0 features (F0 mean, F0 max), and intensity features (Intensity mean, Intensity max). The results of comparison are showed in Table 6-1.

Table 6-1 The comparison of prosodic proximity at conversation level between MC and SAE

Feature	MC	SAE
Speaking-rate	√	√
F0 min	×	—
F0 mean	×	×
F0 max	√	√
Intensity min	×	—
Intensity mean	√	√
Intensity max	√	√

In Table 38, the symbol "√" represents showing similarity, "×" showing difference, and "—" showing no test on this feature.

The comparison in Table 38 shows the similar pattern of proximity in prosodic entrainment at conversation level in two languages. Speakers in Tongji Games Corpus were significantly more similar to their partners than to their non-partners in Speaking-rate, F0 max, Intensity mean, Intensity max.

These four prosodic features show evidence of entrainment in SAE as well. In the study of SAE, no evidence of entrainment at conversation level on F0 mean, which is the same to MC. No evidence of entrainment for Intensity min or F0 min, which the SAE study did not consider.

2. Comparison of convergence

The results of prosodic convergence at conversation level are compared between Mandarin Chinese (MC) conversations in Tongji Games Corpus and Standard American English (SAE) in Columbia Games Corpus. The results of MC come from the analyses in Section 4. 1, and the results of SAE come from the research of Levitan & Hirschberg (2011).

Some differences are found.

For SAE, it is found that Intensity mean is more similar in the second half of the first game than in the first. When similarity features are compared across halves of an entire session, it is found that F0 mean is more similar in the second half. No evidence of convergence is found on F0 max or Speaking-rate in Columbia Games Corpus.

For MC, in the Tongji Games Corpus, each conversation consists of 18 sections, each of which involves the placement or description of a single picture. We compared partner differences over the first nine sections with those in the second nine. We also compared partner differences in the first section with those in the last. The analysis in this section is over 66 conversations (four were omitted from the 70 conversations because some parallel sections could not be found in the interlocutors' speaking over the 4 conversations). No significant differences were found. We therefore cannot conclude that MC speakers globally converge on any of the features we examined.

Through the method of descriptive statistics, it is found in the present research that in the process of Mandarin conversations, both convergence and divergence exist in prosodic entrainment, and convergence and divergence appear alternately.

Therefore, the conclusions of convergence in these two studies are different.

Levitan & Hirschberg (2011) predict a linear entrainment process. There are gradual coordination and more entrainment over the course of English conversations.

The present research predicts a wave entrainment process: convergence and divergence appear alternately in Mandarin conversation. However, the proposal of this wave model is put forward on the basis of descriptive statistics. Therefore, this prediction needs to be tested by more future studies.

De Looze *et al*. (2014) assumed that speech accommodation could actually manifest as both a linear and dynamic phenomenon, because the fact that prosodic accommodation had been shown to increase continuously as well as to vary over the course of the conversation.

This assumption is reasonable, because what makes a conversation an interactive dialogue are the dynamic changes involved in interaction by going through the phrases in conversations such as listening, thinking, arguing, giving feedback, etc. Therefore, it can be assumed that adaptation undergoes dynamic changes in real-life spoken interaction.

However, to capture entrainment dynamic manifestation is not an easy task. The difficulties exist mainly in two sides.

One is that spontaneous conversations involve various factors, and the adaptation of two interlocutors changes with the situation where they are. These changes would be caused by psychological, social, behavioral, or other factors. It is difficult to find a fixed model to capture these changes.

Another difficulty is that the adaptation of partners is not time-aligned. Speakers do not accommodate to each other immediately due to the inherent temporally reactive nature of conversational speech (De Looze *et al*. 2014).

Therefore, it is necessary to do more studies on the model of prosodic entrainment process in conversation in the future studies.

6.2.2 Comparison at Turn Level

Comparison at turn level is accomplished from the aspects of proximity, convergence and synchrony in two languages.

1. Comparison of proximity

The results of prosodic proximity at conversation level are compared between Mandarin Chinese (MC) conversations in Tongji Games Corpus and Standard American English (SAE) in Columbia Games Corpus. The results of MC come from the analyses in Section 4. 2, and the results of SAE come from the research of Levitan & Hirschberg (2011).

The results of comparisons are showed in Table 6 - 2.

Table 6 - 2 The comparison of prosodic proximity at turn level between MC and SAE

Feature	MC	SAE
Speaking-rate	√	√
F0 min	×	—
F0 mean	×	√
F0 max	×	√
Intensity min	×	—
Intensity mean	√	√
Intensity max	√	√

In Table 6 - 2, the symbol "√" represents showing similarity, "×" showing difference, and "—" showing no test on this feature.

Table 39 shows the results of the comparisons of proximity at turn level between the MC in Tongji Games Corpus and SAE in Columbia Games Corpus. Comparing the two sets of results, it is easy to find out one similarity and some differences.

The similarity is that there is proximity at turn level in both MC and in SAE over the prosodic features including Speaking-rate, Intensity mean, and Intensity max.

Two differences are found here. Firstly, in the tests of MC, the prosodic features showing proximity at turn level and conversation level are almost consistent. MC exhibit significant proximity at conversation level over 4 prosodic features (Speaking-rate, F0 max, Intensity mean, Intensity max) and proximity in turn level over 3 prosodic features (Speaking-rate, Intensity mean, Intensity max). On the contrary, in the analyses of SAE, the prosodic features showing proximity at turn level and conversation level are not consistent. SAE exhibit significant proximity at turn level over every prosodic feature, but it exhibits proximity at conversation level only over four prosodic features examined.

The second difference is that in MC conversations, no evidence is found for proximity at turn level in terms of F0 mean and F0 max, but these two variables show proximity at turn level in SAE.

2. Comparison of convergence

The results of prosodic convergence at conversation level are compared between Mandarin Chinese (MC) conversations in Tongji Games Corpus and Standard American English (SAE) in Columbia Games Corpus. The results of MC come from the analyses in Section 4.2, and the results of SAE come from the research of Levitan & Hirschberg (2011).

The results of comparisons are showed in Table 6 - 3.

Table 6 - 3　The comparison of convergence at turn level between MC and SAE

Feature	*r*(MC)	*p*(MC)	MC	SAE
Speaking-rate	0.128	0.000	×	×
F0 min	−0.193	0.000	√	—
F0 mean	−0.218	0.000	√	√
F0 max	−0.238	0.000	√	√
Intensity min	−0.086	0.001	√	—
Intensity mean	0.028	0.295	×	×
Intensity max	0.022	0.418	×	×

In Table 6 - 3, the symbol "√" represents showing similarity, "×" showing difference, and "—" showing no test on this feature.

According to Table 6 - 2, the following similarities present obviously.

In both MC and SAE conversations, F0 mean and F0 max exhibit convergence at turn level over the conversations; Speaking-rate, Intensity mean and Intensity max do not exhibit convergence at turn level over the conversations.

One difference is found in the comparison. It is the correlation value. For MC corpus, the negative correlations between adjacent differences and time are about four times as strong as correlations for the SAE corpus, although both of them are still moderate. This indicates that for the same variable, the convergence at turn level is much more evident in MC than in SAE.

3. Comparison of synchrony

The results of prosodic synchrony at conversation level are compared between Mandarin Chinese (MC) conversations in Tongji Games Corpus and Standard American English (SAE) in Columbia Games Corpus. The results of MC come from the analyses in Section 4.2, and the results of SAE come from the research of Levitan & Hirschberg (2011).

The comparison is showed in Table 6 - 4.

Table 6 - 4 The comparison of synchrony at turn level between MC and SAE

Feature	*r*(MC)	*p*(MC)	MC	*r*(SAE)	*p*(SAE)	SAE
Speaking-rate	−0.048	0.073	×	0.15	0.000	√
F0 min	0.625	0.000	√	—	—	—
F0 mean	0.661	0.000	√	0.28	0.000	√
F0 max	0.610	0.000	√	0.18	0.000	√
Intensity min	0.311	0.000	√	—	—	—
Intensity mean	0.628	0.000	√	0.50	0.000	√
Intensity max	0.551	0.000	√	0.47	0.000	√

In Table 6 - 4, the symbol "√" represents showing similarity, "×" showing difference, and "—" showing no test on this feature.

Table 6 - 4 shows the following similarities and differences. Several similarities are found in the comparison.

One is that in both MC and SAE, except Speaking-rate, all the other prosodic features tested in both of the research (F0 mean, F0 max Intensity mean, and Intensity max) exhibit synchrony at turn exchanges.

The second one is that the correlations for means, the features of both Intensity and F0, are slightly stronger than the correlations for maximums, and the correlation for Speaking-rate is the lowest correlation in both languages.

The third one is that synchrony is possible even without proximity at conversation level or turn level in the analyses of MC and SAE. In MC, F0 min, F0 mean, and Intensity min do not exhibit proximity as measured in Section 4. 1, but do exhibit synchrony at turn level. In SAE, F0 mean do not exhibit proximity at conversation or turn level but exhibit synchrony at turn level.

Two differences are found in the comparison.

The most noticeable difference between the two languages is that, in SAE, correlations between F0 features in adjacent IPUs are weak, while in MC, they are among the strongest.

Another difference is that the analysis of synchrony in SAE shows significant correlation over every feature examined. But the analysis in MC shows 6 significant correlations in most features except Speaking-rate. Speaking-rate does not exhibit synchrony in MC conversations, but it does in SAE conversations.

6. 2. 3 Comparison Among Different Gender Groups

In terms of entrainment and gender, the cross-linguistic comparison covers two aspects: proximity by gender groups, and entrainment degree by gender groups.

1. Comparison of proximity

The results of prosodic proximity over three gender groups are compared between Mandarin Chinese (MC) conversations in Tongji Games Corpus and Standard American English (SAE) in Columbia Games Corpus. The results of MC come from the analyses in Section 5. 1, and the results of SAE come from the research of Levitan *et al*. (2012).

The results of comparison are showed in Table 6 - 5.

Table 6 - 5 The comparison of proximity over gender groups between MC and SAE

	Female-Female		Male-Male		Female-Male	
	MC	SAE	MC	SAE	MC	SAE
Speaking-rate	✓	✓	✓	✓	✓	✓
F0 min	×	—	×	—	×	—
F0 mean	×	×	×	×	✓	✓
F0 max	×	×	×	×	✓	✓
Intensity min	×	—	×	—	×	—
Intensity mean	✓	✓	×	✓	✓	✓
Intensity max	✓	✓	×	✓	✓	✓

In Table 6 - 5, the symbol "✓" represents showing similarity, "×" showing difference, and "—" showing no test on this feature.

Table 6 - 5 shows that the more similarities are found in both languages over 3 gender groups. MC and SAE conversations show the similar patterns of entrainment over 3 gender groups. In detail, the mixed gender pairs entrain over the most of prosodic features, and male pairs over the least in both languages.

One difference is found in this analysis. For SAE, the prosodic features showing entrainment are consistent over 3 gender groups. That is, all the gender groups entrained over Intensity mean, Intensity max, and Speaking-rate. But in MC, the prosodic features showing entrainment are not consistent over 3 gender groups, for example, male pairs entrain only on speaking rate.

2. Comparison of entrainment degree

The results of entrainment degree by gender groups are compared between Mandarin Chinese (MC) conversations in Tongji Games Corpus and Standard American English (SAE) in Columbia Games Corpus. The results of MC come from the analyses in Section 5.1, and the results of SAE come from the research of Levitan *et al*. (2012).

According to the research of Levitan *et al*. (2012), for SAE, it is found that entrainment on Intensity mean and max is strongest for mixed gender pairs and weakest for male pairs; the strength of entrainment on speaking-rate followed this pattern but the differences only approached significance ($p = 0.08$).

The similarity is found in MC and SAE conversations that the male pairs tend to entrain least.

The difference is found that in SAE conversations, entrainment is both strongest and most prevalent in mixed gender pairs, while in MC, it is most prevalent in mixed gender pairs, but not necessarily strongest.

6.3 Absolute Entrainment and Relative Entrainment

Through the comparison of the present research on Mandarin conversations and the previous ones on English conversations, two kinds of entrainment are proposed by the present research: absolute entrainment and relative entrainment.

Relative entrainment is found in mixed gender pairs' production of tones in Mandarin Chinese.

Whether there is entrainment in the relative pitch registers of the corresponding tones produced by female and male pairs is analyzed in the present research. Pearson's correlation analyses are adopted in this analysis. For one speaker, the five-point-scale value of the pitch mean over the tone unit within his pitch range is adopted to represent the pitch register that this tone unit occupies. Pearson's correlation analyses are accomplished between the 161 five-point-scale values of female speakers and 161 values of their male pairs.

Through this analysis, it is found that there is significantly positive correlation between the relative pitch registers of the corresponding tone units produced by female and male subjects, although they are in different pitch ranges in speaking. Therefore, the hypothesis that there is relative entrainment between the relative pitch registers of tones in the conversations of mixed gender pairs is proved.

For the mixed gender pairs, pitch ranges of their speaking are different by nature. How do mixed gender pairs exhibit collaboration in the production of tones? The analysis in this section shows that there is relative entrainment between the relative pitch registers of tones in the conversations of mixed gender pairs. That is, they exhibit significant relative entrainment instead of absolute entrainment in the production of tones to show collaboration.

In collaborative conversations, for the mixed gender pairs, the approach of the relative pitch registers of tones is reasonable, while the approach of their absolute pitch registers sounds weird, because two speakers with gender differences stay within different pitch ranges in speaking.

The entrainment found in previous research on prosody in English conversations (Levitan & Hirschberg 2011; Levitan *et al*. 2012) is absolute. In the analyses of global or local entrainment and the relation between entrainment and social factors, the distance of the pairs is used to measure entrainment. If the distance becomes smaller, entrainment is proved, and if it becomes bigger, entrainment is not proved. Therefore, reduced distance of the pairs in conversation means absolute entrainment. The reason for validity of such absolute entrainment in English is that pairs are always able to find shared references in the production of prosody.

However, for Chinese, as a tone language, in the production of tones, mixed gender pairs can not find shared references in their production of tones. Reduced distances, absolute entrainment, between these pairs do not indicate convergence, but divergence.

Both absolute and relative entrainment is proved in the prosody of Mandarin Chinese conversations. In terms of absolute entrainment, in the present research, the distance of the pairs is also adopted to measure entrainment in the analyses over global and local units (Chapter 4) and of the relation to social factors (Chapter 5) in Mandarin Chinese, and absolute entrainment is found from these aspects in Mandarin Chinese. In terms of relative entrainment, the present research proves that mixed gender pairs exhibit relative accommodation in their production of tones in Mandarin Chinese.

Actually, absolute entrainment belongs to relative entrainment. The former is a special case of the later. If the references are not shared, pairs in conversations converge relatively. When shared references exist, pairs converge absolutely. In this situation, the relative entrainment becomes the absolute one.

6.4 Summary of Comparison

This chapter proposes several findings to this question in global entrainment comparison (based on the analyses of entrainment at conversation level), local entrainment comparison (based on the analyses of entrainment at turn level), and comparison of the relation between entrainment and social factors (based on the analyses of entrainment over different gender groups).

Based on the analyses of proximity at both conversation and turn levels, the similarity and difference are found.

One similarity is found in proximity.

Proximity is found over the same prosodic features at each level in MC and SAE. Holistic similarity between interlocutors at conversation level is found over the same prosodic features in two languages including Speaking-rate, F0 max, Intensity mean and Intensity max. Holistic similarity at turn level is also found over the same prosodic features in two languages including Speaking-rate, Intensity mean, and Intensity max.

One difference is found in proximity.

In MC the prosodic features showing proximity at turn level and conversation level are almost consistent, but in SAE the prosodic features showing proximity at turn level are more than those showing proximity at conversation level. For example, in MC conversations, no evidence is found for proximity at turn level in terms of F0 mean and F0 max, but these two variables exhibit proximity at turn level in SAE.

Based on the analyses of convergence at both conversation and turn levels, the similarity and difference are found.

One similarity is found in convergence.

Similar patterns in convergence at turn level are found in two languages. Interlocutors in both MC and SAE become more and more similar with the turns' progress in conversation over F0 mean and F0 max, and they do not exhibit such convergence at turn level over Speaking-rate, Intensity mean and Intensity max.

Two differences are found in convergence.

The first is that different convergence patterns are proposed at conversation level in two languages. Levitan & Hirschberg (2011) predict a linear entrainment process in English conversations. That is, there are gradual coordination and more entrainment in the course of English conversations. The present research does not find similar convergence pattern, but predicts a wave entrainment process in Mandarin Chinese conversations. That is, there exists convergence and divergence in Mandarin conversation, and the convergence and divergence appear alternately. However, this model is only a rough account based on the descriptive data. It is necessary to find more effective methods to model the prosodic entrainment process in conversation in future studies.

The second is that convergence degree is different at turn levels in two languages. The correlation values, which are used to measure the relation between similarity and time, are different in both languages. For MC corpus, the negative correlations between adjacent distances of two interlocutors and time are about four times as strong as correlations for the SAE corpus, although both of them are still moderate. This indicates that for the same variable, the convergence at turn level is much more evident in MC than in SAE.

Based on the analyses of synchrony at turn level, the similarity and difference are found.

Three similarities are found in synchrony.

Firstly, synchrony over turns are found over the same prosodic features in both MC and SAE including F0 mean, F0 max, Intensity mean, and Intensity max. Secondly, synchrony pattern is similar: the correlations for means, both intensity and F0, are slightly stronger than the correlations for maximums, and the correlation for speaking-rate is the lowest correlation in both languages. Thirdly, local entrainment is possible even without global proximity in both languages. Synchrony at turn level is possible even without proximity at conversation level in both languages. For MC, F0 min, F0 mean, and Intensity min do not exhibit proximity at conversation level as measured, but they do exhibit synchrony at turn level. For SAE, F0 mean does not exhibit proximity at conversation level but exhibits the synchrony at turn level.

Two differences are found in synchrony.

Firstly, synchrony degree is different in two languages. Correlation values are used to measure synchrony degree over turns. The most noticeable difference is that in SAE, correlations between two interlocutors' in adjacent IPUs over F0 features are weak, while in MC, they are among the strongest. This indicates that the functions of pitch in MC more prominent in the exhibition of entrainment than in SAE. This proves that pitch in MC plays a dual role in a tonal language, conveying both lexical and pragmatic information.

Secondly, the analyses of synchrony in SAE show significant correlation over every feature examined. But the analysis in MC shows 6 significant correlations in most features except Speaking-rate. Speaking-rate does not exhibit synchrony in MC conversations, but it does in SAE conversations.

Besides, the absolute entrainment is found in previous research on prosody in English conversations (Levitan & Hirschberg 2011; Levitan *et al*. 2012). In the analyses of global or local entrainment and the relation between entrainment and social factors, the distance of the pairs is used to measure entrainment. Therefore, reduced distance of the pairs in conversation is absolute entrainment.

Differently, both absolute and relative entrainment is proved in the prosody of Mandarin Chinese conversations in the present research. In terms of absolute entrainment, the distance of the pairs is also adopted to measure entrainment in the analyses over global and local units (Chapter 4) and of the relation to social factors (Chapter 5) in Mandarin Chinese, and absolute entrainment is found from these aspects in Mandarin Chinese. In terms of relative entrainment, the present research proves that mixed gender pairs exhibit relative accommodation in their production of tones in Mandarin Chinese.

6.5 Discussion

Cross-linguistic comparison of prosodic entrainment is accomplished in this chapter between Chinese and English. Based on all the results of analyses in this chapter, the present research has obtained some findings for the research questions in this chapter.

How is prosodic entrainment in Mandarin conversation differ or similar to that in English conversation?

The comparisons of prosodic entrainment from at both global and local levels and over different gender groups are accomplished in this chapter to answer this question.

Striking similarities are found in entrainment patterns in both languages.

At conversation level, there are similar proximity patterns in conversation of MC and SAE. Speakers in the Tongji Games Corpus are significantly more similar to their partners than to their non-partners over Speaking-rate, F0 max, Intensity mean and Intensity max. These four features show entrainment in SAE as well. In SAE, no evidence of proximity on F0 mean, and it is the same to MC.

At turn level, in both MC and SAE, holistic proximity between interlocutors over turns is found in the prosodic features including Speaking-rate, Intensity mean, and Intensity max. Similar patterns in convergence at turn level are found in two languages. Interlocutors in both MC and SAE become more and more similar with the turns' progress in conversation over F0 mean and F0 max, and they do not exhibit such convergence at turn level over Speaking-rate, Intensity mean and Intensity max.

Similar synchrony over turns is found in two languages. Firstly, synchrony over turns are found over the same prosodic features in both MC and SAE including F0 mean, F0 max, Intensity mean, and Intensity max. Secondly, synchrony pattern is similar: the correlations for means, both intensity and F0, are slightly stronger than the correlations for maximums, and the correlation for speaking-rate is the lowest correlation in both languages. Thirdly, local entrainment is possible even without global proximity in both languages. Synchrony at turn level is possible even without proximity at conversation level in both languages. For MC, F0 min, F0 mean, and Intensity min do not exhibit proximity at conversation level as measured, but they do exhibit synchrony at turn level. For SAE, F0 mean does not exhibit proximity at conversation level but exhibits the synchrony at turn level.

Over different gender groups, in both languages, the number of prosodic features showing entrainment in the mixed gender pairs is the most, and that is the least in male pairs. The similarity is found in MC and SAE conversations that the male pairs tend to entrain least.

Differences are found in entrainment degree in both languages.

At turn level, differences in convergence and synchrony degree are found in both languages. Convergence degree is different in two languages. The correlation values, which are used to measure the relation between similarity and time, are different in both languages. For MC corpus, the negative correlations between adjacent distances of two interlocutors and time are about four times as strong as correlations for the SAE corpus, although both of them are still moderate. This indicates that for the same variable, the convergence at turn level is much more evident in MC than in SAE. Synchrony degree is different in two languages. Correlation values are used to measure synchrony degree over turns. The most noticeable difference is that in SAE, correlations between two interlocutors' in adjacent IPUs over F0 features are weak, while in MC, they are among the strongest. This indicates that the functions of pitch in MC more prominent in the exhibition of entrainment than in SAE. This proves that pitch in MC plays a dual role in a tonal language, conveying both lexical and pragmatic information.

Over different gender groups, in SAE conversations, entrainment is both strongest and prevalent in mixed gender pairs; in MC, it is most prevalent in mixed gender pairs, but not necessarily strongest.

The similarities of the entrainment patterns in MC from Tongji Games Corpus and SAE from Columbia Games Corpus support not only the view that entrainment is a cross-cultural phenomenon but propose the ways that these two languages entrain similarly. The differences of the entrainment degree in both languages partially are due to the differences in language type.

Besides, the existence of two categories of entrainment in two languages is different.

The present research proposes two categories of entrainment: absolute entrainment and relative entrainment.

Entrainment in previous research on prosody in English conversations (Levitan & Hirschberg 2011; Levitan *et al*. 2012) is absolute. In the analyses of global or local entrainment and the relation between entrainment and social factors, the distance of the pairs in conversation is used to measure entrainment. If the distance becomes smaller, entrainment is proved, and if it becomes bigger, entrainment is not proved. Thus, reduced distance of one pair in conversation means the absolute approach of two speakers, and it indicates absolute entrainment.

Both absolute and relative entrainment is proved in the prosody of Mandarin Chinese conversations.

Absolute entrainment is also found in Mandarin conversations. The present research adopts some methods in the studies of English, among which the distance of pairs in conversation is also used to measure entrainment. In the analyses of entrainment at multiple levels (Chapter 4) and from social aspect (Chapter 5), the present research has found absolute entrainment in Mandarin conversations.

Different from absolute entrainment, relative convergence in tones is proposed by the present research through the analysis of tones produced by mixed gender pairs in Mandarin conversations.

For the mixed gender pairs, pitch ranges of their speaking are different by nature. In this situation, the approach of absolute pitch values in tones of the male and female pair sounds weird or far away from collaborative. For example, for a male speaker, his imitation of his female partner's high pitch in the tones is always perceived not to be cooperative, but strange or ironic.

How do mixed gender pairs exhibit collaboration in the production of tones? The analysis of entrainment over tones indicates that there is convergence of the relative pitch registers of tones in mixed gender pairs' conversations. Therefore, mixed gender pairs exhibit significant relative entrainment instead of absolute entrainment in the production of tones to show collaboration.

Chapter 7
Conclusion

This chapter states the major findings and limitations of this study. The further researches in the future studies are also mentioned at the end of this chapter.

7.1 Major Findings

The present research explores the prosodic entrainment in Chinese conversations. The analyses of prosodic entrainment are accomplished at multiple levels and over different social factors. In addition, cross-linguistic comparison of prosodic entrainment is accomplished between Mandarin Chinese and English. These analyses are the main contents of Chapter 4, 5 and 6.

The analyses in Chapter 4 are expected to answer the first research question: *how is prosody used to entrain in Mandarin conversation?* In this chapter, this question is decomposed into two questions:

Is prosodic entrainment in Mandarin conversation global or local? In Chapter 4, prosodic entrainment is analyzed from the global to the local at three levels, the levels of conversation, turn and tone units. Based on these analyses, at the end of this chapter, cross-level comparisons of the results at these three levels are made in order to find out whether prosodic entrainment in Mandarin conversation is global, local or both, and how prosodic entrainment is made at these levels.

Is prosodic entrainment in Mandarin conversation convergent or constant as time goes on? Different from the static perspective in the question above, this question focuses on the dynamic entrainment process in conversation. The analyses of entrainment process in Chapter 4 aim to find out whether the similarity between the two interlocutors is increased or decreased when a conversation goes on.

Empirical methods are used in these analyses. Firstly, distances of prosodic performances between two interlocutors are calculated for the measurement of entrainment only with a negative correlation between them. Secondly, series of paired T-tests are used to identify entrainment at different levels in conversation, including the tests between partner distances and non-partner distances at conversation level, adjacent IPUs and non-adjacent IPUs at turn level, and corresponding distances and non-corresponding distances over tone units. Thirdly, series of correlation analyses are used to identify synchronous entrainment between two interlocutors at the levels of turn and tone units. Fourthly, series of ANOVA tests are adopted to measure the differences in entrainment degree among the prosodic features showing entrainment at conversation level.

Major findings in Chapter 4 are listed below.

(i) Entrainment in Mandarin conversation is proved to exist in 3 main aspects of prosody.

The analyses in the present research provide considerable evidences for the existence of entrainment in 3 main aspects of prosody: the features of duration, F0 and intensity. 7 variables, Speaking-rate (one feature of duration), F0 min, F0 mean, F0 max (three features of F0) and Intensity min, Intensity mean, Intensity max (three features of intensity) are set as parameters in the present research, over which entrainment in conversation has been proved.

This finding supports the viewpoint that prosody plays roles in keeping effective interaction.

Current research on prosody in spoken interaction covers emotional prosody, prosody in cooperation or affiliation, attitudinal intonation, etc. Speech prosody is used in interaction to express emotions. It is also used to show cooperation or competition, agreement or disagreement, affiliation or disaffiliation in interaction. Prosody also can express attitudes in interaction. In communication, intonation works with other linguistic patterns to express attitudes. The currently contribution to our understanding of attitudinal meaning in intonation is the study of "affiliating and disaffiliating" behavior.

Recently, more and more attention is paid to attitudinal function of prosody because of the need in development of human-machine dialogue systems. The related research is helpful to make machines produce voices that sound cooperative, friendly, or polite, along with the aim to recognize when human customers are irate, frustrated or just plain exasperated.

Entrainment in conversation is both attitudinal and emotional, because it can be considered as cooperation, agreement, or support in communication. However, entrainment emphasizes adjustment and alignment between two interlocutors in cooperation. Therefore, the research of entrainment pays more attention to the coordination or adjustment between two parties in interaction, while the studies of emotional and attitudinal prosody mentioned above pay more attention to a single part. It is from this different perspective that prosody is proved to play crucial roles in interaction.

(ii) For the prosodic features measured in the present research, local entrainment is more evident than global entrainment.

According to the analyses in Chapter 4, more prosodic features exhibit entrainment at relatively local level than at global level. In detail, in terms of proximity, 5 features show entrainment over tone units, and 4 features at conversation level; in terms of synchrony, 7 features show entrainment over tone units, 6 features at turn level. Besides, the features of F0 show more prominent entrainment at relatively local level, in spite of their less evident entrainment at global level.

(iii) Different prosodic features exhibit entrainment at different levels: at both global and local levels, features of intensity exhibit prominent entrainment; the durational feature exhibits more prominent at relatively global level; the features of F0 exhibit more prominent entrainment at relatively local level.

According to the cross-level comparison in Chapter 4, the features of intensity show entrainment at almost all the levels tested, the features of duration show more prominent entrainment at conversation level than turn level, and the features of F0 show evident synchrony at levels of turn and tone unit, while they show less entrainment at the level of conversation.

Therefore, all the three hypotheses made at the beginning of Chapter 4 for the relationship between global entrainment and local entrainment, exist for different prosodic features. The hypothesis that two interlocutors in conversation entrain both globally and locally is proved in the analyses of the Intensity features. For these features, entrainment can be considered as a dynamic and accumulative process of continuous matching from the local units to the local ones. The hypothesis that two interlocutors in conversation entrain globally, but diverge at local positions is proved in the analyses of the durational feature. The hypothesis that two interlocutors in conversation are not similar globally, but entrain locally is proved in the analyses of F0 features.

(iv) With the progress of conversation, increased similarity between two interlocutors is found at turn level, but no increased similarity is found at conversation level or over tone units.

The present research has accomplished the analyses of convergence at three levels. The cross-level comparisons of convergence at three levels show that it is more difficult to capture convergence in conversation than proximity and synchrony, and that convergence is found only at turn level.

Two simple hypotheses for the entrainment process in conversation are made in Chapter 4. One is that two interlocutors become more and more similar when time progresses till the end of conversation. Another is that distances of two interlocutors decreases to fixed distance, and the pair keep this fixed distance to the end of conversation. Through the analyses in Chapter 4, one of the two hypotheses for the entrainment process in conversation is proved at turn level. That is, two interlocutors are proved to be more and more similar with the progress of conversation only at turn level.

It is not an easy task to capture entrainment dynamic manifestation in conversation. The difficulties exist mainly in two aspects. One is that spontaneous conversations involve various factors, and the adaptation of two interlocutors changes with the situation where they are. Any psychological, social, behavioral, or other factors probably trigger the interlocutors' states in conversation. It is difficult to find a fixed model to capture these changes. Another difficulty is that the adaptation between partners is not time-aligned. Speakers do not accommodate to each other immediately due to the inherent temporally reactive nature of conversational speech (De Looze *et al.* 2014: 15).

The difficulty in model the entrainment process causes the inconsistency in relevant researches, in which different models of convergence in conversation are proposed. Levitan & Hirschberg (2011) predict a linear entrainment process. There are gradual coordination and more entrainment over the course of English conversations. De Looze *et al.* (2014: 14) assume that speech accommodation can actually manifest as both a linear and dynamic phenomenon, because the fact that prosodic accommodation has been shown to increase continuously as well as to vary over the course of the conversation.

The present research predicts a wave entrainment process. Both convergence and divergence exist in Mandarin conversation, and they appear alternately. However, this wave model is proposed based on descriptive statistics. Therefore, this prediction needs to be tested by different research methods.

Therefore, it is necessary to do more exploration on the model of prosodic entrainment process in conversation in the future studies.

The analyses in Chapter 5 are made to answer the second research question: *how do social factors affect prosodic entrainment in Mandarin conversation?*

Social factors cover various aspects. It is difficult to control simultaneously several social factors in one experiment. This research focuses on two of them: gender and role. Two kinds of analyses are made in Chapter 5: the analyses of entrainment and gender, and the analyses of entrainment and role. The analyses of entrainment and gender are accomplished from the aspects of the proximity and entrainment degree over the pairs with different gender combinations. The analyses of entrainment and role include Role

Influence Test and Role Direction test.

In terms of the methods in analyses, series of paired T-tests are used in this chapter. Some paired T-tests between partner distances and non-partner distances at conversation level are accomplished among three gender groups. Some paired T-tests are adopted in Role Influence Test to find out the difference in entrainment degree between Picture Ordering Games and Picture Classifying Games. Others are used in Role Direction test to find out the differences between the deviation caused by the role of giver and that caused by the role of follower. Besides these paired T-tests, series of ANOVA tests are adopted in the analyses of entrainment degree over different gender groups.

The major findings in Chapter 5 are listed below.

(v) Entrainment is proved to be closely related to the gender and role of interlocutors in Mandarin conversations.

In terms of gender, the most prosodic features are involved in mixed gender pairs' entrainment, and in both number of features entrained and degree of entrainment, males entrain the least.

In terms of role, it is proved that the roles affect the entrainment degree in conversation over the prosodic features of duration and F0, and that information givers entrain more than followers in conversation.

The findings of entrainment and gender partially support the theories of dominance and perception. In previous studies of entrainment and gender differences, theories of dominance and perception are proposed. Bilous & Krauss (1988) make the male dominance hypothesis, and point out differences in speech between men and women have to do with men's dominant position in society. In addition, according to CAT (Giles *et al*. 1987), it is proposed that when there is an imbalance of power between speakers, the less dominant speaker will entrain more. In terms of perception, perception behavior link (Chartrand & Bargh 1999) states that perceiving something makes people more likely to mimic it and females are known to be more sensitive to perceived differences in speech.

Based on these theories, predictions are made: in mixed gender pairs' conversations, females should entrain more, and there should be more entrainment in female -female pairs' conversations than male-male pairs' conversations. The result that the most prosodic features are involved in mixed gender pairs' entrainment, and in both number of features entrained and degree of entrainment, males entrain the least support partially the theories of dominance and perception.

The findings of entrainment and role supply evidence for the fact that there is directive distinction in entrainment between two interlocutors. That is, the entrainment degree of a pair in conversation is unbalanced. We can feel the entrainment direction in our daily life. For instance, in Child-directed speech or motherese (Fernald *et al.* 1989), which is a term used to describe speakers' accommodation when having conversations with children. It is observed that adults entrain more to children in their conversations. For another example, in foreign talk or foreigness (Ferguson 1975; Zuengler 1991; Smith 2007), which is used when talking with non-native speakers, we observe that native speakers entrain more to the foreigners.

Directive distinction in entrainment between two interlocutors has been investigated in the previous studies. Motivated by the hypothesis of *audience design* (Bell 1984), which means the audience-oriented entrainment, studies have been accomplished to find out to how and what extent speakers adapt to their addressees (Branigan *et al.* 2007; Galati & Brenna 2010). Kristiansen (2008) proposes that there are three possible directions in entrainment between two interlocutors (A, B) in conversation. One is A to B (A→B), the other one is B to A (A←B), and the third one is that both A and B approach to an intermediate state (A→←B).

Different from the analyses in previous studies, the present research has examined the entrainment between information givers and information followers. In chapter 5, Role Influence Test is made to examine whether there is prosodic entrainment between information givers and information followers, based on which, Role Direction Test is made to find out the direction of entrainment between them, that is, whether information givers entrain to information followers, or followers entrain to givers. It is found by the present research that more entrainment is made from givers to followers.

The analyses in Chapter 6 are made to answer the third research question: *how is prosodic entrainment in Mandarin conversation differ or similar to that in English conversation?*

For this research question, the present research has accomplished cross-linguistic comparisons of prosodic entrainment between Mandarin Chinese in Tongji Games Corpus and Standard American English in Columbia Games Corpus in Chapter 6. The results of analyzing prosodic entrainment in Mandarin conversation in the present research are compared with those in English in previous research. The comparison of prosodic entrainment between Chinese and English is accomplished mainly over conversational level, turn level, and gender aspects, on which the parallel work is available in these two languages.

The major findings in Chapter 6 are listed below.

(vi) Striking similarities are found in entrainment patterns in MC and English, and differences in entrainment degree are found in both languages.

The following similarities in entrainment patterns in two languages are found in Chapter 6. At conversation level, those features, which exhibit holistic entrainment in conversation and those which do not, are the same in MC and SAE. At turn level, in both MC and SAE, holistic similarities between interlocutors over turns is found in the same prosodic features including Speaking-rate, Intensity mean, and Intensity max. At the turn level, those features, which show increasing similarities as the conversation goes on and those which do not, are the same in MC and SAE. Similar synchrony over turns is found in two languages. Over different gender groups, in both languages, the number of prosodic features showing entrainment in the mixed gender pairs is the most, and that in male pairs is the least.

The following differences in entrainment degree in both languages are found in Chapter 6. At turn level, differences in convergence and synchrony degree are found in both languages. According to the analyses in this chapter, for the same variable, the convergence at turn level is much more evident in MC than in SAE. The most noticeable difference is that in SAE, synchrony of adjacent IPUs from two interlocutors over F0 features are weak, while in MC, they are among the strongest. This indicates that the functions of pitch in MC more prominent in the exhibition of entrainment than in SAE. This proves that pitch in MC plays a dual role in a tonal language, conveying both lexical and pragmatic information. Over different gender groups, in SAE conversations, entrainment is both strongest and prevalent in mixed gender pairs, while in MC, it is most prevalent in mixed gender pairs, but not necessarily strongest.

The similarities of the entrainment patterns in MC from Tongji Games Corpus and SAE from Columbia Games Corpus support not only the view that entrainment is a cross-cultural phenomenon but propose the ways that these two languages entrain similarly. The differences of the entrainment degree in both languages partially are due to the differences in language type.

(vii) Two kinds of entrainment are proposed in the present research: absolute entrainment and relative entrainment.

Absolute entrainment is found in previous research on prosody in English conversations, and both kinds of entrainment is proved in the prosody of Mandarin Chinese conversations in the present research.

Entrainment in previous research on prosody in English conversations (Levitan & Hirschberg 2011; Levitan *et al*. 2012) is absolute. In the analyses of global or local entrainment and the relation between entrainment and social factors, the distance of the pairs in conversation is used to measure entrainment. If the distance becomes smaller, entrainment is proved, and if it becomes bigger, entrainment is not proved. Thus, reduced distance of one pair in conversation means the absolute approach of two speakers, and it indicates absolute entrainment.

This kind of absolute entrainment is also found in Mandarin conversations. The present research adopts some methods in the studies of English, among which the distance of pairs in conversation is also used to measure entrainment. In the analyses of entrainment at multiple levels (Chapter 4) and from social aspect (Chapter 5), the present research has found absolute entrainment in Mandarin conversations.

Different from absolute entrainment, relative convergence in tones is proposed by the present research through the analysis of tones produced by mixed gender pairs in Mandarin conversations.

Whether there is entrainment in the relative pitch registers of the corresponding tones produced by female and male pairs is analyzed in the present research. Pearson's correlation analyses are adopted in this analysis. For one speaker, the five-point-scale value of the pitch mean over the tone unit within his pitch range is adopted to represent the pitch register that this tone unit occupies. Pearson's correlation analyses are accomplished between the 161 five-point-scale values of female speakers and 161 values of their male pairs.

Through this analysis, it is found that there is significantly positive correlation between the relative pitch registers of the corresponding tone units produced by female and male subjects, although they are in different pitch range in speaking. Therefore, the hypothesis that there is relative entrainment between the relative pitch registers of tones in the conversations of mixed gender pairs is proved.

For the mixed gender pairs, pitch ranges of their speaking are different by nature. In this situation, the approach of absolute pitch values in tones of the male and female speakers sounds weird or far away from collaborative. For example, for a male speaker, his imitation of his female partner's high pitch in the tones is always perceived not to be cooperative, but strange or ironic.

How do mixed gender pairs exhibit collaboration in the production of tones? The analysis of entrainment over tones indicates that there is convergence of the relative pitch registers of tones in mixed gender pairs' conversations. Therefore, mixed gender pairs exhibit significant relative entrainment instead of absolute entrainment in the production of tones to show collaboration.

In summary, the absolute entrainment is found in previous research on prosody in English conversations, and both kinds of entrainment (absolute and relative) is proved in the prosody of Mandarin Chinese conversations in the present research.

It is necessary to discuss the relation of the two kinds of entrainment proposed in the present research.

Two categories of entrainment are different. Absolute entrainment of pairs in conversation means absolute approach of two speakers, which is exhibited by reduced distance of the pair in conversation. Relative entrainment means relative approach of two interlocutors, which can not be exhibited directly by reduced distance or absolute approach of the pair, but by their relative approach. For example, in the present research, in collaborative communication, female and male interlocutors in one conversation exhibit convergence in relative pitch register of Mandarin tones, although speakers with different gender have different pitch ranges in speaking.

In spite of differences, the two categories of entrainment are closely related. Actually, absolute entrainment belongs to relative entrainment. The former is a special case of the later. In the process of collaborative communication, interlocutors are supposed to make coordination with certain references. When the references are similar or shared by both interlocutors, the pair makes absolute convergence. When the references used by each of the pair are different or not shared, both interlocutors achieve relative convergence with respective references.

The reason for validity of absolute entrainment in the present research is that pairs are able to find shared references in the production of prosody at the global levels (conversation level and turn level). However, in Chinese, a tone language, mixed gender pairs can not find shared references in their production of tones. Reduced distances or absolute entrainment over tones between mixed gender pairs do not indicate convergence, but divergence. Therefore, if the references are not shared, pairs in conversations converge relatively. When shared references exist, pairs converge absolutely, and in this situation, the relative entrainment becomes the absolute one.

Absolute or relative entrainment, which one is universal in collaborative communication? This is an open question, which calls for future researches on this topic. In Mandarin collaborative communication, relative entrainment is proved in the production of tones, and absolute entrainment is proved in the production of prosody over more global units (at the levels of conversation and turn) in the present research. Entrainment in previous research on prosody in English conversations (Levitan & Hirschberg 2011; Levitan *et al*. 2012) is absolute, in which, absolute entrainment is proved in the analyses of global or local entrainment and the relation between entrainment and social factors in English collaborative communication. As mentioned above, shared or not shared references are crucial for interlocutors to make absolute or relative entrainment. Studies are needed to explore the situations where the shared or not shared references exist, to verify the existence of both kinds of entrainment, to compare popularity of both kinds of entrainment, and so on.

(viii) The research methods used in the present research are valuable.

Doing analyses of interlocutors' entrainment in conversation is not an easy task. The research methods used in the present research are worth of mention.

Firstly, comprehensive analyses of entrainment over tones are accomplished in different angles.

Section 4.3 in Chapter 4 is about the analyses of entrainment over tone units, which can be divided into two parts. From different angles, the analyses of entrainment over tones are accomplished in these two parts. In the former three sub-sections, absolute entrainment over tone units is proved, and 7 prosodic features from the 3 main aspects of prosody (duration, fundamental frequency, and intensity) are comprehensively investigated. In the last sub-sections, relative entrainment over tone units is proved, and this part focuses on pitch register of tones. The former part is consistent with the method used in more global units, and follows the line in the analyses of the entrainment from the global to the local. The latter part highlight relative pitch registers of Mandarin tones. Therefore, two parts in this section are mutual complementary, and form comprehensive analyses of entrainment over tone units.

Secondly, methods used in analyses of absolute entrainment have reference value for future researches, among which two points need to be mentioned.

The first point is that the present research adopts the distances between two interlocutors to present entrainment. To measure entrainment is not easy. The reason is that entrainment involves dynamic performances of two interlocutors, and there are several possible directions in entrainment between pairs. The present research adopts distances between two interlocutors to present entrainment. In detail, distances of prosodic performances between two interlocutors are calculated for the measurement of entrainment only with a negative correlation between them. That is, when interlocutors' distance becomes smaller, entrainment becomes bigger. Thus, no matter in which direction interlocutors entrain, it is valid that distances of interlocutors' represent entrainment degree. The method that adopting distances between two interlocutors to present entrainment forms the base for other methods used in the analyses of prosodic entrainment in the present research.

The second point is that in the present research, the comparisons between partner distances and non-partner distances are used to identify entrainment in conversation. How to identify entrainment in conversation is also a difficult task. Methods used to test whether two interlocutors become similar or not are not easy to find. The present research adopts the notion of Levitan and her group (Levitan & Hirschberg 2011, Levitan *et al*. 2012) that the comparisons between partner distances and non-partner distances are used to identify entrainment in conversation. If the partner distances between A and B are smaller than non-partner distances between A and C, entrainment can be identified in the conversations of this pair. Here, A and B are two interlocutors in conversation, C is the speaker with the same gender and role to B and never talks with A. Here, the non-partner distance is taken as the baseline in comparison. The present research makes sufficient use of this method.

The similar methods, in which the third party is taken as the reference in the analyses of the relations of two parties, are used sufficiently in the present research. Besides the comparisons between partner distances and non-partner distances in the analyses of proximity at conversation level, the similar methods are adopted in other analyses. For example, in the analyses of proximity at turn level, comparisons between adjacent IPUs at turn exchanges and non-adjacent IPUs are used. As another example, in the analyses of proximity over turn units, comparisons between corresponding distances and non-corresponding distances are used. Although the units in comparisons are different in size, the key point that the irrelevant third party is borrowed in comparisons of two parties is the same.

Thirdly, inspired by the method from Computation Linguistics, the present research makes calculation of the values extracted by Praat, and uses the values computed in analyses. In the research on pragmatic functions of prosody, analyses of the values directly extracted by Praat can't achieve the research goal, because not all the values of effective parameters in analyses can be extracted directly from software. According to the research design, the present research sets effective parameters, makes calculation of the values extracted by Praat, and accomplishes analyses of the values computed.

7.2 Limitations of this Research

The present research analyzes the prosodic entrainment in Mandarin Chinese conversations from 3 main aspects: entrainment at multiple levels, entrainment and social factors, and cross-linguistic comparisons of prosodic entrainment. The present research has limitations, which supply the potential possibilities for the future studies.

Firstly, modeling the entrainment process in conversations should be improved. Capturing dynamic entrainment is difficult. The difficulties exist mainly in two sides. One is that the adaptation of two interlocutors changes with the progress of conversation. These changes might be caused by psychological, social, behavioral, or other factors. It is difficult to find a fixed model to generalize these changes. Another difficulty is that the adaptation partners are not time-aligned. Therefore, it is necessary to find effective methods to model precisely the prosodic entrainment process in conversation in the future studies.

Secondly, more social factors should be involved in the study of prosodic entrainment. The entrainment in conversation involves various social factors of interlocutors: the status, age, gender, role, region, ethnicity, environment features, etc., of which the present research studied the gender and role. In fact, the functions of other social factors are also worth investigating. It is not possible to do research on all the social factors in one study. The difficulty in dealing with these social factors is how to make the target factors prominent and make valid control of other factors in experiments.

Thirdly, the relationship between pitch and prosodic entrainment should be studied further. The present research did a preliminary study, in which prosodic entrainment is analyzed over tone units. Proximity, convergence, and synchrony are tested over all the units. However, for the relationship between tones and prosody in Chinese, majority of literature only supply assumed descriptions rather than explicit explanations. Therefore, it is necessary to make further research on this point.

References

[1] Ang J, Dhillon R, Krupski A, et al. Prosody-based automatic detection of annoyance and frustration in human-computer dialogue[C]//Proceedings of ICSLP-2002, Denver, CO., 2002: 2037-2040.

[2] Aubanel V, Nguyen N. Automatic recognition of regional phonological variation in conversational interaction. Speech Communication, 2010, 52(6): 577-586.

[3] Auer P. Introduction: John Gumperz' approach to contextualization[M]//Auer P, Luxio A D (eds.), The Contextualization of Language. Amsterdam and Philadelphia: Benjamins, 1992: 1-38.

[4] Auer P, Luzio A D. The Contextualization of Language[M]. Amsterdam and Philadelphia: Benjamins, 1992.

[5] Auer P, Couper-Kuhlen E, Muller F. Language in time: The rhythm and tempo of spoken interaction[M]. Oxford: Oxford University Press, 1999.

[6] Babel M, Bulatov D. The role of fundamental frequency in phonetic accommodation[J]. Language and Speech, 2011, 55(2): 231-248.

[7] Bailly G, Lelong A. Speech dominoes and phonetic convergence[J]. In Interspeech 2010, 2010: 1153-1156.

[8] Bandura A. Social learning theory[M]. Englewood Cliffs, NJ: Prentice Hall, 1977.

[9] Baumann S, Grice M. The intonation of accessibility[J]. Journal of Pragmatics, 2006, 38(10): 1636-1657.

[10] Bavelas J B, Black A, Lemery C R, et al. I show how you feel: motor mimicry as a communicative act[J]. Journal of Personality and Social Psychology, 1986, 50(2): 322.

[11] Bavelas J B, Black A, Lemery C R, et al. Experimental methods for studying "elementary motor mimicry"[J]. Journal of Nonverbal Behavior, 1986, 10: 102-119.

[12] Beckman M E, Hirschberg J. The ToBI annotation conventions[D]. Ohio State University, 1994.

[13] Bell A. Language style as audience design[J]. Language in Society, 1984, 13(2): 145 - 204.

[14] Bell L, Gustafson J, Heldner M. Prosodic adaptation in human-computer interaction [C]//Proceedings of the 15th International Congress of Phonetic Sciences (ICPhS), Citeseer, 2003, 3: 833 - 836.

[15] Beňuš Š. Variability and stability in collaborative dialogues: turn-taking and filled pauses [C]//Proceedings of the 10th INTERSPEECH, 2009: 709 - 799.

[16] Beňuš Š, Gravano A, Hirschberg J. Pragmatic aspects of temporal accommodation in turn-taking[J]. Journal of Pragmatics, 2011, 43: 3001 - 3027.

[17] Beňuš Š, Levitan R, Hirschberg J. Entrainment in spontaneous speech: the case of filled pauses in Supreme Court hearings [C]//Proceedings of 3rd IEEE International Conference on Cognitive Infocommunications. Kosice, Slovakia, 2012: 793 - 797.

[18] Bernieri F J, Rosenthal R. Interpersonal coordination: Behavior matching and interactional synchrony[M]//Feldman R S, Rimé B (eds.), Fundamentals of Nonverbal Behavior. New York: Cambridge University Press, 1991: 401 - 432.

[19] Bernieri F J, Davis J M, Rosenthal R, et al. Interactional synchrony and rapport: measuring synchrony in displays devoid of sound and facial affect[J]. Personality and Social Psychology Bulletin, 1994, 20: 303 - 311.

[20] Bigi B, Hirst D. Speech phonetization alignment and syllabification (Sppas): a tool for the automatic analysis of speech prosody[C]//Proceedings of Speech Prosody 2012. Shanghai: Tongji University, 2012: 19 - 22.

[21] Bilous F R, Krauss R M. Dominance and accommodation in the conversational behaviors of same-and mixed-gender dyads[J]. Language, Communication, 1988, 8: 183 - 194.

[22] Black J W. The intensity of oral responses to stimulus words[J]. Journal of Speech and Hearing Disorders, 1949, 14(1): 16 - 22.

[23] Boersma P, Weenink D. Praat: doing phonetics by computer [computer program]. Version 5. 3. 23, retrieved 21 August, 2012 from http://www. praat. org.

[24] Bock J K. Syntactic persistence in language production[J]. Cognitive Psychology, 1986, 18: 355 - 387.

[25] Bolinger D. Generality, gradience and the all or none[M]. The Hague: Mouton, 1961.

[26] Bolinger D. The atomization of meaning[J]. Language, 1965, 41: 555 - 573.

[27] Bolinger D. Accent is predictable (if you are a mind-reader)[J]. Language, 1972, 48 (3): 633 - 644.

[28] Bolinger D. Intonation and Its Parts[M]. Stanford University Press, 1986.

[29] Bolinger D. Intonation and Its Use: Melody in Grammar and Discourse[M]. London:

Edward Arnold, 1989.

[30] Bortfeld H, Brennan S E. Use and acquisition of idiomatic expressions in referring by native and non-native speakers[J]. Discourse Processes, 1997, 23: 119 - 147.

[31] Bourhis R Y, Giles H, Lambert W E. Social consequences of accommodating one's syle of speech: a cross-national investigation[J]. International Journal of the Sociology of Language, 1975, 6: 55 - 72.

[32] Boylan P. Accommodation theory revisited [EB/OL]. [2012 - 9 - 10]. http://www.docin.com/p - 688557528.html.

[33] Branigan H P, Pickering M J, Cleland A A. Syntactic coordination in dialogue[J]. Cognition, 2000, 75: B13 - B25.

[34] Branigan H P, Pickering M J, McLean J F, et al. Syntactic alignment and participant role in dialogue[J]. Cognition, 2007, 104(2): 163 - 197.

[35] Branigan H P, Pickering M J, Pearson J, et al. Linguistic alignment between people and computers[J]. Journal of Pragmatics, 2010, 42: 2355 - 2368.

[36] Branigan H P, Pickering M J, McLean J F, et al. The role of beliefs in lexical alignment: evidence from dialogs with humans and computers[J]. Cognition, 2011, 121: 41 - 57.

[37] Brazil D. Phonology: intonation in Discourse[M]//Van Dijk T (ed.), Handbook of Discourse Analysis, II: Dimensions of Discourse. London: Academic Press, 1985: 57 - 75.

[38] Breazeal C. Regulation and entrainment in human-robot interaction [J]. The International Journal of Robotics Research, 2002, 21(10 - 11): 883 - 902.

[39] Brennan S E. Lexical entrainment in spontaneous dialog [C]//Proceedings of International Symposium on Spoken Dialogue (ISSD), Philadelphia, 1996: 41 - 44.

[40] Brennan S E, Clark H H. Conceptual pacts and lexical choice in conversation[J]. Journal of Experimental Psychology: Learning, Memory, and Cognition, 1996, 22: 1482 - 1493.

[41] Brennan S E, Galati A, Kuhlen A K. Two Minds, One Dialog: coordinating Speaking and Understanding[M]//Brian H R (ed.), The Psychology of Learning and Motivation, Academic Prss, 2010, 53: 301 - 344.

[42] Brown G, Currie K L, Kenworthy J. Questions of Intonation[M]. London: Croom Helm, 1980.

[43] Buller D B, LePoire B A, Aune R K, et al. Social perceptions as mediators of the effect of Speaking-rate similarity on compliance[J]. Human Communication Research, 1992, 19: 286 - 311.

[44] Byrne D. The Attraction Paradigm[M]. New York: Academic Press, 1971.

[45] Cappella J N, Panalp S. Talk and silence sequences in informal conversations: III. Inter-speaker influence[J]. Human Communication Research, 1981, 7: 117 - 132.

[46] Caspers J. Local speech melody as a limiting factor in the turn-taking system in Dutch [J]. Journal of Phonetics, 2003, 31: 251 - 276.

[47] Chambers C G, Tanenhaus M K, Eberhard K M, et al. Circumscribing referential domains in real-time sentence comprehension[J]. Journal of Memory and Language, 2002, 47: 30 - 49.

[48] Chao Y R. A system of tone letters[J]. Le Maîter Phonétuque, 1930, 45: 24 - 27.

[49] Chartrand T L, Bargh J A. The Chameleon Effect: The perception-behavior link and social interaction[J]. Journal of Personality and Social Psychology, 1999, 76(6): 893 - 910.

[50] Chartrand T L, Maddux W W, Lakin J L. Beyond the perception-behavior link: the ubiquitous utility and motivational moderators of nonconscious mimicry[M]//Hassin R R, Uleman J S, Bargh J A (eds.), The New Unconnscious. Oxford: Oxford University Press, 2005: 334 - 361.

[51] Chen M, Bargh J A. Non-conscious behavioral confirmation processes: The self-fulfilling consequences of automatic stereotype activation[J]. Journal of Experimental Social Psychology, 1997, 33: 541 - 560.

[52] Chi-Chun L, Matthew B, Athanasios K, et al. Quantification of prosodic entrainment in affective spontaneous spoken interactions of married couples [C]//Proceedings of Eleventh Annual Conference of the International Speech Communication Association. Makuhari, Japan, 2010: 793 - 796.

[53] Clark H H, Wilkes-Gibbs D. Referring as a collaborative process[J]. Cognition, 1986, 22: 1 - 39.

[54] Cleland A A, Pickering M J. The use of lexical and syntactic information in language production: Evidence from the priming of noun phrase structure[J]. Journal of Memory and Language, 2003, 49: 214 - 230.

[55] Collins B. Convergence of fundamental frequencies in conversation: if it happens, does it matter? [C]//Proceedings of Fifth International Conference on Spoken Language Processing (ICSLP), 1998.

[56] Condon W S, Sander L W. Synchrony demonstrated between movements of the neonate and adult speech[J]. Child Development, 1974, 54: 456 - 462.

[57] Coulston R, Oviatt S, Darves C. Amplitude convergence in children's conversational speech with animated personas[C]//Proceedings of the Seventh International Conference

on Spoken Language Processing. Citeseer, 2002, 4: 2689 - 2692.

[58] Coupland N, Jaworski A. Relevance, accommodation, and conversation: Modeling the social dimension of communication[J]. Multilingua, 1997, 16: 235 - 258.

[59] Couper-Kuhlen E. The prosody of repetition: on quoting and mimicry[M]//Couper-Kuhlen E, Selting M (eds.), Prosody in Conversation. Cambridge: Cambridge University Press, 1996: 366 - 405.

[60] Couper-Kuhlen E. Prosody[M]//Verschueren J, Ostman J O, Blommert J, Bulcaen C (eds.), Handbook of Pragmatics. Amstercam: Benjamins, 2000: 1 - 9.

[61] Couper-Kuhlen E. Prosody[M]//D'hondt S, Ostman J O, Verschueren J (eds.), The Pragmatics of Interaction. Amsterdam: John Benjamins Publishing Company, NLD, 2009: 174 - 189.

[62] Couper-Kuhlen E, Selting M. Towards an interactional perspective on prosody and a prosodic perspective on interaction [M]//Prosody in Conversation. Cambridge: Cambridge University Press, 1996: 11 - 56.

[63] Cruttenden A. Intonation[M]. 2nd Edition. Cambridge: Cambridge University Press, 1997.

[64] Crystal D. Prosodic Systems and Intonation in English[M]. Cambridge: Cambridge University Press, 1969.

[65] Cummins F. Rhythm as entrainment: the case of synchronous speech[J]. Journal of Phonetics, 2009, 37: 16 - 28.

[66] De Looze C, Rauzy S. Measuring speakers' similarity in speech by means of prosodic cues: methods and potential[C]//Proceedings of Interspeech 2011, (publishing), 2011: 1393 - 1396.

[67] De Looze C, Oertel C, Rauzy S, et al. Measuring dynamics of mimicry by means of prosodic cues in conversational speech[C]//Proceedings of ICPhS. Springer, 2011: 1294 - 1297.

[68] De Looze C, Scherer S, Vaughan B, Campbell N. Investigating automatic measurements of prosodic accommodation and its dynamics in social interaction [J]. Speech Communication, 2014, 58: 11 - 34.

[69] Delvaux V, Soquet A. The influence of ambient speech on adult speech productions through unintentional imitation[J]. Phonetica, 2007, 64(23): 145 - 173.

[70] Dijksterhuis A, Bargh J. The perception-behavior expressway: Automatic effects of social perception on social behavior[J]. Advances in Experimental Social Psychology, 2001, 33: 1 - 40.

[71] Edlund J, Heldner M, Hirschberg J. Pause and gap length in face-to-face interaction

[C]//Proceedings of 10th Annual Conference of the International Speech Communication Association, 2009: 2779 - 2782.

[72] Ferguson C A. Toward a characterization of English foreigner talk[J]. Anthropological Linguistics, 1975: 17(1): 1 - 14.

[73] Fernald A, Taeschner T, Dunn J, et al. A cross-language study of prosodic modifications in mothers' and fathers' speech to preverbal infants[J]. Journal of Child Language, 1989, 16(3): 477 - 501.

[74] Firth J R. Papers in Linguistics[M]. Oxford: Oxford University Press, 1957.

[75] Fowler C A. Speech production and perception[M]//Healy A and Proctor R (eds.), Handbook of psychology. New York: John Wiley & Sons, 2003: 237 - 266.

[76] Fowler C A, Housum J. Talkers' signaling "new" and "old" words in speech and listeners' perception and use of the distinction[J]. Journal of Memory and Language, 1987, 26: 489 - 504.

[77] French P, Local J. Prosodic features and the management of interruption[M]//Johns-Lewis C (ed.), Intonation in Discourse. San Diego: College Hill, 1986: 157 - 180.

[78] Friedberg H, Litman D, Susannah B S, et al. Lexical entrainment and success in student engineering groups[C]//Proceedings of 2012 IEEE, Spoken Language Technology Workshop (SLT). Miami, FL, 2012: 404 - 409.

[79] Fujisaki H. Dynamic characteristics of voice fundamental frequency in speech and singing [M]//MacNeilage P F (ed.), The Production of Speech. Springer-Verlag, New York, 1983: 39 - 55.

[80] Fujisaki H. Prosody, Information, and Modeling - with Emphasis on Tonal Features of Speech[C]//Proceedings of Workshop on Spoken Language Processing, 2003: 5 - 14.

[81] Galef B G. Imitation in animals: History, definition and interpretation of data from the psychological laboratory [M]//Zentall T, Galef B G (eds.), Comparative Social Learning. Hillsdale, NJ: Erlbaum, 1988: 3 - 28.

[82] Gallois C, Callan V J. Communication accommodation and the prototypical speaker: predicting evaluations of status and solidarity[J]. Language and Communication, 1988, 8(3): 271 - 283.

[83] Galati A, Brenna S E. Attenuating information in spoken communication: for the speaker, or for the addressee?[J]. Journal of Memory and Language, 2010, 62: 35 - 51.

[84] Gallois C, Ogay T, Giles H. Communication Accommodation Theory: a look back and a look ahead[M]//Gudykunst W B (ed.), Theorizing About Intercultural Communication. SAGE Publications, 2005: 121 - 148.

[85] Gårding E. Sentence Intonation in Swedish[J]. Phonetica, 1979, 36: 207 - 215.

[86] Garrod S, Anderson A. Saying what you mean in dialogue: A study inconceptual and semantic co-ordination[J]. Cognition, 1987, 27: 181-218.
[87] Giles H. Accent mobility: a model and some data[J]. Anthropological Linguistics, 1973, 15(2): 87-105.
[88] Giles H, Powesland P F. Speech style and social evaluation[M]. London: Academic press, 1975.
[89] Giles H, Smith P. Accommodation Theory: Optimal Levels of Convergence[M]//Giles H, Clair S, Robert N (eds.), Language and Social Psychology. Baltimore: Basil Blackwell, 1979.
[90] Giles H, Ogay T. Communication Accommodation Theory[M]//Whaley B B, Samter W (eds.), Explaining Communication: Contemporary Theories and Exemplars. Lawrence Erlbaum Associates, Inc., 2007: 325-344.
[91] Giles H, Taylor D M, Bourhis R Y. Towards a theory of interpersonal accommodation through speech: Some Canadian data[J]. Language in Society, 1973, 2: 177-192.
[92] Giles H, Coupland J, Coupland N. Accommodation Theory: Communication, Context, and Consequence[M]//Giles H, Coupland J, Coupland N (eds.), Contexts of Accommodation. Cambridge: Cambridge University Press, 1991.
[93] Giles H, Mulac A, Bradac J, et al. Speech accommodation theory: the first decade and beyond[M]. Beverly Hills, CA: Sage, 1987.
[94] Goleman D. Social Intelligence: The New Science of Human Relationships[M]. Bantam, 2006.
[95] Gravano A. Turn-taking and affirmative cue words in task-oriented dialogue[D]. Columbia University, 2009.
[96] Gregory S W. Analysis of fundamental frequency reveals co-variation in interview partners' speech[J]. Journal of Nonverbal Behavior, 1990, 14: 237-251.
[97] Gregory S W, Hoyt B R. Conversation partner mutual adaptation as demonstrated by Fourier series analysis[J]. Journal of Psychological Research, 1982, 1: 35-46.
[98] Gregory S W, Dagan K. Evaluating the relation of vocal accommodation in conversation partners' fundamental frequencies to perceptions of communication quality[J]. Journal of Nonverbal Behavior, 1997, 21(1): 23-43.
[99] Gregory S W, Webster S, Huang G. Voice pitch and amplitude convergence as a metric of quality in dyadic interviews[J]. Language and Communication, 1993, 13: 195-217.
[100] Gudykunst W B. Anxiety, uncertainty management theory: Current status[M]//Wiseman R L (ed.), Intercultural Communication Theory. SAGE Publications INC, 1995: 8-58.

[101] Gumperz J J. Discourse Strategies[M]. Cambridge University Press, 1982.

[102] Gumperz J J. Contextualization revisited[M]//Auer P and di Luzio A (eds.), The Contextualization of Language. Amsterdam and Philadelphia: Benjamins, 1992, 39 - 53.

[103] Halliday M A K. Intonation and grammar in British English[M]. The Hague: Mouton, 1967.

[104] Halliday M A K. A course in spoken English: Intonation[M]. Oxford University Press, 1970.

[105] Hartsuiker R J, Pickering M J, Elena V. Is syntax separate or shared between languages? Cross-linguistic syntactic priming in Spanish/English bilinguals[J]. Psychological Science, 2004, 15(6): 409 - 414.

[106] Haywood S L, Pickering M J, Branigan H P. Do speakers avoid ambiguities during dialogue?[J]. Psychological Science, 2005, 16(5): 362 - 366.

[107] Heldner J, Edlund M, Hirschberg J. Pitch similarity in the vicinity of backchannels [C]//Proceedings of Interspeech 2010, 2010: 1 - 4.

[108] Hess U, Blairy S. Facial mimicry and emotional contagion to dynamic emotional facial expressions and their influence on decoding accuracy[J]. International Journal of Psychophysiology, 2001, 40(2): 129 - 141.

[109] Heyes C M. Imitation, culture and cognition[J]. Animal Behavior, 1993, 46: 999 - 1010.

[110] Hirschberg J. Pragmatics and intonation. In Horn L, Ward G (eds.), The handbook of pragmatics. Wiley Online Library, 2004: 515 - 537. http://dx.doi.org/10.1002/9780470756959.ch23.

[111] Hirst D. The analysis by synthesis of speech melody: From data to models[J]. Journal of Speech Sciences, 2011, 1(1): 55 - 83.

[112] Horton W S, Gerrig R J. The impact of memory demands on audience design during language production[J]. Cognition, 2005, 96(2): 127 - 142.

[113] Iwata T, Watanabe S. Influence relation estimation based on lexical entrainment in conversation[J]. Speech Communication, 2013, 55(2): 329 - 339.

[114] Jaffe J. Rhythms of Dialogue in Infancy: Coordinated Timing in Development[M]. Wiley-Blackwell, 2001.

[115] Jaffe J, Feldstain S. Rhythms of Dialogue[M]. New York: Academic Press, 1970.

[116] John-Lewis C. Intonation in Discourse[M]. College-Hill Press, INC, 1986.

[117] Johnson-Laird P N. Mental Models: Toward A Cognitive Science of Language, Inference and Consciousness[M]. Harvard University Press, 1983.

[118] Kelly J, Local J. Doing Phonology: Observing, Recording, Interpreting [M]. Manchester: Manchester University Press, 1989.

[119] Koiso H, Horinchi Y, Tutiya S, et al. An analysis of turn-taking and backchannels based on prosodic and syntactic features in Japaneses Map Task dialogues[J]. Language and Speech, 1998, 41: 295 - 321.

[120] Kooststra G J, Hell J G V, Dijkstra T. Syntactic alignment and shared word order in code-switched sentence production: evidence from bilingual monologue and dialogue [J]. Journal of Memory and Language, 2010, 63: 210 - 231.

[121] Kousidis S, Dorran D, Mcdonnell C, et al. 2009. Convergence in human dialogues time series analysis of acoustic feature [C]//Proceedings of the International Workshop SPEECH and COMPUTER (SPECOM). St. Petersburg, Russian Federation. Retrieved June, 10, 2013, from http://arrow. dit. ie/cgi/viewcontent. cgi? article=1002& context=dmccon.

[122] Kopp S. Social resonance and embodied coordination in face-to-face conversation with artificial interlocutors[J]. Speech Communication, 2010, 52(6): 587 - 597.

[123] Kousidis S, Dorran D, McDonnell C, et al. Times series analysis of acoustic feature convergence in human dialogues[C]//Proceedings of Interspeech, 2008.

[124] Kristiansen G. Style-shifting and shifting styles: a socio-cognitive approach to lectal variation[M]//Geeraerts D, Dirven R, Taylor J R (eds). Cognitive Sociolinguistics. Berlin: Mouton de Gruyter, 2008: 45 - 88.

[125] Ladd D R. Intonational phonology[M]. Cambridge University Press, 1996.

[126] Lakin J L, Chartrand T L. Using nonconscious behavioral mimicry to create affiliation and rapport[J]. Journal of Psychological Science, 2003, 14(4): 334 - 339.

[127] Lakin J L, Jefferis V E, Cheng C M, et al. The chameleon effect as social glue: evidence for the evolutionary significance of non-conscious mimicry [J]. Journal of Nonverbal Behavior, 2003, 27(3): 145 - 162.

[128] Lee C C, Katsamanis A, Black M P, et al. Computing vocal entrainment: A signal-derived PCA-based quantification scheme with application to affect analysis in married couple interactions[J]. Computer Speech & Language, 2014, 28(2): 518 - 539.

[129] Leech G N. Principles of Pragmatics[M]. London: Longman, 1983.

[130] Levelt W J M, Kelter S. Surface form and memory in question answering[J]. Cognitive Psychology, 1982, 14: 78 - 106.

[131] Levitan R. Entrainment in spoken dialogue systems: adopting, perdicting, and influencing user behavior[C]//Proceedings of the NAACL HLT 2013 Student Research Workshop, Atlanta, Georgia, 2013: 84 - 90.

[132] Levitan R, Hirschberg J. Measuring acoustic-prosodic entrainment with respect to multiple levels and dimensions[C]//Proceedings of Interspeech, Florence, Italy, 2011: 3081 - 3084.

[133] Levitan R, Gravano A, Hirschberg J. Entrainment in speech-proceeding backchannels [C]//Proceedings of the 49th Annual Meeting of the Association for Computational Linguistics. Portland, Oregon, 2011: 113 - 117.

[134] Levitan R, Gravano A, Willson L, et al. Acoustic-prosodic entrainment and social behavior[C]//Proceedings of Conference of the North American, Chapter of the Association for Computational Linguistics: Human Language Technologies. Montréal, Canada, 2012: 11 - 19.

[135] Li A J. Chinese prosody and prosodic labeling of spontaneous speech[C]//Proceedings of Speech Prosody. Aix-en-Provence, France, 2002(a): 39 - 46.

[136] Liberman M, Sag I. Prosodic form and discourse function[J]. Chicago Linguistic Society, 1974, 10: 416 - 427.

[137] Local J K, Walker G. Abrupt-joins as a resource for the production of multi-unit, multi-action turns[J]. Journal of Pragmatics, 2004, 36(8): 1375 - 1402.

[138] Local J, Kelly J, Wells W H G. Towards a phonology of conversation: turn-taking in Tyneside English[J]. Journal of Linguistics, 1986, 22(2): 411 - 437.

[139] Matarazzo J D, Wiens A N. Interviewer influence on durations of interviewee silence [J]. Journal of Experimental Research in Personality, 1967, 2(1): 59 - 69.

[140] Maurer R E, Tindall J H. Effect of postural congruence on client's percepton of counselor empathy[J]. Journal of Counseling Psychology, 1983, 30(2): 158.

[141] McGarva A R, Warner R M. Attraction and social coordination: mutual entrainment of vocal activity rhythms[J]. Journal of Psychology, 2003, 32(3): 335 - 354.

[142] Metzing C, Brennan S E. When conceptual pacts are broken: Partner-specific effects in the comprehension of referring expressions[J]. Journal of Memory and Language, 2003, 49(2): 201 - 213.

[143] Meltzoff A N, Moor M K. Imitation of facial and manual gestures by human neonates [J]. Science, 1977, 198(4312): 75 - 78.

[144] Miles L K, Nind L K, Macrae C N. The rhythm of rapport: interpersonal synchrony and social perception[J]. Journal of Experimental Social Psychology, 2009, 45(3): 585 - 589.

[145] Ireland M E, Slatcher R B, Eastwick P W, et al. Language style matching predicts relationship initiation and stability[J]. Psychological Science, 2011, 22(1): 39 - 44.

[146] Müller F. Affiliating and disaffiliating with continuers: prosodic aspects of recipiency

[M]//Couper-Kuhlen E, Selting (eds.), Prosody in conversation. Cambridge: Cambridge University Press, 1996: 131 - 176.

[147] Namy L L, Nygaard L C, Sauerteig D. Gender differences in vocal accommodation: the role of perception[J]. Journal of Personality and Social Psychology, 2002, 21(4): 422 - 432.

[148] Natale M. Convergence of mean vocal intensity in dyadic communication as a function of social desirability[J]. Journal of Personality and Social Psychology, 1975, 32: 790 - 804.

[149] Nenkova A, Gravano A, Hirschberg J. High frequency word entrainment in spoken dialogue [C]//Proceedings of the 46th Annual Meeting of the Association for Computational Linguistics on Human Language Technologies. Ohio, USA, 2008: 169 - 172.

[150] Neumann R, Strack F. "Mood contagion": the automatic transfer of mood between persons[J]. Journal of Personality and Social Psychology, 2000, 79: 211 - 223.

[151] Niederhoffer K G, Pennebaker J W. Linguistic style matching in social interaction[J]. Journal of Language and Social Psychology, 2002, 21: 337 - 360.

[152] Oviatt S. User-centered modeling for spoken language and multimodal interfaces[J]. IEEE Multimedia, 1996, 3(4): 26 - 35.

[153] Pardo J S. On phonetic convergence during conversational interaction[J]. Acoustical Society of America, 2006, 119(4): 2382 - 2393.

[154] Parrill F, Kimbara I. Seeing and hearing double: the influence of mimicry in speech and gesture on observers[J]. Journal of Nonverbal Behavior, 2006, 30(4): 157 - 166.

[155] Pentland A. Honest Signals - How They Shape Our World [M]. MIT Press. Cambridge, 2008.

[156] Pike K L. The Intonation of American English[M]. University of Michigan Press, 1945.

[157] Pierrehumbert J. The phonology and phonetics of English intonation [D]. MIT, published 1988 by IULC, 1980.

[158] Pickering M J, Garrod S. Towards a mechanistic psychology of dialogue[J]. Behavioral and Brain Sciences, 2004, 27: 169 - 226.

[159] Pickering M J, Garrod S. Alignment as the basis for successful communication[J]. Research on Language and Computation, 2006, 4: 203 - 228.

[160] Pickering M J, Ferreira V S. Structural priming: a critical review[J]. Psychological Bulletin, 2008, 134(3): 427.

[161] Putman W B, Street R L. The conception and perception of non-content speech performance: implications for speech-accommodation theory[J]. International Journal

of the Sociology of Language, 1984, 46: 97 - 114.

[162] Reitter D, Moore J D. Predicting success in dialogue[C]//Proceedings of the 45th Annual Meeting of the Association of Computational Linguistics. Prague, Czech Republic, 2007: 808 - 815.

[163] Reitter D, Moore J D. Alignment and task success in spoken dialogue[J]. Journal of Memory and Language, 2014, (76): 29 - 46.

[164] Richardson M J, Marsh K L, Isenhower R W, et al. Rocking together: dynamics of intentional and unintentional interpersonal coordination[J]. Human Movement Science, 2007, 26(6): 867 - 891.

[165] Sacks H, Shegloff E, Jefferson G. A simplest systematics for the organization of turn-taking in conversation[J]. Language, 1974, 50: 696 - 735.

[166] Sag I, Liberman M. The intonational disambiguation of indirect speech acts[J]. Chicago Linguistic Society, 1975, 11: 487 - 497.

[167] Sancier M L, Fowler C A. Gestural drift in a bilingual speaker of Brazilian Portuguese and English[J]. Journal of Phonetics, 1997, 25: 421 - 436.

[168] Scherer K R. Vocal communication of emotion: a review of research paradigms[J]. Speech Communication, 2003, 40: 227 - 256.

[169] Selting M. Prosody in conversational questions[J]. Journal of Pragmatics, 1992, 17: 315 - 345.

[170] Selting M. Prosody as an activity-type distinctive cue in conversation: the case of so-called "astonished" questions in repair[M]//Couper-Kuhlen E, Selting M (eds.), Prosody in Conversation. Cambridge: Cambridge University Press, 1996: 231 - 270.

[171] Selting M. Prosody in interaction: state of art[M]//Weingarten D B, Reber E, Selting M (eds.), Prosody in Interaction. Amsterdam: John Benjamins, 2010: 3 - 40.

[172] Shepard C A, Giles H, Le Poire B A. Communication accommodation theory[M]//The New Handbook of Language and Social Psychology, John Wiley & Sons Incorporated, 2001, 12: 33 - 56.

[173] Shih C, Ao B. Duration study for the Bell Laboratories Mandarin Text-to-Speech System[M]//Van Santen J, Sproat R W, Olive J P, Hirschberg J (eds.), Progressing in Speech Synthesis. Springer-Verlag New York, Inc, 1997: 383 - 397.

[174] Shockley K, Baker A A, Richardson M J, et al. Articulatory constraints on interpersonal postural coordination[J]. Journal of Experimental Psychology: Human Perception and Performance, 2007, 33(1): 201.

[175] Shockley K, Richardson D C, Dale R. Conversation and coordinative structures[J]. Topics in Cognitive Science, 2009, 1(2): 305 - 319.

[176] Smith C. Prosodic accommodation by French speakers to a non-native interlocutor [C]//Proceedings of the XVIth International Congress of Phonetic Sciences, 2007: 313 - 348.

[177] Stanford G W, Webster S. A nonverbal signal in voices of interview partners effectively predicts communication accommodation and social status perceptions[J]. Journal of Personality and Social Psychology, 1996, 70(6): 1231 - 1240.

[178] Street, Richard J L, James N, et al. Speech convergence among talktive and reticent three year-olds[J]. Language Sciences, 1983, 5(1): 79 - 96.

[179] Summers W V, Pisoni D B, Bernacki R H, et al. Effects of noise on speech production: acoustic and perceptual analyses[J]. The Journal of the Acoustical Society of America, 1988, 84(3): 917 - 928.

[180] Suzuki N, Katagiri Y. Prosodic alignment in human-computer interaction [J]. Connection Science, 2007, 19(2): 131 - 141.

[181] Tanenhaus M K, Spivey-Knowlton M J, Eberhard K M, et al. Integration of visual and linguistic information in spoken language comprehension [J]. Science, 1995, 268 (5217): 632 - 634.

[182] Taylor J P, Thomas S. Linguistic Style Matching and Negotiation outcome [J]. Negotiation and conflict management research, 2008, 1(3): 263 - 281.

[183] Thomason J, Nguyen V H, Litman D. Prosodic entrainment and tutoring dialogue success[J]. International Journal of Artificial Intelligence in Education, 2013: 750 - 753.

[184] Tickle-Degnen L, Rosenthal R. The nature of rapport and its nonverbal correlates[J]. Psychological inquiry, 2007, 1(4): 285 - 293.

[185] Tseng C Y, Pin S H, Lee Y L, et al. Fluent speech prosody: framework and modeling [J]. Speech Communication, 2005, 46: 284 - 309.

[186] Turner L H, West R L. Introducing Communication Theory: Analysis and Application [M]. 4th ed. New York, NY: McGraw-Hill, 2010.

[187] Van Der Wege M M. Lexical entrainment and lexical differentiation in reference phrase choice[J]. Journal of Memory and Language, 2009, 60: 448 - 463.

[188] Van Summers W, Pisoni D B, Bernacki R H, et al. Effects of noise on speech production: acoustic and perceptual analyses[J]. The Journal of the Acoustical Society of America, 1988, 84: 9 - 17.

[189] Vandepitte S. A pragmatic function of intonation[J]. Lingua, 1989, 79(4): 265 - 297.

[190] Vaughan B. Prosodic synchrony in cooperative task-based dialogues: a measure of agreement and disagreement[C]//Proceedings of Interspeech. Publisher? 2011: 1865 - 1868.

[191] Vinciarelli A. Capturing order in social interactions[J]. IEEE Signal Processing Magazine, 2009, 26(5): 133 - 152.

[192] Ward N, Nakagawa S. Automatic user-adaptive speaking rate selection for information delivery[C]//7th International Conference on Spoken Language Processing (ICSLP 2002 - INTERSPEECH 2002), 2002.

[193] Webb J T. Subject Speaking-rates as a function of interviewer behavior[J]. Language & Speech, 1969, 12: 54 - 67.

[194] Webb J T. Interview synchrony: an investigation of two Speaking-rate measures in an automated standardized interview[M]//Pope B, Siegman A W (eds.), Studies in Dyadic Communication. New York: Pergamon, 1972: 115 - 133.

[195] Wege M M V D. Lexical entrainment and lexical differentiation in reference phrase choice[J]. Journal of Memory and Language, 2009, 60: 448 - 463.

[196] Welkowitz J, Kuc M. Interrelationships among warmth, genuineness, empathy, and temporal speech patterns in interpersonal interaction[J]. Journal of Consulting and Clinical Psychology, 1973, 41(3): 472 - 473.

[197] Wichmann A. Intonation in Text and Discourse[M]. Pearson Education Limited, 2000.

[198] Wichmann A, Dehé N, Weingarten D B. Where prosody meets pragmatics: Research at the interface[M]//Weingarten D B, Dehé N, Whichmann A (eds.), Where Prosody Meets Pragmatics. Emerald Group Publishing Limited, 2009: 1 - 20.

[199] Wilkes-Gibbs D, Clark H H. Coordinating beliefs in conversation[J]. Journal of Memory and Language, 1992, 31: 183 - 194.

[200] Woodall G W, Burgoon J K. Talking fast and changing attitudes: a critique and clarification[J]. Journal of Nonverbal Behavior, 1983, 8(2): 126 - 142.

[201] Worgan S F, Moor R K. Towards the detection of social dominance in dialogue[J]. Speech Communication, 2011, 53: 1104 - 1114.

[202] Xia Z H, Levitan R, Hirschberg J. Prosodic entrainment in Mandarin and English: A cross-linguistic comparison[J]. The proceedings of Speech Prosody 2014, Dublin, Ireland, 2014: 65 - 69.

[203] Xu Y. Speech melody as articulatorily implemented communicative functions[J]. Speech Communication, 2005, 46: 220 - 251.

[204] Young R D, Frye M. Some are laughing; some are not - why?[J]. Psychological Reports, 1966, 18: 747 - 752.

[205] Yue G. Speakers' topics and major paratones[J]. Lingua, 1980, 52: 33 - 47.

[206] Zebrowitz L A, Brownlow S, Olson K. Baby talk to the baby-faced[J]. Journal of

Nonverbal Behavior, 1992, 16(3): 143 - 158.

[207] Zuengler J. Accommodation in native-non-native interactions: going beyond the "what" to the "why" in second language research[M]//Giles H, Coupland J, Coupland N (eds.), Contexts of Accommodations. Cambridge: Cambridge Press, 1991: 223 - 244.

[208] Zwaan R A, Radvansky G A. Situation models in language comprehension and memory [J]. Psychological Bulletin, 1998, 123: 162 - 185.

[209] 曹剑芬. 汉语声调与语调的关系[J]. 中国语文,2002,(3): 195 - 202.

[210] 曹文. 语调核心单元[C]//第七届中国语音学学术会议暨语音学前沿问题国际论坛,2006.

[211] 陈嘉猷,鲍怀翘. 基于 EPG 的普通话塞音,塞擦音发音过程研究[C]. 第六届全国现代语音学学术会议论文集(上),2003.

[212] 陈怡,石锋. 普通话强调焦点句语调的音高表现[J]. 南开语言学刊,2011,(1): 9 - 19.

[213] 胡伟湘,徐波,黄泰翼. 汉语韵律边界的声学实验研究[J]. 中文信息学报,2002,16(1): 43 - 48.

[214] 贾媛. 普通话焦点的语音实现及音系分析[D]. 南开大学博士论文,2009.

[215] 孔江平. 论语言发声[M]. 北京: 中央民族大学出版社,2001.

[216] 李爱军. 普通话对话中韵律特征的声学表现[J]. 中国语文,2002(b),(6): 525 - 535.

[217] 李爱军. 友好语音的声学分析[J]. 中国语文,2005,(5): 418 - 431.

[218] 李爱军,张利刚,李洋,等. 汉语口语对话中姿态与语音信息关系初探[J]. 清华大学学报(自然科学版),2008,48(S1): 627 - 634.

[219] 李爱军,祖漪清,李洋,等. 汉语普通话篇章语速变化模式初探[J]. 语音、通信及信号处理,2007,26(4): 242 - 247.

[220] 粟进英,李经伟. 言语适应理论与身份研究述评[J]. 外语教学,2010,31(6): 38 - 41.

[221] 林茂灿. 2002, 汉语韵律结构和功能语调[R/OL]. [2013 - 1 - 5]. 中国社会科学院语音室研究报告,http://ling. cass. cn/yuyin/report/report_2002_2. htm.

[222] 林茂灿. 汉语语调与声调[J]. 语言文字应用,2004,(3): 57 - 68.

[223] 林茂灿. 2005,语调理论与汉语语调[R/OL]. [2013 - 1 - 5]. 中国社会科学院语音室研究报告,http://ling. cass. cn/yuyin/report/report_2005_1. htm.

[224] 林茂灿. 疑问和陈述语气与边界调[J]. 中国语文,2006,(4): 364 - 384.

[225] 刘虹. 会话结构分析[M]. 北京: 北京大学出版社,2004.

[226] 刘源,梁南元. 现代汉语统计词典[M]. 北京: 宇航出版社,1990.

[227] 刘正光. 言语适应理论研究述评[M]. 语言文字应用,2001,(2): 57 - 64.

[228] 沈炯. 汉语语调模型刍议[J]. 语文研究,1992,(4): 16 - 24.

[229] 沈炯. 汉语语调构造和语调模型[J]. 方言,1994,(3): 221 - 228.

[230] 沈炯. 关于韵律和语调的一些看法[C]. 第三届全国现代语音学学术会议文集,1996.

[231] 沈晓楠. 关于美国人学习汉语声调[J]. 世界汉语教学,1989,(3):158 - 168.

[232] 石锋. 天津方言双字组声调分析[J]. 语言研究,1986,(1):66 - 83.

[233] 王初明. 语言学习与交互[J]. 外国语,2008,31(6):53 - 60.

[234] 王茂林. 汉语自然话语韵律组块的优选论分析[J]. 暨南学报(哲学社会科学版),2005,(4):85 - 87.

[235] 吴宗济. 1981,普通话语调的实验研究——兼论现代汉语语调规则问题[C]. 中国语言学会第1届学术年会论文,改订为"普通话语句中的声调变化",吴宗济语言学论文集,商务印书馆,2004.

[236] 吴宗济. 1998,普通话四字组韵律变量的处理规则[R/OL]. [2013 - 1 - 5]. 中国社会科学院语音室研究报告,http://ling. cass. cn/yuyin/report/report_1998_3. htm.

[237] 吴宗济. 2003,试论普通话中的韵律规则与其他若干学科中的韵律规则的共性[R/OL]. [2013 - 1 - 5]. 中国社会科学院语音室研究报告,http://ling. cass. cn/yuyin/report/report_2003_1. htm.

[238] 吴宗济. 2004,面向普通话高自然度合成的韵律研究综述[R/OL]. [2013 - 1 - 5]. 中国社会科学院语音室研究报告,http://ling. cass. cn/yuyin/report/report_2004_1. htm.

[239] 夏志华,穆凤英. 中国英语学习者话轮转换过程中边界调的使用分析[J]. 解放军外国语学院学报,2008,(1):48 - 54.

[240] 夏志华. 中心理论——话题与韵律接面研究的新方法[J]. 山东外语教学,2012,(2):36 - 40.

[241] 夏志华. 英语学习者口语中话题结构上的韵律实现[J]. 外语教学与研究,2013,45(3):413 - 425.

[242] 熊子瑜. 自然语句边界的韵律特征及其交际功能[D]. 中国社会科学院,2003.

[243] 徐俊,蔡连红. 面向情感转换的层次化韵律分析与建模[J]. 清华大学学报(自然科学版),2009,49(S1):1274 - 1277.

[244] 杨晓红,赵建军,杨玉芳,等. 汉语语篇层级性对焦点声学表现的影响[J]. 声学学报,2011,(5):542 - 549.

[245] 于剑,黄力行,陶建华. 汉语对话语气韵律建模方法[J]. 清华大学学报(自然科学版),2008,48(S1):658 - 663.

[246] 赵建军,杨晓红,杨玉芳,等. 音高和时长在语篇语句重音中的作用[J]. 声学学报,2011,(4):435 - 443.

[247] 赵元任. 赵元任语言学论文集[M]//吴宗济,赵新那编. 北京:商务印书馆,2002.

[248] 赵元任. 汉语的字调跟语调[M]//赵元任语言学论文集,北京:商务印书馆,1933.

[249] 郑秋豫. 语篇的基频构组与语流韵律体现[J]. 语言暨语言学,2010,11(2):183 - 218.

[250] 钟毅平,范伟,赵科,等. 情感韵律在真假句子加工上的差异:来自 ERPs 的证据[J]. 心理科学,2011,34(2):312 - 316.

Appendix (A–L)

Appendix A Givers' Pictures in Picture Ordering Game

Appendix B Followers' Pictures in Picture Ordering

1 书包

2 飞机

3 沙滩

4 花灯

5 乌龟

6 山坡

7 司机

8 鲜花

9 西瓜

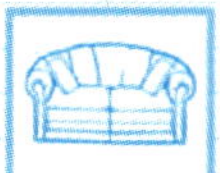
10 沙发

11 山峰

12 乡村

13 青蛙

14 咖啡

15 公鸡

16 医生

17 烟花

18 军官

Appendix C One Interlocutor's Pictures in Picture Classifying Game

1 书包

2 飞机

3 沙滩

4 花灯

5 乌龟

6 山坡

7 司机

8 鲜花

9 西瓜

10 沙发

11 山峰

12 乡村

13 青蛙

14 咖啡

15 公鸡

16 医生

17 烟花

18 军官

Appendix D The Other Interlocutor's Pictures in Picture Classifying Game

1 书包

2 飞机

3 沙滩

4 花灯

5 乌龟

6 山坡

7 司机

8 鲜花

9 西瓜

10 沙发

11 山峰

12 乡村

13 青蛙

14 咖啡

15 公鸡

16 医生

17 烟花

18 军官

Appendix E

Praat Script for Data Extraction

(Written and modified by Professor Daniel Hirst)

```
# Praat script
script_name$ = "analyse_tier.praat"
# author:Daniel Hirst<daniel.hirst@lpl.univ-aix.fr>
version$ = "[2013-04-05]"
date$ = date$ ()

# purpose:Analyse a folder of Sound files
#         and a folder of TextGrid files
#         The folders can be selected by giving their path or by using the browser

#  For each interval or point on selected tier the script calculates:
#   - duration
#     and, depending on the options selected,
#   - mean/min/max pitch (using Hertz/octaves/semitones and 1, 100, 200, 440 or median as reference)
#   - intensity
#   - Speaking-rate
#         this assumes that the labels on the analysis tier have one symbol per syllable as in Hanzi transcription
#  the results are output to the Info window
#  and can be saved as a.txt file which can be read directly by
#  a statistics package such as R

        ######### define parameters used in the script #########
```

```
form Analyse tier
    sentence investigator<Put your name here>
    comment Give the path to the folders or leave empty to select them
with the browser
    sentence Sound_folder
    sentence TextGrid_folder
    word Analysis_tier syllable
    word Sound_extension. wav
    word TextGrid_extension. TextGrid
    real Time_step 0 (=automatic)
    word Undefined_value NA
    boolean calculate_speech_rate yes
    boolean calculate_pitch yes
    boolean automatic_min_max yes
    natural left_Pitch_range 60
    natural right_Pitch_range 750
    optionmenu pitch_units:1
        option Hertz
        option octaves
        option semitones
#   comment For log scales:
    optionmenu pitch_reference:1
        option 1
        option 100
        option 200
        option 440
        option speaker_median
    boolean calculate_intensity yes
#   comment For formants
    boolean calculate_formants yes
    natural Number_of_formants 5
    natural Maximum_formant 5500
```

```
    positive Window_length 0.05
    positive Pre_emphasis 50
#   comment For point tier
    positive Analysis_window 0.1 (= seconds)
endform

            ######### main #########
debug = 0

clearinfo
default_minimum_pitch = 60
default_maximum_pitch = 750
min_pitch = left_Pitch_range
max_pitch = right_Pitch_range

if sound_folder$ = ""
    sound_folder$ = chooseDirectory$ ("Choose the folder containing the
Sound files")
endif
if textGrid_folder$ = ""
    textGrid_folder$ = chooseDirectory $ ( " Choose the folder
containing the TextGrid files")
endif

  #### Read in list of sound files ####
mySounds = Create Strings as file list... sounds
... 'sound_folder$'/*'sound_extension$'
nSounds = Get number of strings
item = 0

myTextGrids = Create Strings as file list... TextGrids
... 'textGrid_folder$'/*'textGrid_extension$'
```

```
    nTextGrids = Get number of strings

    if nSounds>0 and nTextGrids>0
        nSounds = Get number of strings

        #### print header of output file ####
        printline #File created by'script_name$ 'version'version$ '
        printline #Author:Daniel Hirst<daniel.hirst@lpl-aix.fr>
        printline #Analysis carried out by ['investigator$ '] on'date$ '
on tier ['analysis_tier$ ']
        printline #
        printline #Parameters:

        if calculate_pitch
            if automatic_min_max
                printline # 'tab$ 'pitch:Automatic min max
            else
                printline # 'tab$ 'pitch:min ='min_pitch'; max ='max_pitch'
            endif
            printline # Pitch units:'pitch_units$ '
            if pitch_units ! = 1
                printline Pitch_reference:'pitch_reference$ '
            endif
        endif
        if calculate_intensity
            printline # intensity:
        endif
        printline #

        #### print column names ####
        print'tab$ 'file'tab$ 'label'tab$ 'duration
        if calculate_speech_rate
```

```
        print'tab$ 'speech_rate
    endif
    if calculate_pitch
        print  'tab$ 'f0_min'tab$ 'f0_mean'tab$ 'f0_max
    endif
    if calculate_intensity
        print  'tab$ 'int_min  'tab$ 'int_mean  'tab$ 'int_max
    endif
    printline

#check if TextGrid file exists for each sound
# and call treatment
    for iSound from 1 to nSounds
        select mySounds
        sound_name$  = Get string... iSound
if debug
    printline ******* treating sound'sound_name$ '***********
endif
        textGrid_name$  = sound_name$  - sound_extension$
        ... + textGrid_extension$
        sound$  = sound_folder$  + "/"  + sound_name$
        textGrid$  = textGrid_folder$  + "/"  + textGrid_name$
        if fileReadable(textGrid$ )
            call treatment
        else
            printline # Cannot find TextGrid file
            ... ['textGrid_name$ ']
        endif
    endfor
else
    if nSounds = 0
        printline Folder ['sound_folder$ '] doesn't contain
```

```
        ... any files with extension ['sound_extension$']
    elsif nTextGrids = 0
        printline Folder ['textGrid_folder$'] doesn't contain
        ... any files with extension ['textGrid_extension$']
    endif
endif

#Remove file lists
select mySounds
plus myTextGrids
Remove

exit

##################   subroutine treatment of each file ###
###############

procedure treatment
    Read from file...'sound$'
    mySound = selected("Sound")
    name$  = selected$ ("Sound")
    sound_duration = Get total duration
    Read from file...'textGrid$'
    myTextGrid = selected("TextGrid")
    textGrid_duration = Get total duration
    if sound_duration ! = textGrid_duration
        plus mySound
        Scale times
        printline # TextGrid and Sound have different durations
        printline # TextGrid has been scaled to the duration of Sound
    endif
```

```
    #find number of analysis tier
    select myTextGrid
    call find_analysis_tier
    if tier

    #create analysis objects
        select mySound
        printline # file :'name$ '

    #  - pitch
        if calculate_pitch
if debug
    printline ******* calculating pitch ***********
endif
            if automatic_min_max
                myPitch = To Pitch... time_step
                ... default_minimum_pitch default_maximum_pitch
                call automatic_min_max_pitch
            else
                myPitch = To Pitch... time_step
                ... min_pitch max_pitch
            endif
            median_pitch = Get quantile... 0 0 0.5 Hertz
            printline # min_pitch:'min_pitch:0';
            ... median_pitch:'median_pitch:0'
            ... max_pitch'max_pitch:0';
            if pitch_reference$  = "speaker_median"
                pitch_reference = median_pitch
            else
                pitch_reference ='pitch_reference$ '
            endif
        endif
```

```
    # - intensity
        if calculate_intensity
if debug
    printline ******* calculating intensity ***********
endif
            select mySound
            myIntensity = To Intensity... min_pitch
            ... time_step Yes
        endif

    # Get time values of beginning and end of each interval
        select myTextGrid
        if isIntervalTier
            nIntervals = Get number of intervals... tier
if debug
    printline ******* tier has 'nIntervals' intervals ***********
endif
        else
            nIntervals = Get number of points... tier
if debug
    printline ******* tier has 'nIntervals' points ***********
endif

        endif
        for iInterval from 1 to nIntervals

            select myTextGrid
            if isIntervalTier
                label$ = Get label of interval... tier iInterval
                start = Get starting point... tier iInterval
                end = Get end point... tier iInterval
```

```
                else
                    raw_label$  = Get label of point... tier iInterval
                    #### remove any spaces from label ####
                    label$  = replace$ (raw_label$ , " ","",0)
                    mid = Get time of point... tier iInterval
                    start = mid  -  analysis_window/2
                    if start<0
                        start = 0
                    endif
                    end = mid  +  analysis_window/2
                    if end>sound_duration
                        end = sound_duration
                    endif
                endif
    if debug
        println ******* treating interval'iInterval'['start:3'-'end:
3'] ***********
    endif

        #calculate parameters for each non empty interval
    if debug
        printline ******* label:'label$'***********
    endif
                if label$ ! = "" and label$ ! = "#"
                    item = item + 1
            #  -  duration
                    duration_s = end  -  start
                    duraton_ms = round(1000 * duration_s)
                    call set_undefined duraton_ms
                    duration$  = value$

            #  -  Speaking - rate
```

```
        if calculate_speech_rate
            nSyllables = length(label$)
            speech_rate = nSyllables/duration_s
            call set_undefined speech_rate
            speech_rate$  = value$
        endif
# - pitch
        if calculate_pitch
            select myPitch
            f0_min = Get minimum... start end Hertz Parabolic
            call convert_F0 f0_min
            f0_min = value
            call set_undefined f0_min
            f0_min$  = value$
            f0_mean = Get mean... start end Hertz
            call convert_F0 f0_mean
            f0_mean = value
            call set_undefined f0_mean
            f0_mean$  = value$
            f0_max = Get maximum... start end Hertz Parabolic
            call convert_F0 f0_max
            f0_max = value
            call set_undefined f0_max
            f0_max$  = value$
        endif

# - intensity
        if calculate_intensity
            select myIntensity
            intensity_min = Get minimum... start end Parabolic
            call set_undefined intensity_min
            intensity_min$  = value$
```

```
            intensity_mean = Get mean... start end energy
            call set_undefined intensity_mean
            intensity_mean$  = value$
            intensity_max = Get maximum... start end Parabolic
            call set_undefined intensity_max
            intensity_max$  = value$
        endif

#print out results
        print'item''tab$ ''name$ ''tab$ ''label$ '
        ...'tab$ ''duration$ '
        if calculate_speech_rate
            print'tab$ ''speech_rate$ '
        endif
        if calculate_pitch
            print'tab$ ''f0_min$ ''tab$ ''f0_mean$ '
            ...'tab$ ''f0_max$ '
        endif
        if calculate_intensity
            print'tab$ ''intensity_min$ '
            ...'tab$ ''intensity_mean$ '
            ...'tab$ ''intensity_max$ '
        endif
        printline
    endif
endfor

#Remove objects
if calculate_pitch
    select myPitch
    Remove
endif
```

```
        if calculate_intensity
            select myIntensity
            Remove
        endif
    else
        #print warning if TextGrid has no analysis tier
        printline ###TextGrid ['name$'] has no tier ['analysis_tier$']
    endif
        #Remove Sound and TextGrid
    select mySound
    plus myTextGrid
    Remove
endproc

            ########  subroutine convert F0 value to selected
scale ########

procedure convert_F0.value
    .value = .value/pitch_reference
    if pitch_units$ = "octaves"
        .value = log2(.value)
    elsif pitch_units$ = "semitones"
        .value = 12 * log2(.value)
    endif
    if pitch_units$ = "Hertz"
        value = round(.value)
    else
        value = .value
    endif
endproc

            ########  subroutine replace numeric value by
```

```
string #########
        #### Uses undefined symbol if the value is undefined
    ####
        #### otherwise integer has no decimal figures and real values
have three figures. ####
    procedure set_undefined.value
        if.value = undefined
            value$  = undefined_value$
        elsif.value = floor(.value)
            value$  = "'.value:0'"
        else
            value$  = "'.value:3'"
        endif
    endproc

                  ######### subroutine automatic maximum and minimum
for pitch detection #########

    procedure automatic_min_max_pitch
        q25 = Get quantile...  0 0 0.25 Hertz
        q75 = Get quantile...  0 0 0.75 Hertz
        min_pitch = 0.75 * q25
        max_pitch = 1.5 * q75
        Remove
        select mySound
        myPitch = To Pitch...  time_step min_pitch
        ... max_pitch
    endproc

                  #########   subroutine get number of analysis tier
from name #########
    procedure find_analysis_tier
```

```
        nTiers = Get number of tiers
        tier = 0
        for iTier from 1 to nTiers
            tier_name$ = Get tier name... iTier
            if tier_name$ = analysis_tier$
                tier = iTier
                isIntervalTier = Is interval tier... tier
            endif
        endfor
    endproc


    # Version history

    # 2013-04-05      removes any spaces from label
    #                 added option to calculate Speaking-rate in syllables
per second
    #          - this assumes that the labels on the analysis tier have one
character per syllable (as in Hanzi/Kanji)

    # 2012-10-30    added option to select folders with browser
    # 2011-12-29    added optional log scale for pitch
    # 2009-08-07    declared time_step as real with default value 0
( = automatic)
    # 2009-05-28    first version
```

Appendix F Computation Program 1

1) Program for Weighted average calculation:

```
int Account::balance_average (CString org_file, CString des_file)
```

the core part of calculation in program:

```
double averages = 0;
double sum = 0;
double sumcol1 = 0;

//for(j = 0; j<MAXCOL - 3; j++)
//   result[0][j] = array[0][j];

for(j = 0; j<MAXCOL - 3; j++)
{
sum = 0;
sumcol1 = 0;
for(i = 0; i<MAXLINE - 1; i++)
{
sum += fabs(array[i][0] * array[i][j]);
sumcol1 += array[i][0];
}

result[0][j] = sum/sumcol1;
}
```

2) One example of calculation over one turn.

	file	duration	Speaking_ rate	F0_ min	F0_ mean	F0_ max	Int_ min	Int_ mean	Int_ max
turn2	IPU1	2 022	5. 44	175	234	313	10. 33	56. 60	64. 35
	IPU2	1 320	6. 06	193	232	277	12. 11	55. 70	64. 64
	IPU3	719	6. 95	206	234	312	26. 13	56. 33	63. 73
	IPU4	925	6. 49	213	233	291	9. 25	51. 34	58. 83
	IPU5	490	8. 16	175	224	258	38. 49	52. 78	58. 96
turn2	weighted average		6. 21	189. 83	232. 454	295. 6	15. 17	55. 12	62. 92

Appendix G Computation Program 2

1) Absolute distances between target unit and a sets of randomly selected units

```
int Account::abs_values (CString org_file, CString des_file)
```

the core part of calculation in program:

```
double averages = 0;

for(j = 0; j<MAXCOL - 3; j + + )
result[0][j] = array[0][j];

for(i = 1; i<MAXLINE - 1; i + + )
for(j = 0; j<MAXCOL - 3; j + + )
result[i][j] = fabs(array[0][j] - array[i][j]);
```

2) One example of calculation

	Speaking_rate	F0_min	F0_mean	F0_max	Int_min	Int_mean	Int_max
Target	3. 68	153. 37	205. 04	280. 53	30. 28	65. 71	72. 72
other1	4. 88	122. 89	148. 26	186. 37	21. 97	48. 84	56. 27
other2	4. 18	182. 00	229. 25	290. 03	10. 03	48. 07	55. 36
other3	5. 15	138. 68	163. 06	115. 90	22. 32	48. 08	54. 13
other4	5. 64	113. 61	136. 11	163. 23	23. 21	46. 67	53. 39
other5	4. 11	105. 41	125. 68	150. 22	21. 43	48. 85	55. 60
other6	6. 01	88. 51	110. 15	133. 80	25. 45	50. 25	57. 23
other7	4. 25	121. 48	154. 64	200. 01	16. 77	53. 44	61. 57
other8	4. 30	102. 54	121. 64	146. 92	23. 39	49. 53	57. 00

(continued)

	Speaking_rate	F0_min	F0_mean	F0_max	Int_min	Int_mean	Int_max
disnp1	1.21	30.47	56.78	94.17	8.31	16.87	16.45
disnp2	0.50	28.63	24.21	9.50	20.25	17.64	17.36
disnp3	1.47	14.69	41.98	164.63	7.96	17.63	18.59
disnp4	1.96	39.76	68.92	117.30	7.06	19.03	19.33
disnp5	0.43	47.95	79.36	130.31	8.85	16.86	17.12
disnp6	2.34	64.86	94.89	146.73	4.83	15.46	15.49
disnp7	0.58	31.89	50.40	80.52	13.50	12.26	11.15
disnp8	0.63	50.83	83.40	133.61	6.89	16.18	15.72

Appendix H

1) Values of *disa* in Formula 4

	Speaking_ rate	F0_ min	F0_ mean	F0_ max	Int_ min	Int_ mean	Int_ max
1	0.333	72	103	141	8.925	4.698	4.69
2	0.003	55	63	71	1.473	3.466	4.079
3	1.033	52	76	103	0.514	3.846	0.336
4	0.452	82	92	105	1.665	2.819	2.974
5	0.313	97	97	129	7.974	2.262	1.362
6	0.281	80	67	88	7.908	4.543	4.563
7	1.677	111	114	125	1.519	1.269	3.363
8	0.078	55	72	51	2.548	4.577	7.846
9	0.348	93	102	108	3.521	1.507	3.463
10	0.915	118	145	181	4.123	4.438	3.284
11	0.142	71	96	180	14.294	0.569	2.247
12	0.078	2	2	17	12.118	4.225	6.759
13	0.311	18	2	23	13.864	1.785	4.708
14	0.751	14	16	23	1.567	2.184	0.587
15	0.317	10	19	30	3.937	1.786	0.066
16	0.273	3	10	19	0.942	0.198	0.006
17	0.01	22	19	62	15.54	0.531	2.98
18	0.836	5	3	6	3.73	3.973	3.035
19	0.28	5	2	30	0.263	2.425	2.311
20	0.313	42	68	114	7.393	1.448	1.902
21	0.14	20	16	19	16.356	1.646	3.315
22	0.219	33	23	1	4.244	7.256	8.502
23	0.365	8	27	51	0.891	0.608	2.453

(continued)

	Speaking_ rate	F0_ min	F0_ mean	F0_ max	Int_ min	Int_ mean	Int_ max
24	0.126	74	46	27	5.112	4.447	4.72
25	0.175	29	6	85	16.96	5.854	3.251
26	0.144	15	34	41	20.757	3.176	3.033
27	1.471	4	3	2	6.12	9.11	12.622
28	0.794	6	23	52	14.23	0.738	0.347
29	0.311	31	11	17	12.384	4.677	3.018
30	1.995	6	13	3	9.6	1.495	2.316
31	0.706	23	13	22	10.812	2.617	2.757
32	0.151	12	9	92	0.93	1.696	1.571
33	0.465	5	30	32	0.071	0.515	2.239
34	0.394	71	59	27	8.047	1.871	0.351
35	0.478	3	44	130	0.182	5.422	3.106
36	0.336	27	8	31	8.439	3.2	2.153
37	0.704	15	13	11	17.457	2.096	2.424
38	0.445	17	29	43	27.024	1.895	0.143
39	1.298	38	59	166	14.165	6.313	3.869
40	0.359	14	25	82	3.078	3.053	4.934
41	0.009	16	60	92	13.487	3.645	3.844
42	2.583	6	10	14	13.738	4.03	3.224
43	0.202	24	16	41	15.077	0.781	0.724
44	1.367	38	27	3	6.688	1.825	3.452
45	0.855	0	29	32	29.44	5.849	5.706
46	1.588	19	17	18	13.772	12.865	10.892
47	1.15	9	37	68	15.687	15.819	17.371
48	0.316	21	12	11	8.313	0.317	2.899
49	1.764	8	10	7	8.05	9.335	9.621
50	1.413	10	50	58	23.385	6.25	4.387
51	0.029	18	63	72	5.423	9.506	10.469

(continued)

	Speaking_ rate	F0_ min	F0_ mean	F0_ max	Int_ min	Int_ mean	Int_ max
52	0.145	4	10	18	0.069	1.483	2.723
53	0.491	65	74	74	16.681	12.019	10.487
54	0.689	57	66	90	13.272	0.264	5.329
55	2.799	67	120	167	29.076	4.538	0.335
56	1.738	58	121	202	2.26	6.039	6.302
57	3.018	52	61	59	16.981	2.215	7.958
58	1.233	32	97	198	5.949	3.917	0.553
59	1.239	80	132	223	38.567	6.524	4.452
60	0.532	103	124	139	12.24	2.319	2.633
61	1.436	104	115	157	21.609	3.46	3.864
62	1.624	62	107	148	14.639	5.332	0.731
63	2.269	43	65	89	29.419	3.017	4.416
64	1.737	46	92	134	5.971	5.08	5.301
65	1.154	69	107	138	7.234	7.772	7.376
66	0.364	56	64	76	11.242	3.892	4.569
67	1.62	77	95	112	19.243	1.852	4.58
68	0.467	106	97	101	23.035	3.223	7.154
69	2.503	75	82	119	12.214	7.558	8.834
70	3.1	105	115	151	16.794	0.702	1.508

2) Values of *disna* in Formula 5

	Speaking_ rate	F0_ min	F0_ mean	F0_ max	Int_ min	Int_ mean	Int_ max
1	1.025 6	51.8	56.3	80.7	11.148 1	4.977 4	4.318 9
2	1.332	75.9	84.2	97.6	4.609 8	6.271 7	7.457 3
3	1.332	75.9	84.2	97.6	4.609 8	6.271 7	7.457 3
4	1.332	75.9	84.2	97.6	4.609 8	6.271 7	7.457 3
5	1.275	97.1	98.4	125.5	10.344 6	2.960 8	3.066 4

(continued)

	Speaking_ rate	F0_ min	F0_ mean	F0_ max	Int_ min	Int_ mean	Int_ max
6	0.561 2	86.2	69.2	85.5	8.398 6	4.88	5.064 6
7	1.009 9	98.3	118.6	162.3	9.634 6	1.580 8	1.630 7
8	0.916 5	41.1	68.2	92	14.540 6	9.236 5	10.245 7
9	1.246 4	70	92.4	141.1	16.872 2	6.937 5	6.898 1
10	0.911 9	83.2	109.4	148.5	13.895 5	2.978 1	4.127 1
11	1.034 8	71.4	113.2	157.5	8.211 1	3.846 2	4.218 5
12	0.720 3	5.9	7.7	10	13.032 9	2.886 9	3.170 9
13	1.711 2	13.2	4.8	24.2	9.238	2.105 6	4.780 6
14	2.537 4	23.1	25.4	30.7	6.417 4	2.279 4	2.778 1
15	0.460 9	17.6	16	23.5	6.684 3	2.127 3	1.845 9
16	1.678 4	7.2	6	13.5	8.642	3.086 5	4.361 6
17	1.689	18.7	12.3	43.8	11.083 9	3.719	3.562
18	1.604 5	13.3	7.1	18.9	6.536 3	2.320 6	2.897 4
19	1.139 3	7.3	8	38.1	5.586 1	2.043 6	2.221 9
20	0.959 7	56.1	63.7	79.7	5.710 4	1.226 2	2.131 1
21	1.126 1	19.8	23	13.9	6.150 6	2.235 4	3.819 4
22	0.452 3	28.7	22.7	21.3	6.546 4	7.349 5	7.247 5
23	0.690 8	28.6	34.2	42.3	3.457 2	2.718 8	2.720 8
24	0.683 2	43.2	39.6	20.2	3.734 4	3.970 8	4.062 2
25	0.583 1	17.7	15.7	42.3	4.201 8	2.562	3.057 9
26	0.641 9	36.3	47	76	11.747 6	4.934 7	5.519 3
27	0.669 9	6.8	13.2	41	7.528	3.372 2	3.723 8
28	0.782 4	14.6	36.4	81.6	11.177 6	2.675	3.194 1
29	0.576 5	29.2	17.6	48.6	5.069	4.055 9	4.062 9
30	1.258 3	8.9	6.9	10.8	8.255 2	4.202 2	3.100 8
31	1.255 9	21.4	37.3	82.2	23.441 3	3.705 3	5.068 9
32	0.742 9	22.7	8.2	105.4	7.872 4	1.556 5	3.389 5
33	0.963 5	18.3	21.8	41.5	5.842	2.692 1	2.602 7

(continued)

	Speaking_ rate	F0_ min	F0_ mean	F0_ max	Int_ min	Int_ mean	Int_ max
34	0.983 6	36.5	29.8	21.3	6.124 6	3.610 6	2.069 1
35	1.025 7	10.6	35.4	85.7	5.094 4	4.406	3.955 7
36	0.419 9	21.7	5.9	34.4	10.439 5	4.151 5	3.822 6
37	1.105 5	10.5	9.9	22.8	10.094 5	1.894 9	3.375 4
38	1.547 6	8.5	9.9	30	18.181	1.157 6	4.036
39	0.905 7	28.6	58.9	94.7	16.825 1	6.868 9	2.494 4
40	0.871 8	10.5	31.2	57.3	15.812 1	3.849 4	5.395 4
41	1.179 1	16.2	27	41.7	7.697 1	3.093 7	2.839 1
42	2.242 3	10.8	12.6	19.2	7.085 2	4.652 8	4.579 9
43	0.602 3	6.4	8.8	32	2.817 5	2.440 8	3.079 1
44	0.783 2	41.6	29.5	26	12.436 1	1.511 9	4.153 7
45	1.341 6	28.5	35.6	55.3	29.371 8	8.457 6	10.370 2
46	0.869 5	7.4	35.6	59	6.360 8	10.313 2	8.031 1
47	1.375 9	15.1	28.8	46	7.962 5	13.039 3	14.381
48	1.038 1	19.6	11.5	14	9.224 8	2.964 3	5.258 1
49	1.255 1	16.2	15.4	12.2	11.994 2	11.544 8	11.956 2
50	0.900 2	3.9	43.7	65.7	6.679	6.008 8	5.579 3
51	0.781 3	31.1	51.8	67.9	4.774	9.187 1	11.603 8
52	0.668 3	9.8	9	15.3	5.438 3	1.714 9	2.578
53	0.444 5	82.4	85.3	84.5	13.188 4	13.495 9	12.574 2
54	1.566 2	44.6	57.6	89.2	6.752 6	4.559 9	6.449 7
55	3.490 5	72.4	118.9	160.7	26.062 5	4.946 9	2.438 5
56	1.666 6	75.7	115.5	165.2	5.625 6	6.032 2	5.783 2
57	1.923 8	58.8	55.7	40.5	10.443 7	2.120 1	6.493 9
58	0.964 2	38.7	84.7	154.3	14.802 1	5.468 2	3.207 6
59	0.622 2	90.6	132.2	204.8	20.607 8	6.217 5	8.813 4
60	0.800 7	99.7	119.1	127.7	21.716 2	5.414 7	5.168
61	0.826 7	96.9	105.4	132.3	22.114	7.040 3	6.662 6

(continued)

	Speaking_ rate	F0_ min	F0_ mean	F0_ max	Int_ min	Int_ mean	Int_ max
62	0.911 3	59.8	97.8	167.3	10.621 2	7.878	4.679 1
63	1.295 3	35	61.9	79.6	23.529	4.240 8	6.144 4
64	1.112 1	41.7	74.6	90.9	5.626 2	5.091 4	5.644 4
65	0.743 9	70.7	116.8	149.8	7.839 8	7.547 3	8.443 1
66	0.796 6	70.5	72.6	64	5.832	4.005 7	6.741 1
67	1.309 1	67.7	81.7	85.8	16.074 5	4.739 6	6.11
68	1.374 4	102.5	90.8	92.5	4.199 2	5.062 9	7.779 3
69	3.388 2	76.2	92.1	167.7	7.339 8	8.243 6	8.351 3
70	1.965 957	87.057 14	93.371 43	118.428 6	14.128 5	4.483 014	6.330 943

Appendix I

1) Values of *disc* in Formula 6

	Speech_ rate	f0_ min	f0_ mean	f0_ max	int_ min	int_ mean	int_ max
1	0. 39	29. 00	31. 00	87. 00	15. 09	4. 04	0. 53
2	0. 03	32. 00	25. 00	22. 00	1. 11	7. 21	5. 67
3	0. 11	25. 00	23. 00	4. 00	0. 20	1. 05	0. 14
4	0. 27	23. 00	15. 00	12. 00	0. 56	0. 50	0. 19
5	0. 09	1. 00	5. 00	6. 00	3. 20	7. 37	6. 21
6	0. 19	14. 00	12. 00	7. 00	10. 32	1. 48	1. 79
7	0. 66	49. 00	26. 00	64. 00	5. 49	0. 63	1. 49
8	0. 00	19. 00	23. 00	9. 00	0. 97	0. 71	0. 89
9	0. 05	13. 00	14. 00	32. 00	4. 06	1. 15	0. 83
10	0. 74	99. 00	40. 00	45. 00	11. 28	4. 60	0. 59
11	0. 21	103. 00	65. 00	76. 00	1. 39	4. 67	1. 12
12	0. 29	85. 00	86. 00	106. 00	8. 88	0. 40	0. 51
13	0. 54	67. 00	107. 00	125. 00	4. 88	2. 03	1. 58
14	0. 40	54. 00	62. 00	74. 00	2. 60	4. 21	5. 10
15	0. 43	94. 00	105. 00	104. 00	5. 80	0. 94	1. 69
16	0. 11	126. 00	133. 00	151. 00	19. 94	3. 17	3. 39
17	0. 09	100. 00	111. 00	118. 00	13. 15	1. 08	1. 99
18	0. 81	63. 00	78. 00	77. 00	16. 96	7. 26	6. 96
19	0. 70	57. 00	79. 00	91. 00	18. 95	2. 40	2. 81
20	0. 32	129. 00	118. 00	122. 00	4. 50	10. 13	9. 82
21	0. 19	4. 00	6. 00	19. 00	3. 37	1. 52	1. 18
22	0. 64	26. 00	20. 00	34. 00	2. 46	0. 34	0. 42
23	0. 59	16. 00	17. 00	14. 00	6. 31	2. 56	2. 11

(continued)

	Speech_ rate	f0_ min	f0_ mean	f0_ max	int_ min	int_ mean	int_ max
24	0. 75	3. 00	33. 00	48. 00	1. 22	2. 96	0. 02
25	0. 47	8. 00	4. 00	9. 00	0. 76	2. 57	4. 24
26	0. 30	0. 00	2. 00	11. 00	5. 54	1. 33	1. 03
27	0. 23	6. 00	5. 00	12. 00	2. 87	0. 68	0. 14
28	0. 34	33. 00	64. 00	84. 00	7. 21	2. 05	2. 48
29	1. 47	20. 00	17. 00	14. 00	6. 03	1. 83	0. 55
30	0. 50	9. 00	10. 00	19. 00	3. 63	10. 62	10. 82

2) Values of *disnc* in Formula 7

	Speaking_ rate	f0_ min	f0_ mean	f0_ max	int_ min	int_ mean	int_ max
1	0. 54	32. 75	32. 75	102. 00	7. 80	5. 71	3. 13
2	0. 18	57. 88	23. 63	39. 38	13. 40	2. 80	2. 46
3	0. 38	9. 88	6. 50	7. 50	14. 32	0. 92	1. 85
4	0. 43	8. 25	6. 50	11. 25	8. 32	2. 41	2. 16
5	0. 20	16. 38	7. 75	9. 13	4. 80	7. 73	8. 27
6	0. 43	18. 75	19. 75	11. 50	6. 57	6. 00	6. 53
7	0. 91	11. 25	30. 50	65. 25	11. 22	4. 16	4. 57
8	0. 34	24. 88	35. 13	38. 00	11. 16	1. 83	2. 53
9	0. 48	26. 03	28. 66	44. 06	7. 21	1. 83	2. 37
10	0. 35	97. 25	34. 25	40. 63	8. 92	5. 69	3. 42
11	0. 42	70. 75	54. 25	80. 50	5. 93	3. 84	1. 93
12	0. 22	81. 75	89. 25	105. 00	17. 61	1. 39	2. 00
13	0. 65	79. 75	109. 88	133. 88	13. 95	4. 27	3. 51
14	0. 91	74. 88	72. 38	73. 25	5. 07	4. 92	7. 78
15	0. 86	88. 75	96. 00	102. 88	7. 37	3. 99	5. 15
16	0. 44	132. 25	137. 00	159. 50	18. 42	4. 85	5. 44
17	0. 82	89. 00	101. 00	131. 00	18. 59	4. 52	5. 80

(continued)

	Speaking_rate	f0_min	f0_mean	f0_max	int_min	int_mean	int_max
18	0.58	88.38	92.25	85.13	17.75	9.89	8.23
19	1.31	62.63	76.13	89.63	17.64	7.94	8.38
20	0.98	125.75	121.25	118.00	19.29	11.31	11.32
21	0.66	9.25	10.75	20.00	9.39	2.53	1.90
22	1.01	22.88	22.25	30.88	2.29	1.88	2.44
23	0.45	17.00	25.00	27.25	4.30	2.47	2.89
24	0.59	20.25	24.00	28.13	14.07	2.42	1.39
25	0.30	7.25	5.88	5.25	4.49	3.54	4.31
26	0.55	12.13	10.13	14.38	3.83	2.32	3.44
27	0.66	2.75	4.13	6.75	3.90	1.81	2.00
28	0.66	37.17	60.67	87.83	5.25	2.05	2.82
29	1.60	26.40	21.20	16.20	10.75	2.97	2.44
30	0.74	5.25	12.75	25.75	5.24	9.20	8.69

Appendix J

(male)

number of tones	relative pitch	number of tones	relative pitch	number of tones	relative pitch	number of tones	relative pitch
1	2.551 478	23	2.865 569	45	2.149 846	67	2.866 994
2	3.064 859	24	2.932 854	46	2.201 752	68	3.023 551
3	2.899 321	25	2.865 569	47	2.405 237	69	2.706 087
4	2.693 429	26	2.797 398	48	2.354 973	70	2.945 801
5	2.515 374	27	2.966 172	49	2.405 237	71	2.279 725
6	3.064 859	28	2.831 595	50	2.044 747	72	2.279 725
7	2.865 569	29	2.728 318	51	2.044 747	73	2.393 488
8	2.932 854	30	3.256 767	52	2.201 752	74	2.163 753
9	2.865 569	31	3.064 859	53	2.013 651	75	2.336 877
10	2.797 398	32	3.319 188	54	2.540 583	76	2.560 17
11	2.966 172	33	4.062 366	55	2.665 152	77	2.104 911
12	2.831 595	34	3.871 792	56	2.582 405	78	2.045 484
13	2.728 318	35	2.304 308	57	3.361 059	79	2.279 725
14	3.256 767	36	2.405 237	58	2.540 583	80	1.801 679
15	3.064 859	37	2.455 107	59	2.540 583	81	2.104 911
16	3.319 188	38	2.405 237	60	2.456 023	82	2.560 17
17	2.551 478	39	2.602 411	61	2.326 822	83	2.279 725
18	3.064 859	40	2.405 237	62	2.706 087	84	2.449 567
19	2.899 321	41	2.650 764	63	2.582 405	85	2.393 488
20	2.693 429	42	2.304 308	64	2.827 184	86	2.336 877
21	2.515 374	43	2.097 514	65	3.062 037	87	2.336 877
22	3.064 859	44	1.774 137	66	2.706 087	88	2.336 877

(continued)

number of tones	relative pitch	number of tones	relative pitch	number of tones	relative pitch	number of tones	relative pitch
89	1. 797 735	108	2. 461 685	127	2. 190 423	146	1. 982 992
90	1. 956 316	109	2. 100 695	128	2. 265 414	147	1. 686 304
91	1. 743 929	110	2. 258 214	129	2. 433 503	148	2. 298 03
92	1. 851 062	111	2. 228 03	130	2. 809 423	149	2. 027 858
93	1. 956 316	112	2. 627 461	131	2. 624 168	150	2. 851 907
94	2. 161 439	113	2. 376 243	132	1. 982 992	151	2. 899 758
95	1. 634 848	114	2. 485 144	133	2. 717 453	152	2. 350 602
96	1. 851 062	115	2. 592 184	134	2. 624 168	153	2. 556 297
97	1. 797 735	116	2. 265 414	135	1. 930 961	154	2. 402 706
98	1. 743 929	117	2. 800 926	136	1. 930 961	155	2. 755 017
99	2. 110 812	118	2. 190 423	137	2. 187 065	156	2. 402 706
100	1. 956 316	119	2. 302 575	138	2. 336 041	157	2. 350 602
101	2. 059 754	120	1. 881 141	139	2. 034 611	158	2. 705 965
102	2. 261 43	121	2. 037 691	140	2. 481 693	159	2. 298 03
103	2. 211 643	122	2. 228 03	141	2. 085 825	160	2. 350 602
104	2. 161 439	123	2. 697 425	142	2. 034 611	161	2. 402 706
105	2. 161 439	124	2. 228 03	143	1. 825 639		
106	2. 211 643	125	2. 376 243	144	2. 187 065		
107	2. 848 043	126	2. 190 423	145	1. 982 992		

(female)

number of tones	relative pitch	number of tones	relative pitch	number of tones	relative pitch	number of tones	relative pitch
1	2. 560 632	5	2. 430 691	9	2. 216 304	13	2. 509 017
2	2. 611 775	6	2. 712 682	10	2. 534 884	14	2. 712 682
3	2. 483 03	7	2. 534 884	11	2. 509 017	15	2. 637 173
4	2. 377 859	8	2. 377 859	12	2. 377 859	16	2. 885 009

(continued)

number of tones	relative pitch	number of tones	relative pitch	number of tones	relative pitch	number of tones	relative pitch
17	4.652 93	44	2.432 932	71	1.799 689	98	2.064 354
18	4.836 905	45	2.406 773	72	2.138 23	99	2.413 86
19	4.512 925	46	2.510 75	73	2.138 23	100	2.253 433
20	5.062 678	47	2.301 012	74	2.344 007	101	2.678 741
21	4.882 428	48	2.354 12	75	2.078 099	102	2.569 873
22	5.414 652	49	2.837 041	76	2.285 94	103	2.391 217
23	4.972 918	50	2.301 012	77	2.078 099	104	2.413 86
24	4.606 457	51	2.301 012	78	2.108 241	105	2.206 751
25	4.275 597	52	1.772 252	79	2.197 756	106	2.458 874
26	4.512 925	53	2.188 448	80	2.227 297	107	2.122 259
27	5.371 259	54	2.431 025	81	2.401 511	108	1.839 779
28	5.017 889	55	2.587 19	82	2.514 871	109	1.692 542
29	4.371 137	56	2.535 609	83	2.017 351	110	2.006 426
30	4.275 597	57	2.215 916	84	2.430 055	111	3.150 641
31	3.983 959	58	2.638 309	85	2.256 691	112	2.814 516
32	4.371 137	59	2.788 971	86	2.168 068	113	2.342 723
33	4.179 231	60	2.638 309	87	2.197 756	114	2.594 467
34	4.465 863	61	2.587 19	88	1.799 689	115	2.572 012
35	2.432 932	62	2.483 557	89	2.391 217	116	2.504 14
36	2.688 59	63	2.688 973	90	2.230 14	117	2.435 491
37	2.193 403	64	2.612 807	91	2.040 27	118	2.458 461
38	2.380 503	65	2.688 973	92	2.299 734	119	2.504 14
39	2.327 623	66	2.788 971	93	2.112 218	120	2.771 146
40	2.274 285	67	2.483 557	94	2.436 412	121	2.878 989
41	2.000 443	68	2.638 309	95	2.064 354	122	2.984 929
42	2.638 3	69	2.714 138	96	2.230 14	123	2.319 305
43	2.638 3	70	2.270 459	97	2.299 734	124	2.705 499

(continued)

number of tones	relative pitch	number of tones	relative pitch	number of tones	relative pitch	number of tones	relative pitch
125	2.792 87	135	2.411 914	145	2.497 799	155	2.999 724
126	2.594 467	136	2.469 306	146	2.324 793	156	2.831 745
127	2.412 433	137	2.383 012	147	2.658 751	157	2.454 505
128	2.771 146	138	2.324 793	148	2.480 433	158	2.807 345
129	2.554 386	139	2.206 647	149	2.454 505	159	2.904 333
130	2.236 4	140	2.176 746	150	2.454 505	160	2.506 245
131	2.146 698	141	2.324 793	151	3.023 328	161	2.683 782
132	2.206 647	142	2.693 583	152	2.733 524		
133	2.353 973	143	2.383 012	153	2.928 328		
134	2.440 678	144	2.440 678	154	2.633 61		

Appendix K Formulas

1. Formula 1 in section 4. 1. 1

$$disp = | A_f - B_f |$$

2. Formula 2 in section 4. 1. 1

$$disnp = \frac{\sum_i | A_f - Xi_f |}{| X |}$$

3. Formula 3 in section 4. 1. 3

$$sim = 1 - \frac{disp}{disnp}$$

4. Formula 4 in section 4. 2. 1

$$disa = | IPU_t - IPU_p |$$

5. Formula 5 in section 4. 2. 1

$$disna = \frac{\sum_{i=1}^{10} | IPU_t - IPU_i |}{10}$$

6. Formula 6 in section 4. 3. 1

$$disc = | TU_t - TU_c |$$

7. Formula 7 in section 4. 3. 1

$$disnc = \frac{\sum_{i=1}^{8} | TU_t - TU_i |}{8}$$

Appendix L　One Conversation in Corpus

19－1　刘鹏-邓威_giver

file	contents	file	contents	file	contents
1	好的	24	就是济和哎去	47	是的
2	第一个图标是书包	25	嗯	48	在哎和币之间也就是书包的
3	嗯	26	下一个图标是		
4	书标在	27	沙滩	49	左下方
5	第二行的	28	沙滩在	50	好
6	第二列	29	第一行的第四列	51	下一个图标是
7	第二列	30	对	52	山坡
8	呃	31	就是在	53	山坡在
9	在	32	杰和恺之间	54	最
10	第和	33	好了吗	55	左上角
11	哎	34	好	56	在第一行第一列
12	亿之间	35	下一个图标是	57	对
13	亿之间第二行第二列	36	花灯	58	在书包的左上方
14	好了吗	37	花灯在	59	嗯
15	好的	38	第二行的第五	60	下一个图标是司机
16	下一个图标是	39	五列	61	司机在
17	飞机	40	对	62	最右
18	飞机在书包的	41	对 在	63	最右上角
19	右下方 在	42	嗯和哎木之间	64	第对
20	第三行	43	下一个图标是乌龟	65	在屁和酷之间在第一行的最后一个
21	第三列	44	乌龟在		
22	对	45	第三行的	66	好
23	第三行第三列	46	第一列	67	下一个图标是

(continued)

file	contents
68	鲜花
69	鲜花在
70	第三
71	行的第四列
72	在飞机的后面
73	对
74	飞机我们在
75	第三列
76	鲜花在第三行第四列
77	第三行第四列
78	飞机刚才的位置不对吗
79	飞机
80	飞机刚才不是在
81	济和哎去之间
82	飞机在第三行的
83	第三列
84	没有找到吗
85	第二个图标飞机
86	还是没有吗
87	噢好
88	呃没有飞机的下方飞机在第三行的第三列
89	对
90	然后鲜花在第三行的第四列
91	对
92	在飞机的后面吗

file	contents
93	对
94	好
95	下一个图标是西瓜
96	西瓜在
97	第三行的
98	最后一个
99	对也就是在最右下角
100	在屁和酷之间恩
101	好
102	下一个图标是
103	第十个沙发
104	嗯
105	沙发在第三行的第二列
106	对在第和亿之间 在
107	乌龟和飞机中间
108	下一个图标是山峰
109	嗯
110	在第一行的第二列
111	第一行
112	嗯
113	在
114	在山坡后面对
115	下一个图标是乡村
116	乡村在
117	第
118	二行的
119	第四列

file	contents
120	对
121	在
122	沙滩的下面
123	和鲜花上面
124	好
125	下一个图标是青蛙
126	在第一行的
127	第五列
128	第一行第五列
129	对
130	在沙滩的后面
131	司机的前面
132	嗯
133	好
134	下一个图标是
135	咖啡
136	对
137	咖啡在
138	第二行的第三列
139	嗯
140	嗯
141	不
142	不在沙滩 沙滩在
143	第一行的第四列
144	第二行的第三列
145	对
146	它在飞机的上面
147	嗯

(continued)

file	contents	file	contents	file	contents
148	好	171	烟花在	195	嗯
149	下一个图标是公鸡	172	第	196	我们对一遍吧
150	公鸡在	173	二行的最后一个	197	呃我按照顺序横着来
151	第三行的	174	嗯	198	呃
152	第五列	175	它的上面是司机吗	199	山坡
153	五列对	176	烟花的上面是司机吗	200	山峰
154	在	177	鲜花在	201	医生
155	鲜花和西瓜	178	第三行的第四列	202	沙滩
156	中间	179	嗯	203	青蛙
157	好了吗	180	乡村	204	司机
158	好	181	嗯	205	好
159	下一个图标是	182	然后	206	第二行是军官
160	医生	183	司机现在是在最	207	书包
161	嗯	184	右上角了吗	208	咖啡
162	医生	185	好	209	乡村
163	找到了吗	186	那烟花下面是西瓜吗	210	花灯
164	医生在第一行的第三列	187	上面是司机	211	烟花
		188	呃	212	接着是
165	对	189	好	213	乌龟
166	对	190	下一个图标是军官	214	沙发
167	在咖啡的上方然后前面是山峰吗	191	嗯	215	飞机
		192	军官在第二行的第一个	216	鲜花
168	好的			217	公鸡
169	下一个图标是烟花	193	对	218	还有西瓜
170	嗯	194	好的	219	好的

20–1 邓威-刘鹏_follower

file	contents	file	contents	file	contents
1	第一个图标是书包	27	好	54	之间
2	十三到十七	28	下一个图标是山坡	55	在
3	在	29	第一行	56	书包的下方
4	第和亿中间	30	第一列	57	好的
5	好的	31	也就是在第一个	58	下一个图标是山峰
6	下一个图标是飞机	32	好的	59	嗯嘛也就是第和亿
7	飞机在	33	下一个图标是司机	60	好的
8	济和	34	好的找到了	61	下一个图标是乡村
9	济和哎去之间	35	第一行的最后一个	62	好的
10	二十三到二十七	36	好的	63	在
11	好的	37	下一个图标是鲜花	64	鲜花和沙滩的中间噢
12	在书包的右下方是吧	38	好的找到了	65	在花灯的
13	好	39	在	66	左方
14	下一个图标是沙滩	40	飞机的	67	也就是杰和恺
15	沙滩在杰和恺之间恩	41	好的它的	68	好的
16	三到七	42	纵坐标是杰和恺是吗	69	下一个图标是青蛙
17	好	43	好	70	在沙滩和
18	下一个图标是花灯	44	##	71	司机中间花灯之上好的
19	沙滩的	45	下一个图标是西瓜		
20	右下方	46	好的找到了	72	下一个图标是咖啡
21	好的	47	在	73	在书包和乡村中间飞机的正上方
22	呃是	48	第三行的最后一列		
23	哎木和嗯这	49	司机的	74	它的上方是公鸡吗
24	嗯 好	50	正	75	哦哦哦
25	下一个图标是乌龟	51	嗯好的	76	那它的
26	横坐标就是在街三行是吗	52	下一个图标是沙发	77	下方是飞机
		53	在乌龟和飞机	78	好的 在

(continued)

file	contents
79	济和哎去之间
80	好
81	十三到十七对
82	嗯
83	下一个图标是公鸡
84	在
85	第三行
86	哎木和哎嗯之间
87	好的
88	下一个图标是医生
89	好的
90	在咖啡上方山峰和沙发中间
91	下一个图标是烟花
92	在第二行最右边
93	一列
94	好的它的上方是司机
95	是
96	西瓜好
97	最后一个图标是
98	下一个图标是军官
99	军官在山坡和乌龟之间就是第二行第一个
100	好的
101	呃嗯
102	对
103	对
104	嗯
105	嗯
106	对
107	是的
108	嗯
109	嗯
110	好
111	对
112	对
113	对
114	对
115	对
116	对
117	是的
118	嗯
119	是的

Afterwords

My sincere appreciation should go to the people who help me to make this research and dissertation possible.

First of all, I would like to express my deepest gratitude to my supervisor, Professor Ma Qiuwu. He gave me the chance to be his PhD student, which set a milestone in my life. Professor Ma inspires my interest in both Phonetics and Phonology. With his international horizon, Professor Ma directs me to recognize the uniqueness of Chinese, and encouraged me to do research on it, although I majored in foreign language learning and teaching for 17 years. The expansion of research interest makes the present thesis on prosodic entrainment in Chinese conversation possible. Professor Ma teaches us how to do research correctly, how to produce profound and valuable papers, how to make balance between work and life, etc. All he teaches me will make far-reaching influence on my learning and research in the future.

I appreciate greatly the help from teachers and students in Speech Lab of Columbia University who are friendly and generous to give me tremendous favor in doing this thesis during my one-year visiting program in New York City. In particular, the most sincere appreciation goes to Professor Julia Hirschberg, my supervisor in Columbia University. She spared time to have meetings with me every week, gave me instructions in my work, and encouraged me to keep on working when I faced challenges. Special thanks should go to Rivka Leviton, who did the parallel research on prosodic entrainment in Standard American English. She supplied amazing ideas in research methods and valuable suggestions in my work on entrainment in

Mandarin.

Great thanks should be given to Professor Daniel Hirst. I am so lucky to be one of his students since 2011, when he is an invited professor of Tongji University. From theories to research methods, Professor Hirst teaches us comprehensive knowledge of speech prosody.

I will remember forever the teachers in Tongji University and Fudan University who supplies me help. Professor Jie Liang, Professor Hongwei Ding, Professor Delu Zhang and Professor Zhongmin Chen gave me patient instructions and suggestions when I turned to them for help.

I would like to express my gratitude to all the friends who have assisted me in the research work and life. Yong Wang, who is a computer science engineer, helped me in making computer programs for automatic calculations in this research. Hong En, Ariane Brotto, and Mei-Vern Chen gave me help in my life during my stay in New York City. Doctor Lijuan Chen and Doctor Limin Gu provided wonderful ideas and suggestion for me when I had difficulties in my research and life.

Finally, how can I express my gratitude to my family? Without their support and love, I couldn't accomplish any tasks. Every step forward is made with holding my husband's hands. My lovely baby daughter is always doing excellence in her own life. Any progress and happiness she gets forms the tremendous encouragement for me to move on.

I feel grateful to all the people who give me hands and raise me up. Thank you!

Zhihua Xia